THE DATING PLAYBOOK FOR MEN

A PROVEN 7 STEP SYSTEM TO GO FROM SINGLE TO THE WOMAN OF YOUR DREAMS

ANDREW FEREBEE

Founder of KnowledgeForMen.com

The Dating Playbook for Men – A Proven 7-Step System to
Go From Single to the Woman of Your Dreams

By Andrew Ferebee

© 2019 Knowledge For Men, LLC All Rights Reserved.
Revised Edition. Printed in the United States of America.

ISBN-13: 978-0692678671
ISBN-10: 0692678670

This book is dedicated to the man who suffers in silence.
May this book help you create a better life.

And to my dad who unexpectantly passed away days
before I published this book. He taught me discipline and
how to live a simple life.

CONTENTS

HOW THIS BOOK WILL HELP YOU
ACHIEVE YOUR GOALS

I've laid out the entire program in seven chapters, each with very specific and sequential lessons that build upon one another to help you get results as quickly as possible. You'll be tempted to skip ahead and read about the things that most interest you. *Fight that temptation.* This book has been written and rewritten to deliver you just the right information at the right time. Trust the process or you'll jeopardize your success.

In Chapter 1, I will teach you the core lessons about masculinity, revealing a simple archetype that will turn you into that rare breed of man capable of penetrating the world, achieving his greatest ambitions, and sparking irresistible attraction in women.

Chapter 2 will fundamentally alter the way you view women and the social dynamics between the sexes, revealing core mindsets and internal processes that will allow you to approach women from a place of total authenticity. You'll no longer feel like you have to prove yourself or that you are somehow "taking" something from attractive women. Instead, you will feel total confidence in yourself and enter into your interactions from a place of pure value and freedom.

Chapter 3 reveals the truth about what women want based on more than a decade of experience and hundreds of expert interviews. You'll gain a concrete understanding of what makes women choose one man over another, what turns them on, and how you can spark uncontrollable attraction—even if you're not a male model or millionaire.

Chapter 4 delivers tactical steps and strategies you need to effortlessly approach the attractive women that terrify other men. You'll learn how to hook her interest within the first few minutes, create engaging conversations that make her feel like you "get her," and become so memorable that she is begging you to take her out on a date.

In Chapter 5, I'll show you how to avoid the "friend zone" by establishing a man-to-woman vibe in your interactions, owning your masculine desires, and effortlessly escalating your interactions from the initial introduction to dating to the bedroom and beyond.

Chapter 6 teaches you one of the most important skills you'll learn: how to filter out the wrong women from your life and ensure that you are only dating and entering relationships with the highest quality women. This chapter teaches you how to recognize and avoid women who will waste your time, energy, and resources.

Finally, Chapter 7 shows you how to master the entire process by breaking down this system into manageable phases. I'll bring together the most critical elements of each chapter to progress from beginner to intermediate to advanced so that you can break through plateaus, stop wasting precious time, and achieve your goals faster.

The chapters are carefully ordered, so go in order even if you believe you have one area mastered. After you read through it once, go back and refer to specific sections you would like to concentrate on as you take action in the real world. The workbook will provide additional exercises and bring everything together to ensure you're progressing quickly and effectively.

You can download the workbook here: knowledgeformen.com/dating-toolkit

Now, it's time to begin your journey to find, attract, and keep the woman of your dreams.

WARNING: This book will challenge many of your long-held beliefs about life, women, and relationships. There will be times when you disagree with me, curse at me, and want to hurl this book through an open window. Good. This is how you're supposed to feel.

The frustration and anger you may experience are all a part of the road to transformation that has been meticulously laid out before you. The truth will sting. But the pain is a catalyst for growth and when you experience discomfort or disagreement, I challenge you to continue reading with an open mind. Counterintuitive and confounding as much of the content in this book may be, it has been used by thousands of successful men before you and will be used by thousands after you.

The only question is, will *you* use it? Or will you let fear and discomfort prevent you from living the life of your dreams?

The choice is yours.

THE DAY I LOST EVERYTHING

"You know, I loved you… but I just don't feel it anymore."

She said it so softly and quietly, yet each word hammered me like a blow to the face. I had no idea what to say. *Wasn't I picking her up for our weekly dinner date?* My jaw dropped and my hands gripped the steering wheel, knuckles white like I was speeding even though I was frozen still.

I was speechless. Moments ago, I would have told you that I was going to spend the rest of my life with this woman. She tried to fill the silence, but her awful words would haunt me for years to come.

"I can't do this anymore, Andrew. It hasn't felt right for a while now."

It hasn't? Am I getting dumped? My eyes drifted away from her, looking for answers but finding none, wondering how I had missed the signs. *Had I?* Couldn't she remember all the good times we had? I thought we had been doing so well… Suddenly, I was out of breath.

"Is this really happening? Fuck. It is." What was life going to be like after this? Looking at her hurt my spirit even more. She looked so confident, so sure of her decision. Those beautiful, brown eyes were indeed set on this terrible new direction.

In the heat of the moment, I couldn't help but notice how gorgeous she looked sitting beside me, even as she was ripping out my heart and throwing it onto the sizzling pavement outside. On the drive over, I had actually been thinking, "The only thing good in my life is this girl."

Just looking at her, I could tell that she wasn't thinking the clichéd, "It's not you, Andrew. It's me." No, she fully believed the problem was me. She was moving on. She'd experienced dating me and it wasn't good enough. *I wasn't good enough.*

I sat in silence for an eternity that couldn't have been more than thirty seconds. When I finally worked up the courage to mumble any words at all, they were a complete lie. I blurted bullshit I didn't really believe, all to just get through this awful moment, to try to figure out how the hell I was going to survive this: "Ugh, you're right. I think we both knew this was coming anyways… maybe we can connect later down the road again? I- I love… loved… you too, but I agree we-we should just end it."

My internal thoughts couldn't believe the words coming out of my mouth. She breathed a sigh of relief and a small smile broke at the corners of her lips. My lies were just what she needed to hear to make herself feel better. She could sleep better tonight… with whomever this beautiful woman chose.

With a gentle sadness in her voice, she tried to let me down softly and respectfully. "Andrew, you're one of the sweetest men I've ever met, and you deserve a great woman."

Although well-intentioned, her futile attempt to salvage some remnant of my dignity did little to soften the harsh blow. The condescending tone—and the realization that she wasn't going to be that woman—boiled an emasculated confusion in me. I didn't want to be a "sweet" guy alone. I wanted to be the man she wanted. *That she loved.*

She obviously didn't want that anymore. She slowly opened the car door, her foot out the door, but turned back to me as a final courtesy: "You're okay, right? I mean… this is for the best."

"Of course," I lied further, even putting together a half-hearted smile for her. "I think we both knew this was coming. We've been drifting apart for a while. This is good for both of us."

I didn't believe a word of it. It was all a lie to remain "strong," to look like I had it all together even when everything was falling apart. I didn't want her to know how deeply I was hurting. I know now that I was never open emotionally with her, even about how much she really meant to me. I wish I had been more open and honest about my feelings with her all those years ago.

Stepping out of the car, we hugged one last time. I walked her toward her building, just like I had done at the end of our first date. "Take care of yourself," she said softly, after giving me a farewell kiss that felt like a dagger ripping through my cheek.

I went back to my car and stood outside, watching her walk away. Even there, wondering if it was all really over, I still hoped that maybe she would suddenly look back at me in despair, run back to me crying, and tell me that she had just made a horrible mistake. She'd tell me she wanted to make things work, that she was willing to fight for me. That she still cared. That she still loved me.

But she didn't... She kept walking away, in full certainty, knowing that she had made the right choice. As I watched the door to her building shut behind her, I started tearing up uncontrollably. That would be the last time that I would ever see her. And just like that, "the love of my life" was gone.

I got in my car and closed the door, still processing the shock of the interaction, but a greater shadow fell over me more than just a break-up. It was that look in her eye, the one that said she was making the right decision.

That feeling shook the very foundation of my masculinity. It wasn't just losing a relationship, it was having someone else be so certain that I wasn't the right choice. I started to believe that I wasn't "good enough" either. *Maybe she was right?*

I looked in the rearview mirror of my beat up ten-year-old coupe. I was a loser, living in my mom's condo with a stepdad who eagerly wanted me out, working a retail job that drowned my inner soul. And I had to ask myself, "Why would a woman like her—hell, any woman—want to be with a guy like me?"

I've known what pain is. I've had my arm nearly ripped off and have been choked unconscious training Brazilian Jiu Jitsu many times. I've broken ankles playing sports and hyperextended my neck in whiplash accidents. Of all the wounds I've ever suffered, nothing hurt as much as that short conversation.

Within 10 minutes, a woman that I loved dearly kicked my self-confidence right out from under me. Just a few words was all it took before *I started to believe I wasn't good enough.*

Afterward, I was a mess emotionally and physically. I cried so much in pain that I barely had the energy to go through the motions each day. I locked myself away from the world, calling in sick to work, sitting silently in my little bedroom. I wasn't eating or sleeping, just drinking and re-running scenarios of how I could have done better and strategizing how I could get her back.

"Where did I go wrong?" I blamed myself for months, numbly attempting to re-create a sense of normalcy in my life. My work performance suffered. My friends grew worried about me. I battled depressive episodes and fleeting thoughts of suicide.

This calamity revealed how much of my happiness was rooted in her and, once taken away, that foundation was broken. I thought I'd had it hard in the past with previous relationships and challenges in my life, but this was truly rock bottom. Sometimes, however… rock bottom is where you have to go to find your true path in life. When there's nowhere to go but up, you're free to recreate your life.

Months had gone by and one night I was up late, unable to sleep, tossing and turning alone in my bed. I was lost in despair with a deep pain in my stomach… when I started to think about what's next. Suddenly, a great epiphany struck me:

"What if I turned this great pain into the greatest opportunity to fuel me towards the life I want?"

This simple question sparked a flurry of emotion as I jumped out of bed, grabbed a pen, and started journaling some of the very words you're going to find in this book, some of what you're reading right now, in fact. The ideas that flowed that night would become a roadmap for an epic adventure in personal transformation, self-development, spiritual growth, and the kind of success with women I never thought imaginable.

That fateful night, right when my entire world felt like it was crumbling down around me, I furiously scribbled as the thoughts came to me. Writing those pages was like planting a proverbial flag in a new discovery: I was DONE.

- Done being rejected by the women I desired.
- Done living my life on the sidelines as a single man.
- Done settling for subpar relationships as I watched other men achieve romantic success.
- Done allowing my lack of confidence and low self-esteem to sabotage my relationships and prevent me from having the life I wanted to experience.
- Done doing nothing while attractive women passed me by every day.
- Done being a submissive "nice" guy who put others' needs first before my own.

For the first time in my life, I was truly committed to growing into the man I needed to be to have the relationships and life I wanted. The funny thing they don't tell you about commitment, however, *is how extremely horrifying it really is.*

When I decided I was going to overcome my challenges with not just women and dating, but also living an exceptional life, my options were simple: face my fears, or live the rest of my life in pain and regret. I knew I had to make a change, but my epiphany was only a fraction of the equation. I still didn't know how to do it, not at first, anyway. In fact, when I first started the journey, I was utterly *terrified.*

What if I really wasn't good enough? Maybe I was too much of a "nice guy" to attract the kinds of women I desired. I was nervous about other people judging my masculinity and sensing my lack of self-worth and lost in the very real fear that I didn't know what women wanted and worse, that I couldn't give it to them. The most terrifying part was the fear that I would be rejected by every beautiful woman I approached.

Though everything about this process frightened me, I also knew that I didn't have any other choice. I had to feel the fear and use it to take action anyway. I would do it scared, because doing nothing would be worse than living in regret for the rest of my life.

I wish that I could tell you that my fears about the struggle were unfounded, that I went out that night to meet new women and instantly began attracting the most beautiful and intelligent women everywhere I went with ease. My journey—like yours will be—wasn't one of those idyllic self-help fairytales where you listen to some guru and success instantly happens.

No, becoming the man I am today was anything but easy. Your journey won't be either, but mark my words – it will be worth it. After all, I had a lot to learn about understanding what makes a strong man, about social dynamics, and more importantly, about what women want. Achieving real results took patience and it often felt like I was making no progress at all.

I read hundreds of books about dating and relationships. I went into debt buying online courses, hiring life coaches, and attending every seminar I could find. If I couldn't afford a seminar, I would find a way to be allowed in to get the training I needed. Sometimes that meant cleaning up the conference room afterward or assisting with videography work without pay. I took everything I learned and took action in the real world. I talked to every woman I could, asking more women out in a single week than I had in the previous decade. No, I didn't just improve my success with women. I rebuilt my entire life from the ground up.

- I quit my soul-sucking job and started my own podcast, blog, and online business.
- I trained at the gym four days a week.
- I built a powerful social circle of men that I respected and admired and quit hanging out with the toxic people who undermined my growth.
- I focused on personal development, interviewing hundreds of experts on life, relationships, and success.

The results compounded to give me the momentum I needed to achieve more success with women and skyrocket my overall sense of confidence, taking it higher than it had been in my entire life. It's been a wild ride filled with ups, downs, love, heartbreak, and more lessons than I thought possible...and I've condensed it all into the book you hold in your hands.

This book is your first step—a huge one, don't get me wrong—toward accomplishing the same kind of life-changing growth that I and thousands of other men now enjoy. I've dated women whom I'd always thought were "out of my league," and you can, too. You'll have the freedom to choose who you want to date instead of hoping to be chosen by happenstance.

I no longer drag out sour, toxic relationships that the old me used to put up with and think were normal. I no longer settle out of scarcity and fear. I freely express myself, cultivating an environment of radical self-love and acceptance. I've removed all doubt and the false personas I wore for so many years in order to please women. Now I trust the right women will be drawn to me and feel the mutual attraction. The wrong ones naturally filter themselves out of my life with no more games. Women and relationships, however, are only the tip of the iceberg. The confidence and self-esteem I built along the journey has given me the toughness and certainty I needed to dominate in other areas of my life as well.

Remember who I was at the start of this journey (and, believe me, I'm not down playing it). Working retail by day, living at my mom's house at night, driving a broken-down car. My ex-girlfriend breaking up with me was only part of the problems I faced, but I couldn't see it then since she filled the void.

The decision to take action and go against the grain has led me to live a life of freedom, confidence, and power that I never knew was possible. This book is my journey, and I'm excited for you to use it to start yours.

Understand this: your journey before today is irrelevant. You might be single, recently divorced, settling for a relationship that you know isn't serving you any longer. Like me, whatever pain brought you here,

I promise you'll learn to see it as the greatest gift you've ever received because it's what brought you here.

**Whoever you are, I understand your pain
and I'm here to help you eradicate it.**

To begin, we need to understand how we got here and why what you've tried in the past has consistently failed you.

THE BILLION DOLLAR WAR THAT MEN ARE LOSING

In the 21st Century, the dating landscape has been irrevocably changed by the inception of social media, dating apps, and the rapid rise in mass advertising backed by the largest corporations in the world. Just a few decades ago, men learned what it meant to be a man from their fathers, grandfathers, and other men in their communities.

Today, we've experienced a dramatic shift in our culture and societal standards around masculinity, dating, and sex. We've been brain washed into thinking our self-worth is determined by the bulge of our biceps, the balance of our bank account, the beauty of our women, and the amount of horsepower in our cars. There is little value placed on being a man of character or real substance. We've become confused about what it means to be a man. These shifts have been detrimental to men, but they've also been doubly so for women.

Women in large cities are now directly and indirectly offered sex hundreds of times each month from men in person, on social media and dating apps. Women can receive more (solicited and unsolicited) offers for sex in a month than even the most famous women in past decades would receive in their *lifetime*.

Although few women entertain any of the propositions they receive from men, this unsubtle shift in their ability to boost their egos and gain instant gratification and validation with the post of a photo or swipe on an app has resulted in a massive shift regarding *who* women will date.

Through their smartphones, women today have a greater level of abundance and more options in the dating world than ever before in human history. And unbeknownst to most men, there is a growing population of women who have actually taken this opportunity to the extreme and turned to Sugar Baby and Sugar Daddy apps where they charge "successful" men absurd amounts of money to go on dates, show up to parties, and well… other activities. How did we get here?

The sexual liberation movement of the 1960s has led women in the 21st century to be more sexually free and open than ever before in human history. And with this unprecedented level of sexual freedom, fueled by societal reform and widespread access to effective contraception, we have encouraged women to be more attractive and sexually appealing to great extremes.

Women now have access to a plethora of operations and products to help them ~~improve~~ *perfect* their appearance. Breast implants, plastic surgery, butt augmentation, lip injections, cosmetics, and countless other solutions allow women to effectively make themselves as attractive as they want, more or less, on command.

As such, they've grown to expect a caliber of man to whom most guys can't even begin to compare. They expect a fictitious man they've been conditioned to believe in, *regardless* of their own social status or the level of inner value that *they* can bring into a relationship.

Entitlement and narcissism run rampant, creating an unprecedented tension between men and women that is continually encouraged and fueled by our growing addictions to ego and validation boosting apps.

Billion-dollar advertising and social media brands gleefully exacerbate this tension, using it to their advantage to push more products, peddle more pills, and make bold promises upon which they rarely deliver. They have declared war on our generation's attention and ability to authentically connect with other humans. Men are losing in this battle, as they're being force fed a lie that *they're* not good enough for what women and society expects of *them*.

In the near future, it will be impossible for any man who is not heavily invested in his masculine development, personal growth, and social skills to meet or date women… especially attractive and high-quality women.

While men sedate their connectionless lives with video games, television marathons, and disturbingly bizarre porn (a trend that is rapidly getting out of hand), we are slowly but surely losing our once innate abilities to meet and maintain relationships with the women we desire in the real world.

Yet instead of *accepting* these problems, rising to the occasion, and addressing them head on... most men hide from them. There is a growing community of men who claim to "go their own way" and ignore these problems, opting to remain single because they bought into the lie that *all* women are "evil," "heartless," or "crazy." These same men refuse to acknowledge *their* own shortcomings and weaknesses, the ones that equally contributed to their relationship problems in the first place.

Then there is the Red Pill crowd that fights fire with fire and treats women as entitled and spoiled objects of sexual conquest instead of human beings with whom they should connect with, adore and love.

And finally, there's the pickup community... While this might seem like the most innocent of the three, the tenants of pickup bring with them their own unique dangers and pitfalls—ones I've experienced firsthand. Though pickup culture does bring some value to the table and is at least an actionable plan, it is certainly *not* the solution.

Here's why...

THE DANGEROUS PROBLEM OF THE "PICKUP" INDUSTRY

Now, before I neg on it, I want to make something very clear... pickup is *not* a bad thing. When used appropriately, it provides men with a basic understanding of psychology and seduction, teaching them the basic tactics required to get quick results with women.

But relying solely on pickup does not lead to lasting relationships with the women you desire most.

It's like trying to start a business when you only know how to sell. Your product sucks, your marketing sucks, and your customer service sucks, but hey! You can still make a quick buck by manipulating people into giving you their credit card number. The only problem is that none of those customers will ever return.

Pickup techniques teach you how to master different situations, so that when she does X you do Y. Yes, sometimes this is enough to score a one-night stand or set up a date, but it's all fleeting. At your core, you're still the same insecure guy who is trying to mask his problems by influencing women into doing things that benefit only you. It doesn't teach you how to become the kind of man who is a true win-win for a woman.

No matter how well you pickup, your life is still the same. Your income, confidence, self-esteem, fitness, social life, and overall character remain unchanged. Without a transformation on the inside, you'll never experience lasting results on the outside with high quality women. If you don't believe me, just look at the leaders of pickup itself. The biggest gurus in the industry make millions off of you, pretending they have the "hot new" strategies (even though the core biological and psychological principles of success with women remains unchanged). However, those same men rarely have long term relationships with high-quality women.

They scream from their pulpits to do things that sound proactive like, "Cold-approach random women for the next ten years in a loud club!" Meanwhile, a small yet growing number of men understand the real game being played, and they achieve their desired results with only the most basic understanding of pickup tactics and techniques.

Let me be clear: you do not need to be a master of "cold approaching." You simply need to have the foundations of social psychology and enough experience so that you are proficient at bringing new women into your life. That's it. Once you're competent in the basics, shift your focus to endeavors that will yield greater returns and improve your overall quality of life: fitness, for example, or improving your social life, investing in your passions, or becoming financially free.

The men I know who are truly happy and fulfilled in every area of their lives—not just with women—are the guys who have built a well-rounded life from the inside out. They are men, whether single or in a relationship, who understand that women are merely a part of their life, not the guiding force of their existence.

Within these pages, I'm going to teach you the basics of "game" and seduction and instruct you on some of the core social and psychological tenants that will dramatically improve your success with women. These tactics are merely the sides, however; they aren't the main course. To rely on these tactics alone is to stunt your own growth as a man and settle for a life of meaningless sex and lackluster connections.

The purpose of this book isn't to help you increase your "lay count," though that's a great goal if you want to ruin your life with an STD, unexpected pregnancy, or years of child support and legal battles. No, the true goal of this book is to change the very fabric of who you are and transform you into the kind of man that women highly desire and other men respect. To achieve this transformation, you must commit to walking the path that you'll learn here all the way to your new life.

I know you're probably thinking, "This all sounds great, but I don't know if I'm ready. I've tried improving my dating life before, why will this time be any different?" I understand your concerns.

In the next section, I'm going to walk you through a simple set of exercises that will help you eradicate those feelings of hesitation, uncertainty, and anxiety. Then we can replace them with a burning passion to go out, kick ass, and have the best time of your life.

THE PATH TO SUCCESS OR THE PATH TO COMFORT: CHOOSE WISELY

There was once a time in the not-so-distant past where the price for inaction was death. Our ancestors were born into a "do or die" world where the slow, timid, and weak were excised from the gene pool by either Mother Nature or rival tribes. This was a time when men were forced to make hard decisions and commit to their chosen journey with a fiery intensity.

Today, men have lost that fire. We live with an endless list of "shoulds," "it'd be nice tos," and "someday I wills." We lack conviction and clarity of purpose to make a real commitment to changing our lives. This ends now for you. Achieving the results you desire is possible, but it starts with taking a stand and deciding for yourself that you will go all in, make time to do the work, and reap rewards that last a lifetime.

To start, you must be brutally honest with yourself about the answers to three critical questions:

1. Why Are You Committed to This Journey?

If you don't have crystal clear clarity on why you are undertaking this journey, you will quit the second that challenges arise and, trust me, they will. So right now, this very second, I want you to write down exactly why you are 100% committed to this journey.

Take your time with it. Search your soul. This is NOT the time to BS your way through with half-assed answers—you'll only be hurting yourself. Really get into the raw and gritty details of why, in the famous words of the lyricist Marshall Mathers, "Success is your only motherf*cking option, failure's not."

What will happen if you go all in on this journey? Will you...

- Meet the woman of your dreams? Someone who is your best friend, your closest ally, and the person with whom you will build your empire and craft a lasting legacy?
- Find a partner with whom you can share life, start a family, and enjoy a lifelong bond?
- Enjoy the mind-blowing, body-shaking sex and deeply intimate connection you've been craving for so many years?

Now, I want you to go deeper. How will these changes benefit your life and make you a better man? Will you...

- Feel confidence and certainty in your abilities to attract the women that you desire and eradicate the feeling that you're not "enough" or that she's "out of your league?"
- Finally overcome your limiting beliefs and teach yourself that you are capable of ten times more than you believe?
- No longer feel like you are "settling" in your relationships and have the confidence that you are choosing your partner from a position of abundance?

Be as detailed in your answers as possible. The point of this exercise is to help you stack the positives of this journey so that you have your eyes on the prize and a powerful list of goals that you can turn to when adversity arises.

The goals are life changing on their own. I can promise you that, but only you have the power to determine *why* it's worth it.

2.   What will happen if you don't take this seriously?

With an understanding of the rewards from seeing this journey through, I want you to flip this script and ask yourself, "What negative consequences will I face if I don't take this seriously?" The answer shouldn't be as simple as, "I'll be single and lonely." Vividly imagine the absolute worst-case scenario that could happen if you don't take action. What's really at stake? Imagine…

- Watching porn and masturbating for the next twenty years and still being single.
- Seeing all of your friends getting married and having children while you wake up each morning with no one beside you.
- Seeing both of your parents pass without ever getting to experience the joy of having grandchildren because you weren't willing to take your relationships seriously today.
- Dying alone with no family, children, or loved ones to support you in your final days, with no one to pass on your legacy or even to show up at your funeral.
- Settling for a mediocre relationship and spending everyday fighting about trivial and insignificant matters with a woman and to whom you aren't attracted.
- Filing for divorce after divorce, losing half of your net worth each time. Sacrificing the custody of your children to your ex and her new partner and losing your dignity.
- Never experiencing what it feels like to truly be in love with the woman of your dreams and to wake up excited that you get to spend another day with the love of your life.

All of those are very realistic scenarios for men today. In fact, I'd argue that they are quickly becoming the norm. The good news, however, is that the growth you experience from this book can prevent that from happening, if you find the dedication to implement everything it teaches—even when you don't "feel" like it.

This is your life, and it's ending one second at a time. So get off your ass and stop waiting for the "perfect" time to take action... the time is now. You deserve to know what you are truly capable of and to transform into the most powerful version of yourself, a man capable of bending the world to his will and achieving the success and abundance he desires with high-quality women in his life. What could possibly be more important?

3. What are you willing to sacrifice to achieve your goal?

The reason that most people never achieve the goals they set is NOT because...

- They didn't write their goal the right way.
- They didn't chant their affirmations consistently enough.
- They didn't visualize their goal daily in front of a mirror.

These might help, but they aren't the determining factor. The reason people don't achieve the goals they set is because they aren't willing to put in the work and make the sacrifices required to achieve them. You should never set goals based on what you want, but upon *what you're willing to sacrifice to achieve them.*

You have the capacity to achieve anything you want in life, as long as you're willing to pay the price. Consider this: no matter what, you are going to experience pain in your life. You alone have the power to choose what pain that is, the pain of action or the pain of regret.

So right now, I want you to get VERY clear on the price you're willing to pay and the sacrifices you're willing to make to achieve the success you want with women. In order to live an incredible life and date the woman you desire, you will be forced to many sacrifices like:

- Your time: You will have to find the time to go out and socialize when you're tired, don't feel like it, or have other priorities that arise.
- Your money: Whether you're paying for a coach or entertainment expenses like travel, food, drinks for dates, or moving to a better location, you will have to invest money in this journey.
- Your energy: You can't go through the motions and expect extraordinary results. You must invest energy and effort into learning new skills, identifying your weaknesses and taking action to improve.
- Your ego: You will face rejection. You will be told "no" by women of lower social status. You will have to humble yourself and act as a student regardless of the success you've experienced in other areas of life.
- Your comfort: This journey is not easy. It will be as challenging as it is exciting. You will have to step out bravely and learn to take risks outside of your comfort zone.

These sacrifices must be acknowledged and accepted now so that you'll be ready for them when they arise on the journey. Accepting this will help you remain steadfast in your commitment to your goals. There's no price you can put on having the right woman to support you through your biggest challenges in life, who really "gets" you and pushes you to grow as a man. Now that you're sold on why you must take action now, let's dive into the basic strategy to help you meet the women you want.

YOUR NO B.S STRATEGY TO DATING THE WOMEN YOU WANT

This book is not filled with theory that sounds good in practice but has never been implemented in the real world. It is a proven strategy based on years of results that has been used by me and thousands of other men before you. This program is ready for you to use and reap its benefits.

All that is required from you is to show up and take action. To make the most out of this journey, it's important that you understand how this book was designed to be consumed. It's not meant to be read once, left on a bookshelf, and easily forgotten. This is an ongoing action guide to help you meet, attract, and keep the woman of your dreams.

I recommend that you read through the book once to gain a basic understanding of the framework behind it, then revisit each chapter after you begin your first 90-day sprint.

The goal of this "sprint" is incredibly straightforward. For ninety days, you're going to go out every week with one goal: to have two meaningful interactions with attractive women, exchange contact information, and follow up to ask her out.

The math here is shockingly simple. Two interactions a week for twelve weeks will lead to high quality interactions with twenty-four women. From there, you'll use what I share with you throughout this book to follow up and turn an average of ten of those interactions into actual dates. Of those dates, my experience has shown that you'll likely connect with five of those women on a deeper, more intimate level.

Then you'll "filter" through those women identifying the best match using strategies I'll reveal in Chapter six. If they pass your tests, you'll enjoy an ongoing casual relationship with three very high-quality women, allowing you to make decisions from a place of abundance and options, a place that most men have never experienced.

From there, you can continue filtering down until you find the one woman whom you want to date exclusively. This process will ensure that you are entering relationships with only the highest quality women who are the best fit for your life.

At the end of that ninety-day sprint, you can decide to either deepen the relationship with your existing partner(s) or you can take a short break then start a new sprint to achieve even higher levels of abundance (recommended).

After your first sprint, each successive sprint becomes easier and will lead to greater results because you are beginning it from a place of abundance with quality women *already* in your life. You'll feel less needy, freer, and more confident in your abilities, appealing to even more attractive women the second or third time around and beyond.

It will be much easier to have higher standards about the quality of women you allow into your life and you'll no longer have to endure flakey BS or pointless games from women. Instead, you can confidently walk away because you already have many other quality women in your life who have proven themselves to be more worthy of your time and energy. Each sprint will further this cycle and bring higher-level women into your life, compounding your abundance, skills and allowing you to attract the highest quality women possible.

At the conclusion of each sprint, you will complete the "Post Sprint Debrief" (Contained in the dating toolkit: knowledgeformen. com/dating-toolkit) to help you assess your progress, review what went well, decode what didn't, and prepare for your next sprint so that you experience even more growth the next time around. Then, simply rinse and repeat, enjoying an abundant dating life until you find a woman that you are ready to be exclusive with.

Now you might be thinking, "This sounds too simple. It can't really work for me, right?"

Well, it can. You see, most books tell you to go out indefinitely until you find a girlfriend. In my experience, however, this is unrealistic and unsustainable. You're likely a busy man with goals and aspirations that supersede your desire to meet new women—or at least, you should be if you're actively living an interesting life.

To go out every day is a prescription for burnout and boredom, not consistent results. Instead, you must remember that this is a skillset that can be learned step-by-step. By breaking down your journey into manageable phases, taking deliberate action, and reflecting on the process, you'll be able to discover what works for you and what doesn't.

This journey won't be perfect, and you won't have high-quality interactions with every woman that you encounter. However, if you will commit to it, I can promise that you will achieve greater results than you ever thought possible.

And for those of you who want additional support on what I believe to be the most exciting journey a man can ever embark on to get results faster, save time and have more fun adventures with attractive women then watch this presentation and learn more about how I can help you expedite your journey: knowledgeformen.com/live

CHAPTER 1

THE GROUNDED MAN

"Nobody can save you but yourself and you're worth saving. It's a war not easily won but if anything is worth winning then this is it."

- CHARLES BUKOWSKI

There is a silent cry from women all over the world: "Where have all the real men gone?"

Women are searching, *begging*, now more than ever for strong men who are willing to show up fully and lead them on the journey of a lifetime. Yet their cries go unanswered. As Thoreau said, "The masses of men lead lives of quiet desperation."

Today, real men—men with grit, backbone, and true "aliveness"—are a dying breed. The average man simply wakes up and clocks in at a 9-to-5 job that only pays the bills. He may even be a business owner drowning in stress and starving for connection. Then he comes home and buries his debilitating dissatisfaction with an endless stream of sports games, social media, porn, television, and video games. Men today aren't living, they're simply existing. And women have painfully noticed.

As bleak as it may sound, it's not entirely our fault. In the past 100 years, social, political, and economic forces have conspired together to create what is now a tragic reality for the modern man. Although feminism has helped women achieve much-needed and long overdue equality in the workforce, social and political spheres, it's also led to consequences we couldn't have foreseen.

Women are rising through the ranks of society at an unprecedented pace. They are graduating college at a higher rate than men, earning more money than ever before, and are no longer reliant on men for protection or financial support. Let me be clear, *these are all good things*! I do not wish to go backwards, and this rise in equality is, by far, one of the most important social achievements of the 20th and 21st centuries.

Although these changes in gender equality have led to a more egalitarian society and true freedom for both sexes, they have also led to an unexpected and, as of yet, unaddressed change in gender *roles*.

Now, more than ever before, men are confused about their place in society and how they are supposed to enter into relationships. What used to work in past generations no longer works, and men all over the world are left wondering what to do. They end up settling for subpar relationships or have completely given up.

It's no longer enough for a man to make a good salary and provide a house with a white picket fence for his future wife and 2.3 kids. Women can support themselves. They want more than a bread winner who will come home, turn on the TV, and call it a day. They *need* more than that.

Women don't just want a man who will pay the bills and provides a home, they want a man of character and substance who brings strength, adventure, and aliveness into their everyday realities.

The problem is that most men have lost their masculine edge that women deeply crave. We've become emotionally senile, mentally impotent, and spiritually castrated by the monotony of daily life.

We have no great wars to fight, no higher purpose to serve, and no great battles to win. Instead, we find ourselves lost, aimless, and lacking the "fire in the belly" that our forefathers used to overcome the challenges of life.

Our greatest war is a silent spiritual war for our own lives. We're not the heroes of our lives. We're zombies who devote little time or energy into building an incredible life, let alone meeting women. According to Professor Helen Fischer at Rutgers University, new research shows that men are, more than ever before, willing to knowingly settle into relationships with women whom they do not love (and in some cases can barely tolerate) in order to check the box "in a relationship" and be done with it.

But hope is not lost. From the ashes of old masculinity, there is a new breed of man emerging, a man filled with passion, vibrancy, and "aliveness." This is a man with purpose, backbone, and a mission that supersedes his own basic desires.

More importantly, it's a man that women are uncontrollably drawn to and other men begrudgingly respect. These old ways of being and showing up in the world are outdated, ineffective, and have long since run their course. I'm going to show you these archetypes for what they are so that you can consciously and definitively make the decision to choose the third and only viable path forward for men.

But for me to do this, we must first understand and examine the common archetypes within which most men mistakenly fall: the "Nice Guy" and the "Bad Boy."

THE THREE PATHS OF MODERN MASCULINITY

Men in the 21st century have been force-fed a lie through years of social and familial conditioning that there are only two types of men. We errantly believe that a man can only be a Nice Guy or a Bad Boy.

You don't need to look far to see evidence of how this false dichotomy has taken over the average man's life and led to years of frustration and stagnation. Everywhere I look I see men making comments like, "*I've always been a nice guy and I'm getting sick of being single and looked over. How can I become a "bad boy" so I can finally get women to notice me?"*

On the surface, this seems to make sense. If you take a quick look at the social dynamics in the modern dating game, there's plenty of evidence that assholes often *do* finish first.

"Nice guys" seem to continually come up short, maybe getting a few dates, a kiss, and—on those rare drunken nights—a phone number from an attractive woman. But they seem totally incapable of finding, attracting, and keeping a beautiful woman for the long term.

"Bad boys," on the other hand, seem to enjoy high levels of success and abundance in their dating lives, so much so that they regularly cheat on women most "nice guys" can't even imagine talking to. But when you peel back the layers of this issue, you will quickly realize that the picture that has been painted by society and the media is far from the reality.

Women don't *want* bad boys, they settle for them because they are the only men they can find who showcase *some* of the raw masculine qualities which they're uncontrollably attracted to. What women truly want, and what I'm going to teach you how to become in the ensuing chapters, is a third type of man. He's a man who marries both the empathy and compassion so readily exuded by the "nice guy" with the raw, masculine, primal characteristics and attitudes personified by the "bad boy."

I call this emerging breed of males the "Grounded Man."

A NICE GUY, BAD BOY, AND GROUNDED MAN WALK INTO A BAR...

To understand the true difference between these three types of men, we must go beyond a superficial glance and understand the core motives and mindsets behind each one.

The Nice Guy:
Potentially the greatest misnomer of our time, the "Nice Guy" is anything but nice. Although his outward actions and behaviors are personified by his people-pleasing nature and genial attitude, when you look under

the hood, you quickly realize that his "niceness" is nothing more than a socially acceptable manifestation of extreme selfishness and insecurity.

A "Nice Guy" isn't nice because that's who he is. His others-focused behavior is driven by his *need* to be liked and approved of by others at the expense of his own self-worth. He operates under the mindset that, "If I do enough nice things, people will like me and then covertly I can get what I want from them." This behavior is characterized by the men who shower women with being overly agreeable, free drinks, expensive gifts, and an inability to stand up for himself. He is unwilling and unable to set healthy boundaries and as a result becomes a walking doormat for others to abuse.

He does not respect himself and instead looks to others for validation, hoping that others will approve of him and thus validate his self-worth. He lacks the core backbone and sense of self-confidence that is required to be a healthy, masculine man. He puts the needs of others before his own, not because he *wants* to but because he believes this is the only way to get his needs met. Ironically, it is these very behaviors and attitudes that cause the nice guy to lose the respect of other men and of course—ding, ding, ding!—attractive women.

Instead of respecting him, valuing him, and seeing him as an ally, other men view the "nice guy" as a weak errand boy. He serves no other purpose than to satisfy their own desires and be used as a tool to get what they want.

Instead of feeling attracted to him and having the "spark" of sexual chemistry that nice guys believe their behavior will result in, women view him as an emasculated man who lacks the grit and backbone they crave. Thus, he stands no chance of creating long-term attraction.

Nice guys do not love, respect, or care for themselves enough and as a result, other people do not love, respect, or care for them, either. He's caught in a vicious trap and thinks that if he can do enough nice things for others, then other people will finally like him. But sadly, this is not the case. He fails to realize that women cannot *feel* attraction for men they can easily control and manipulate. And after enough pain, nice guys start to believe the polar opposite must be the path to getting what they want.

The Bad Boy:

Unlike the nice guy, a true bad boy doesn't care about other people. He focuses only on himself, his own desires, and his own aims. Ironically, this bastardized sense of self-worth and respect is exactly what draws women to him. It's also what turns all of his relationships over time into a smoldering pile of rubble.

The bad boy, much like the nice guy, lacks a true and deep sense of self-worth, respect, and love. He believes this is a "dog eat dog" world and that the only way to achieve lasting success is to take from others and manipulate them into doing his will at their expense. A key difference between the nice guy and the bad boy is that the bad boy *owns* his selfish and egocentric desire with verbal and sometimes physical force.

Whereas the nice guy attempts to "earn" the approval of others through favors, niceties, and blatant lies ("no really, those shoes look *great* on you!"), the bad boy owns and accepts his selfish desires and takes them to the extreme ("those things are absolutely awful, do you have no sense of style?"). He cares only about himself and his own well-being; worse, he's well aware and often *proud* of it. His modus operandi is, "I look out for myself and I use other people to get what I want in this world. I don't care if they like me or not as long as I'm able to win."

I'll be the first to say it. This personality style works in the short-term. Bad boys are often more successful in their careers, business, and with women. But over the long term, their self-centered attitude compounds and the weight of their backstabbing, selfishness, and ego-driven subterfuge become an unbreakable chain. It will eventually prevent them from achieving lasting satisfaction, deep personal connection, and fulfillment in the long term.

They treat women as objects of sexual conquest, rarely if ever enjoying meaningful connection. They treat other men as pawns in their own game and have no qualms about using manipulation, subversion, and sometimes sociopathic social strategies to accomplish their aims.

They don't care about achieving win-win scenarios for others as they only want a win for themselves, often at the detriment of others. A bad boy is just as insecure and lacking as the nice guy. However, their insecure attitude manifests as a polar opposite.

Desperately trying to feel like he's enough, the bad boy will use every tool at his disposal to elevate his status and appear externally like he's winning at the game of life. Ultimately, it leads him to lose close relationships along the way, but as long as he's "ahead," it's justified.

The Grounded Man:

Finally, we arrive at third path. Unlike the Nice Guy or Bad Boy, the Grounded Man does not enter into any conversation or interaction with the desire to get *anything*. Instead, he shows up to give because he is already fulfilled internally.

A Grounded Man has cultivated high levels of self-love, esteem, and confidence, and he doesn't need the approval of anyone (man or woman) to validate his self-worth. He knows who he is, what he stands for, and what he wants. And he lives these values every day without shame or compromise.

He comes from a place of such deep emotional and spiritual abundance that he no longer needs to take from others to get what he wants. Instead—because he has taken care of himself first in a healthy and productive way—he is able to give to others freely while still upholding appropriate boundaries for himself. He is not an asshole like the Bad Boy who will do anything in his power to get what he wants. Nor is he a Nice Guy who will bend over backwards or let others walk over him to get what he wants.

Instead, he tries to make every situation a win-win. He doesn't want to win at the expense of others and he knows that life is a team sport that cannot be won in isolation. He genuinely wants to see others thrive because he knows when everyone around him is thriving, so is he. His guiding principle in life is simple.

"I am enough. I am complete. I am worthy. I give to others because I'm already fulfilled and I seek win-win in all interactions."

The Grounded Man respects himself, respects others, and therefore, is respected by others. He offers more value than he takes value, which makes him non-needy, approval-seeking, or clingy to other people, especially women. He strives to give to others and not always get from others, yet he is comfortable with receiving as well.

Imagine a group of people stranded on an island. The first one to die would be the nice guy because he would let himself get taken advantage of in order to get approval; the bad boy would show promise in the beginning with his boldness and ability to loftily stand up for himself but then the group would quickly realize he only cares about himself. Like a lone wolf, he would be cast out by the group. However, the Grounded Man would be prized as the leader since he comes from a position of strength yet focuses on the success of the entire group, not just himself.

The Grounded Man is a man of action and confidence. He's bold, direct, and clear in his wants and intentions. Now, which man would you want your daughter or niece to date?

- The Nice Guy who is walked over by women to gain approval.
- The Bad Boy who walks over women to feed his damaged ego.
- The Grounded Man who walks with women to lead them.

The answer is obvious. The Grounded Man makes a woman feel safe and secure, which allows her to fall into her feminine, the place where deep attraction and even love can grow. In the following sections of this chapter, I'm going to share the core characteristics and traits that allow *any* man to transition from a nice guy or bad boy into a Grounded Man.

RALPH WALDO EMERSON'S GREATEST LESSON ON BECOMING A GROUNDED MAN

Not too long ago, our ancestors faced death on a regular basis. To survive during the harsh times in which our forefathers resided, self-reliance wasn't optional, but rather it was mandatory for survival. They either hunted and killed their own food or bartered for it with things they'd handcrafted. They learned to defend themselves or they were eaten by a predator in their sleep. They had the strength and autonomy to fight for themselves or died at the hands of stronger men. The self-reliant survived and the weak perished. It was literally do or die.

Today, in every developed country, technological advancements and organized social constructions have all but eliminated the need for self-reliance. Failure is no longer fatal, comfort is commonplace, and strength is no longer a necessity. Don't get me wrong, this progress is great, and I am eternally grateful to have clean running water, modern medicine and first responders. The 21st century is a truly great time to be alive.

However, instead of *using* these technological advancements and treating them as tools designed to complement and streamline a self-reliant life, we've become *controlled* by them, weakening our resolve and eroding our capacity for independence as men.

As the saying goes, "*Hard times create strong men. Strong men create good times. Good times create weak men. And weak men create hard times.*"

Today, we have become weak men. We no longer feel the pull of self-reliance and the call of adventure and exploration. We are content to rest our heads in a cradle of socially constructed safety nets while mainstream culture and incessant consumerism from billion-dollar corporations coddle us into spiritual castration. We have given our power away to others, turning to everyone except ourselves when faced with deep adversity and challenges... or even trivial ones.

Instead of responding to boredom with the spirit of creative energy that lead our forefathers to build monuments, create works of art, and tame vast swathes of wilderness, we pull out our smartphones and begin mindlessly scrolling our lives away glued to a little screen.

Instead of conquering, building, and learning, we spend our finite hours double-tapping pictures of women we'll never meet, places we'll never visit, and things we'll never own. Rather than addressing our challenges head on, we flee from them, sedating our miseries with drugs, alcohol, TV, video games, and streaming porn, all of which are more accessible than ever. And through the centuries of seemingly innocuous concessions and comfort-driven compromises, men have become convinced that the solution to their problems lies outside of themselves and that they are victims in society. But they don't, and you aren't.

To become a Grounded Man, you must embrace the fact that you—and you alone—hold the key to your own liberation. You are both the jailor and the prisoner, and to free yourself from your mind-made prison you must cultivate radical self-reliance. You must become self-reliant in your own thoughts, capabilities, and judgements. You have to be willing to take total responsibility for yourself and your actions and become the sole arbiter of your future and fate. Although this might sound lofty, esoteric, and even unattainable, I assure you it's not. In its simplest form, self-reliance means that you believe *you* are responsible for yourself, your successes, and yes, even your failures.

You cannot blame external circumstances on your lack of results, or praise "luck" and fortune when you achieve your goals. You know that you and only you are responsible for your actions and their outcomes. You must think for yourself, have your own place, handle your finances, take care of your body, and make decisions based on *your* values and vision, not the designs of others.

Yes, you can turn to friends and mentors for wisdom and feedback, but the word of others must not be taken as gospel. You must always have the final say.

The rewards for adopting this mindset, although not immediately obvious, are incalculable. By becoming totally self-reliant, you remove all neediness and validation-driven behavior. When a man lacks self-reliance, the actual ability to care for himself, he enters into interactions with attractive women while exuding neediness. In turn, she senses his ulterior motives. He has not given himself happiness, validation, and worthiness and, as a result, cannot give these positive emotions to the individuals with whom he interacts.

Instead, he tries to take them from others, using them as tools to help him finally feel as if he's "enough." When a man's frame of mind is needy and validation-driven, he has literally nothing to offer others, eliminating all chances of connection, long-term attraction, and intimacy.

By cultivating and practicing an uncommon degree of self-reliance, you will stand out from the masses of men wandering aimlessly through life with no control over themselves or their futures. When you embrace your individuality and authentically express who you are to the world without any fear of reprisal—since you no longer need the approval of others for happiness and fulfillment—you will achieve true freedom and the type of success that cannot be purchased or gained from material items.

You must own who you are, imperfections and all, and love yourself for who you are today while taking responsibility for who you will become in the future. From this frame, you will experience a complete shift in the way that you perceive and interact with the women who interest you.

You want the girl, but you don't need the girl.

You will no longer be dependent or reliant on any one person, relationship, or encounter for validation because you will be capable of creating new relationships if necessary. *You validate yourself.*

The worry, anxiety, and dread that you used to feel will be gone, and in its place, you'll find a quiet confidence and strength giving you permission to be, do, and say the things that are authentically and uniquely *you*. When you can show up authentically and with a feeling of total self-reliance, attraction becomes a forgone conclusion.

The right women will be pulled into your life like flecks of iron to a magnet, and the wrong women—those whose values and personalities are incongruent with your own—will filter themselves out, saving you years (no really, *years*) of pain and heartache. From this place, a man can achieve true abundance and lasting success with the women for whom you yearn. However, that's only a small piece of the puzzle of becoming a Grounded Man.

Because self-reliance, like anything that is taken to an extreme, becomes dangerous when left unchecked and can lead to a transition into the Bad Boy. When you become totally self-reliant but lack a higher purpose beyond your own pleasure, then isolation, narcissism, and an over-inflated ego are inevitable.

To counteract these darker elements of independence and autonomy, you must step into the light and find your purpose.

LIVE YOUR PURPOSE OR DIE TRYING

For millennia, the purpose of every individual in our species was simple… survive long enough to reproduce. We didn't sit in our caves for hours fretting about our place in the universe or how our actions impacted some grand cosmic scheme against us. That sort of mental masturbation did not exist. Instead, we hunted and foraged for food, fought off rival tribes and hungry predators, had sex in hopes of passing on our genes, and—if we were lucky—made it through the night so we could wake up and do it all over again.

Today, with the creature comforts of the industrial and technological revolutions, we have the unprecedented opportunity to contemplate and create a purpose that is, more or less, unique to us. And that's the most important part.

Your purpose is something that *you* create, something upon which *you* decide, something that is unique, exciting, and engaging to *you.* Your purpose is your mission, your life's work, your reason for waking up in the morning and for staying awake late into the night. It is something important, noble, and beautiful enough to possibly die for.

This quest of developing your purpose *is* a task to which you must fully commit yourself. Without a concrete purpose intentionally crafted and meticulously decided upon by *you,* your purpose becomes purely biological. Instead of having a grand goal to work for with high ambition, your purpose defaults into nothing more than sex and survival. A limited, bland, and unfulfilling purpose if there ever was one.

Ironically, this biology-driven purpose makes men weak. Neediness and scarcity run rampantly through their daily lives, leaving them to think only about their next lay or next paycheck or next "hit" that will briefly pull them out of their shallow existences. They're focused solely on what they can get for themselves, stuck in a survival mentality and the thought of giving to others or creating anything of value rarely enters their minds. From this frame, attracting high quality women is impossible.

Without a purpose, you walk through the world reacting to society, falling for vices like entertainment, alcohol,

drugs, and the easiest "lay". You're searching for pleasure, instant gratification, and ways to kill time because— when it's all said and done—your life is meaningless.

And make no mistake, the very act of killing time signifies that you are declining and preparing for an early grave. But it doesn't have to be this way. You can decide *today* to create a purpose for yourself and begin living a 10/10 life in pursuit of a higher calling. It all starts by gaining crystal-clear clarity on who you are and what you want out of your *one* life.

Questions to contemplate deeply:

- What do you want to create?
- Who do you want to help?
- What problem makes you angry that you would like to solve?
- What makes you come alive?
- How do you want to be remembered?
- What is something bigger than yourself? Something so viscerally important and significant to *you* that you would be willing to die for it?

Greatness mandates purpose. Without a strong purpose that inspires you and livens your soul, the hard work, time and discipline required to rise through the ranks will feel like a chore instead of a purpose. Your desire for a greater life, greater abundance of women, more money, more success, and more pleasure are the spark that will ignite a fire under you. But understand this: *a strong purpose* is the fuel that will keep that fire burning for years and decades to come. It serves not only as a fuel for your life and ambition, but a fuel for the flame of attraction.

Women are drawn to men of purpose, and with good reason. Purposeful men are the movers, shakers, and leaders of the world. They are the men who move mountains, carve canals from the earth, explore the deepest recesses of the planet, and create the most magnificent works of art and companies the world has ever seen. *And attractive women find them deadly irresistible. Why?*

Purpose eradicates neediness and approval-seeking behavior because a man is no longer dependent on any social interaction for approval, from men or women. He's on a mission, one that is more important than a relationship, and that makes women value him even more.

Furthermore, men of purpose tend to lead lives that are far more interesting and engaging than men who follow the societal script of "9 to 5 and get by." Instead of sitting behind a screen watching other men live and pursue their best lives, a man of purpose is out in the world creating, building, and transcending the banalities of human existence by turning his life into the grandest of adventures.

And women want to be a part of the adventure. But the question still remains, "How do you create this sense of purpose in your life?" Despite what the self-help gurus and purported "experts" would have you believe, the answer is quite simple: *Take risks and try new things as often as possible.*

If you like it, you stick with it through the tedious plateaus. You get mentors with years of experience. Slowly, this new thing grows to the point where you care deeply about it. Then, you get better at it, try to master it, and it becomes a part of who you are.

Or it doesn't. But you still gained a wealth of knowledge from having tried. You move on to another new thing as a more interesting, more educated, and more experienced man.

You will never create a purpose without attempting different activities and vocations that you *don't* love. You'll never know the things which *could* become your purpose until you first try them. But remember, there is never a moment wasted that was spent in learning and developing, even if it turns out not to be your purpose.

You cannot find your purpose by researching it online. You only discover it by experiencing it in the real world. So set sail, start the adventure, and enjoy the roller coaster of life. Stop being frustrated that you don't know your purpose and go create one by living your life and doing the things you've only imagined doing.

Now, if you are still struggling to determine *a* purpose (because there is no singular purpose that will lead your life), the ambiguity you feel is likely rooted in your lack of concrete values and a fundamental lack of self-awareness.

Let's change that.

THE BACKBONE OF YOUR MASCULINITY

A Grounded Man does not draw his strength and fortitude from his physical dominance, intellectual superiority, or a long history of impressive accomplishments. While he may pride himself on for those things, they are not the backbone of what makes him the man he is. Instead, a Grounded Man pulls his strength and predicates all of his decisions on one thing and one thing only. His values.

Unlike the masses of men who aimlessly wade through life lacking both purpose and backbone, the Grounded Man consciously decides what is important to him and then builds his life around those things. He knows what he wants out of life and what he is willing to do in order to achieve it. At the same time, he understands what he isn't willing to do or tolerate. A strong value system improves and simplifies your life in every way possible.

For example, my values in no particular order are:

- Aliveness and adventure
- Love
- Financial freedom
- Friendship and family
- Health
- Personal growth
- Impact and contribution
- Creativity

These values are my guiding light. They determine what I will and will not allow and how I live on a daily basis. Believe it or not, your values are not only the driving force in your life, they are also your filtration system for determining the type of women that you will allow into your life.

We'll talk more about understanding the right woman in chapter six, but suffice to say, the women you are dating *must* share similar values or be removed from your life. Never settle for a woman with unequal values simply because she is attractive. Without compatible values, the relationship won't work in the long run and she won't respect you because you don't stand up for your own values.

And this is where most single men have it completely wrong. They desperately search for a relationship with someone who will like *them* then try to mold them into their life and force their values onto her instead of finding someone who naturally and happily fits into their lives.

If you believe that "any attractive woman will do" (thinking with your penis is always a recipe for long-term disaster), you probably bounce from relationship to relationship, unable to find a woman who is a good match.

If you fall for a woman simply because she has nice breasts and a sexy butt you will always be frustrated. To date the woman of your dreams, you must look beyond her outer beauty and see her for who she really is. It's unfair to her and fruitless for you to do otherwise.

Doing so, however, requires that you first deepen your understanding of who *you* are. You must cultivate radical self-awareness—hacking away at the social conditioning and subconscious clutter that has directed your life until this point and leaving only that which is authentically *you*.

By developing this uncommon level of self-knowledge, you will be able to show up in the world, not as Mr. Agreeable or Mr. Forceful but as a strong Grounded Man who knows exactly what he wants, who he is, and what he stands for in life. From this place, you can clearly see who people are at their core and refuse to tolerate bullshit, low-class behavior, or disrespect that prevents you from reclaiming the power that is rightfully yours. This is the place from which all attraction—and indeed, all *happiness*—is born.

In addition to being aware of your *values*, you must live in alignment to them and understand that this is also a great deal of *value* to offer to a woman; that's something most men forget the second an attractive woman walks into a room. Right now, before you move on to the next section, write down a list of the character traits, skills, interests, and accomplishments that make *you* a win for *her*.

For example:

1. I'm highly alive, constantly trying new things, and pursuing new interests and hobbies.
2. I own a business that I *love,* provide a high-level of financial security, and can work from anywhere in the world while helping other people transform their lives.
3. I have a well-rounded social circle filled with amazing friends, mentors, family members, and other people that any woman would be lucky to meet.
4. I prioritize my health, treating my body like a temple on weekdays and a playground on weekends. I'm fit, stable, and capable in mind, body, and spirit.
5. I am committed to my own personal development and improving the lives of everyone around me personally and professionally.

When you know who you are, what you offer, what you stand for, and are willing to live your life by *your* values, you show up more powerfully in the world. From this frame and with this level of energy, you will not walk around wondering what to say, how to act, or if someone likes you.

Instead, you will know your value and simply *be.* You will have a deep, visceral belief that your presence improves the lives of others and that you offer value that other people need. This belief and certainty in yourself will make a lasting impression on the women with whom you interact.

As you continue down this path, you will begin to deepen your masculine energy and become the type of man to whom women are irresistibly drawn. To enhance this further, you must understand the power of polarity and the unconscious dance of the masculine and feminine that is at play in every interaction.

If you fail to embrace this, you miss the gold right in front of you—the real *her.*

EMBRACING YOUR
MASCULINE ENERGY

Masculinity, taken to negative extremes, is now viewed as toxic. Political pundits and social justice warriors claim that masculinity is the poison that is corroding Western society. Yet all of these individuals lose sight of the forest through the trees.

There is a difference between genuine masculinity and this "toxic" masculinity that keyboard warriors argue about. Real, healthy, society-advancing masculinity has been hijacked and bastardized into something about which we only speak in hushed tones, while *true* masculinity is at the very heart of all attraction.

When I refer to masculinity, I am not referring to the violent, chest-beating, war-mongering masculinity with which our culture is simultaneously enamored and repulsed. Toxic masculinity, as the term defines it, is the worst of everything about being a man, the attempt to use "boys will be boys" as an excuse for everything from lack of performance to domestic abuse to sexual assault.

Instead, I'm referring to the masculine *energy*, the driving force that causes men and women alike to take bold action, embrace risk, and become creators and captains of their destinies. Masculine energy—although possessed by both men and women—is the very core of what attracts feminine women. It's being on your path, taking action, and driving towards the life you want.

> **By embracing your masculine energy, you open the doors for the women in your life to offer their feminine energy, where true attraction begins.**

When you advance your masculine energy, you subconsciously communicate to those around you—both men and women—that you are capable of handling whatever shit storm may arise. The presence of strong masculine energy puts others at ease and allows women to feel safe enough to let down the false front the toxic masculinity causes and embrace their feminine energy.

They no longer need to have their guard raised or feel as if they must lead the interaction. Instead, they are free to be themselves. Sensual. Playful. Beautiful. Caring. Nurturing. It is in this state and *only* in this state that true attraction can occur. Of course, having masculine energy is not the only element of attraction. Rather that it allows for attraction to unfold.

When a woman is in her masculine state, it's because she feels the need to protect herself. She is fearful, unsure of the character and quality of the men around her. That means she is unable to *experience* attraction because she does not feel safe in her surroundings. The only way for a woman to escape her masculine is to be in the presence of a man who is fully in *his* masculine.

Healthy masculine energy is primarily driven by two factors: freedom and dominance. It is in your nature as a man to be free, primal, and wild while exercising self-control. When you cultivate true masculinity and develop the self-reliance required to bring it into the world, you will stop searching for validation and approval outside of yourself. Your ego will dissolve in the vat of raw masculine energy and you will become truly free.

Dominance is another term that has been corrupted by a society hell-bent on stripping away what is good and strong in men, but—in its simplest, purest form—it means having power and influence to achieve a desired goal.

Everything you do in your life should move you towards a more empowering future and the attainment of your goals (improve health, wealth, relationships, personal growth, adventure, etc). If a person or activity does not match your values or push you towards a greater future, then you use your power and influence to remove it from your life. Eliminate the unnecessary and do *only* the things that bring you fulfillment and satisfaction in order to make you a better man. *That* is dominance.

If your actions are met with a bad reaction, you don't change your actions. Rather, you maintain them and keep going. The disdain and disapproval of other people along your path is inevitable but as long as you show respect and empathy, you have every right to make your opinions known and stand up for yourself.

The way to cultivate dominance and a strong masculine energy is with time, awareness and persistence. Slowly start to assert yourself more in social interactions to get your needs met in a respectful way.

If your boss makes an unreasonable request, stand up for yourself and refuse to allow them to take advantage of you. If you show up to the doctor's office for a scheduled appointment and are forced to wait for 30 minutes or longer, get up and say something; barring a life-threatening emergency that has taken the doctor's time, there's no excuse to sit back and silently wait.

If a woman expresses an opinion or acts in a way that is unacceptable, call her out on the bad behavior. If she is mean to the service staff or makes disparaging remarks about a particular group or individual, *say something*. In short, if she acts in a way contrary to your values, let her know.

The great irony is that many women are so used to having their way with men that the very act of standing up to her unconsciously deepens her attraction for you. At least, that will be true of a woman of worth and quality. Only a shallow, selfish person would respond negatively to a polite but direct message about your values.

It can be difficult to fully embrace your masculine side when you don't feel worthy of being dominant and free. You fear that others won't respond well if you assert your boundaries, thoughts, and feelings.

This becomes natural and effortless once you shift from telling yourself that you *are* this type of man to growing into the man that you *want* to become. Here's how to do that...

THE #1 INVESTMENT THAT DELIVERS THE HIGHEST RETURNS

Over the past few centuries, we've experienced the rise and fall of different assets and investments. Gold, oil, stocks, real estate, and cryptocurrencies have all risen and fallen with market fluctuations and changing times. However, there is one investment—an investment used by a small group of men—that *never* loses its value. Its value is not contingent on the market, social structures, or the political ecosystem.

It simply compounds day in and day out, appreciating in value indefinitely. Sounds like a great investment, right? It's investing in…you. The better you become, the more value you can offer to others and the less needy you will be. By investing in yourself—no, I don't mean buying a new watch or fancy car—you are growing and improving your life. You are unlocking new skills, talents, and abilities and gaining access to networks, locations, and resources that you previously could not. Every personal investment you make increases your experience and grants you access to new levels of success.

In your own life, you are the most important person there will ever be. Therefore, you should prioritize *your* life: your health, finances, education, relationships, and personal growth, everything that is important to you. You cannot put the needs of others before your own or go out to meet women in hopes that one of them will *make* you happy and finally fulfill you.

You need to make yourself happy first so that you're coming from a place of non-neediness and self-love. This investment allows you to offer her pure value versus taking value from her (and the weight is not all on your shoulders as she should be investing in herself too).

Always invest in yourself, not selfishly in order to one up others and boost your ego, but in a healthy way that recognizes you have more value to offer the world. If people think you're boring, then it's because you don't do enough with your life and you're not challenging yourself. Stop sitting around doing the same things and start embarking on new adventures!

You become a more interesting person by trying new things, respectfully making your opinions known, trying things most people haven't done, going places where others haven't been, doing things differently, reading more books, expanding your horizons, and always pushing yourself to the edge of your comfort zone.

Life is meant to be lived, not watched from the sidelines or on a little screen. Read philosophy by Aristotle, Seneca, and Lao Tzu. Listen to different styles of music and learn to appreciate art. Try martial arts. Live in a new city or country. Try a new job or start a side hustle you're passionate about. Do whatever interests you and develop a wide breadth of skills and knowledge. Travel as frequently and intensely as you can. Traveling exposes you to challenges, cultures, and opportunities that would require a lifetime to have in one location.

Adopt the mindset of ABL, which stands for *always be learning*. Wherever you are, there is something to learn, whether you're in traffic, walking to your car, or in the gym working out. I'm not just talking about listening to a podcast but viewing the world through the lens of a student, someone with fresh, innocent eyes. This one trick will make the world a much more interesting place, and boring locations will suddenly become areas of exploration and growth.

If you want to be successful at dating, you've got to become curious about the world around you so that you become a more well-rounded and interesting person. Start by dating yourself; get lost in your own curiosity and share your adventures with others as you go through life.

However much you invest in yourself and your growth, the more interesting you will become and the more value you can ultimately share with others. And the more value you offer, the more attractive you are to higher quality men and women.

> **Success with women isn't about manipulating them to like you. It's about genuinely being a win for her by living an interesting and adventurous life that she's happy to join.**

You're probably thinking that you don't have the time to embark on these adventures or really change your life. You're too busy focusing on growing your business or advancing your career, and those things are the 80/20 that will attract women. Right?

Women seem to think differently.

CHASING MONEY IS NOT THE ANSWER

One of the most common objections from other men when I share the importance of this journey is, "That all sounds nice, Andrew, but I'm focusing on my career right now and I don't have time for women."

I used to think the same way, so I understand. Through decades of social conditioning, we've been led to believe that women crave a wealthy man. If you don't have at least six-figures in the bank and a high net worth, you might as well just keep walking. No woman of substance is going to be interested, right?

Wrong. You don't need to have a high income or net worth to attract quality women. You simply need to have your life together, be grounded, live an adventurous life, and continually take action to propel you towards the life you want. It's okay if you're making $50k per year or less. It doesn't mean you can't date quality women today. However, you must not be content with earning a low wage or living in stagnation forever; you must be actively growing and climbing a ladder that you've built for yourself.

That's the key point. Not the ladder designed by society, some corporate company or self-proclaimed social media "guru" but one designed uniquely *by yourself for yourself,* to fulfill you the way you want to be fulfilled. You might be stocking shelves, working in a small cubicle, or doing something that pays well yet drains your soul, but you can still build something on the side. It's this very drive, hunger, and ambition that women are attracted to—more so than success itself.

I know men with greater net worth's than Hollywood celebrities, yet they still struggle with women and in their relationships. Believe it or not, it's hard to find a rich man who also has a stunning, intelligent woman by his side. Being successful in career or business doesn't necessarily translate to instant success with women contrary to what most men believe. Remember, dating and social dynamics is a skill set, if it's not developed then a poor dating life follows.

What women can find attractive is seeing you grow and progress as a man. A man going from a 400-square foot-apartment in a so-so job to a sprawling beach house and a thriving career is incredibly attractive for a woman to witness. Now, many men will claim that they "aren't ready" for a woman until they hit a certain benchmark in their career or have a certain figure in the bank. This is bullshit, nothing more than an excuse to put off this journey, experiencing rejection, and avoid shaking up their lives. What's worse, this excuse leads men down a dark path of workaholism and ego-fueled overachievement that leaves them with fewer dating options, less time to develop this skill, which likely leads to settling or subpar relationships.

Think about it like this: when men delay investing in their romantic lives, they end up selecting the first woman who's "good enough" or worse, they stay single because their inflated egos let them believe that attractive women should come to them solely because they have money—without questioning the type of man they are. Again, women can provide for themselves just fine today, so leading with money as your main value proposition to a quality woman is becoming increasingly less effective.

By settling for a subpar relationship, everything else in their lives suffer. The stress from their relationships damages the quality of their work, their decision-making ability, and the growth of their income. Their health starts to suffer through junk food, tobacco, drugs, or alcohol to numb the pain of a shoddy romantic life.

Eventually, the decision to settle compounds until one day it implodes. The wife files for divorce, is entitled to half of his net worth, and leaves him to pay child support for years while his children are raised by another man. Decades of hard work and dedication focused on a career and financial success amounts to very little in the end and can leave the man worse off than when he started.

Settling is a short-term escape into comfort followed by years of pain, misery, and regret. Nothing will have a more profound impact on your life, happiness, income, and career than finding the right partner in life.

With the right woman by your side, everything flows. You have the ability to focus deeper on your work with her support and love, you won't have to spend every weekend night trying to "get some" through shallow interactions, you won't face the never-ending stream of emotional nonsense found in toxic relationships.

Don't believe me? You'd rather work harder, spend more time in the office, and chase more zeros, thinking the highest quality women are waiting for you and it will solve your romantic problems?

Then I implore you to read this next section very carefully.

THE MOST IMPORTANT DECISION
A MAN CAN EVER MAKE

The Grounded Man understands that the right woman will fuel an even greater life, *not* take away from it. I know men who will avoid going on this journey and undertaking this rite of passage because they "don't have the time."

They are pursuing their career, business, or passions with such fire and enthusiasm that they never slow down, look around, and consider the value that the right woman would have in their life versus the current project or next deal they're working on. Men often forget that our lives are built on relationships, not around them.

There's nothing wrong with deciding that you don't want a committed relationship, enjoying an abundance of new women and experiences, and living the bachelor lifestyle for a time. I know a lot of men who enjoy this type of life and wouldn't have it any other way.

However, most of us don't fall into this category. We *want* someone with whom we can share our lives. We want someone with whom we can build a real future. We want someone to be there on the journey to support us when times are hard and celebrate with us when they're good.

Yet so many men put off one of the most important decisions they'll ever make in order to add another zero to their bank balance or have a "C" before their job title and have the corner office. But they're missing the point entirely.

Your relationships are the foundation of your life, and there's no more important relationship than the person with whom you choose to share your life with. There is no decision that is more profound and life changing than finding an individual with whom you're in love.

With the right woman by your side, your entire life experience is amplified. You will regain your fire and motivation. She will make your day-to-day life easier and more fulfilling. She will support you when you encounter obstacles. You aren't just picking a romantic lover. You're picking a cofounder in the most important venture you'll ever take part in... your life.

You're free to focus all of your time and attention on building an amazing life together and creating an exciting future. Why put off one of the most important decisions of your life until "someday?" Why wait until everything else is perfect to pursue the right woman when the right woman is the very thing that will help you magnify the rest of your life?

No, you shouldn't settle for the first relationship that presents itself or date any woman who meets the minimum standards. What you sacrifice when you commit to another person is just as immense as what you gain.

So you'd better be damn sure that it's the right person. It must be a win-win scenario where you are both loyal, committed, and able to operate independently of one another, otherwise your relationship will devolve into a toxic, codependent mess that will make every aspect of your life a living hell. Being with the wrong woman is a surefire way to defeat your mission, making you feel further lost and out of touch with yourself as a man. The wrong woman will not assist you, support you, or inspire you to achieve your full potential. She will drain you of your life force, energy, and resources.

Think about the times in your life that you've been broken up with, or when you dated women who weren't the right fit. You likely suffered simultaneously in life, too. You didn't perform at your highest level with an excitement for life and a clear reason why you got out of bed. Something was always lacking, a weight inside your core dragging you down.

But if you follow the path I will lay out for you, if you're willing to embark on this journey, commit to solving this area of your life, and find the woman that you want to build a life with, *life becomes better.*

You don't need to make more money before you can enter an incredible relationship. You don't need the promotion. You don't need half a million in the bank. You simply need to commit to going all in and trust that, if you do it intentionally, you'll come out the other side a stronger, more capable, and more Grounded Man. You can go through the journey of life with the best partner, friend and lover that you could ever hope for.

But to successfully accomplish this goal, you'll need the right team around you. You will need to build a powerful social circle that will support your goals and help you achieve your aims. Fortunately, this is easier than most people imagine.

HOW TO AMPLIFY YOUR ATTRACTIVENESS AND VALUE AS A MAN

The men I know who have the most attractive, high-quality women are the men who have an abundant social life and have strong social skills with both men and women. Women are attracted to men in a position of leadership within a group of men and women. Social proof is one of the most powerful forms of sexual preselection for women. Social proof is *the* fastest way to hack attraction because it instantly makes women feel safe with you and see you as a man of power, authority and leadership.

And the best part? You don't have to be an extroverted life of the party type of guy. She simply wants to see that others respect, value, and have approved of you already. She wants *some* sort of proof that you aren't a creep who will end up stalking her like men in her past have.

Now, you still need to initiate, meet, and interact with the women you desire—and you *can* achieve an abundant dating life by yourself—but having an established, fun social circle which you can bring her into will dramatically streamline the process. You will rarely see a man who lacks social skills and good friends also have a high-quality partner. When you avoid working on this area of your life or you prioritize your romantic life *before* your social life, you are fighting an uphill battle.

If you struggle to make friends with other men or women in whom you have no sexual interest, you will also struggle with adding value to the women you desire. View your social life as your training ground to develop your social skills. It's a low-stakes environment where you have the opportunity to add value, express yourself, and share your unique views and values with others without the pressure of attraction.

When you are around friends, male or female, you gain firsthand experience at adding value to others without expectations. You learn how to assert yourself in an appropriate way and how to express your authentic self without fear or shame. Furthermore, a healthy and abundant social life directly improves the quality of your romantic life. Human beings are hardwired to get happiness, connection, and validation from their social circle and romantic partners. When you lack these things from your social circle, you will compensate by getting all of these needs met by your romantic partner. Inevitably, that will lead to neediness, clinginess, and weakness.

A strong social life is a like a balanced investment portfolio. It keeps you grounded and prevents you from falling into scarcity, weak behavior, and neediness in your romantic life. You have a constant flow of positive emotions coming from a variety of different sources, making you less reliant on any one particular source. This directly increases your attractiveness to women and is a positive unconscious signal that you are someone worth spending time with since many other people already are. And the higher quality men and women in your social circle, the more you are valued by the women you bring into this network.

Are you more interested in eating at the restaurant with the line out the door and thousands of five-star reviews or the restaurant with no line and very few reviews and low ratings? The answer is quite obvious and similar to how women think too.

Building a strong, diverse social circle is one of the most important things you can do as a single man because it makes your life more fulfilling, more balanced, and more fun. Every man needs friends with whom he deeply connects who will support and challenge him on his journey. Life is only worth a damn because it's shared and magnified by experiencing it with others.

When you combine the character traits of the Grounded Man with a social life filled with high-quality people, it allows you to attract the highest quality women with much less effort. As you continue on this journey of becoming a more Grounded Man, it's inevitable that you're going to encounter other interesting men. When you do, invite them into your life and bring them along for the journey. And if you meet an amazing woman whom you aren't physically attracted to, is in a relationship, or simply isn't the right person to be romantic with, invite her along for the ride as well.

Your goal should be to fill your social circle with as many incredible, inspiring people as possible. But you shouldn't simply have them in your life, you must add value into their lives as well. Host regular social events and coordinate people together. If you have your own place or a nice patio, throw parties, mixers, or barbeques to get people together and grow your social influence with quality people.

If you're struggling to build your social life, it's because you aren't doing enough interesting things or extending enough invitations to the people in your network. Everyone else is simply waiting around for something interesting to happen. Your job as a Grounded Man is to *make* those things happen and bring people together.

Although you should always be expanding your network and consistently meeting new people, there's no need to have a huge pool of friends. This isn't a college fraternity. Instead, invest most of your time and energy into three to five high-quality friends. Yes, you can regularly host events with many more people, but you only need to have a few deep friendships (and that's likely all you're capable of maintaining in the long run).

Find men who will be in your corner and push you to be your best self, men who are on a similar path, who have grand visions, and who are of a higher caliber. If you aren't able to build an abundant social circle because of your geography, *get out of there as quickly as you can.* Move to a new city, the biggest one you can, and set up your new life. It's easier today than ever before to move around the country and travel the world.

Don't let geography prevent you from meeting new like-minded people, having genuine connections, and creating memorable experiences. It's better to live in the right location with a lower standard of living (such as a less expensive car, smaller apartment, and higher cost of living) than it is to have an enormous house, a luxury sedan, and a two-car garage at the cost of living in a small town with fewer options.

At the end of your life, you won't remember the extra cabinet space you had, the walk-in closet, or that spare bedroom that was rarely used. You'll remember the experiences that you had and the people you shared them with. Focus on living in the best location that you can that allows you to maximize your overall life experience.

So how does having good friends help you with women?

Having a strong social life with quality people makes you less needy and clingy to attractive women. You are not in need of connection and companionship with new women since you already have it, which puts you in a position to offer pure value.

There are guys out there who can take a lot of action and by sheer numbers date women in the short term, but they don't have the lifestyle to keep them engaged for the long term. Women can sense when something is missing in a man's life, and they don't want to feel like they're the only thing that is important to him or their only source of connection.

"But don't women want to be the only important thing in a man's life?" you ask. On some levels, maybe. But at her core, she doesn't really want to be. She'll never tell you this, but she doesn't want to be the main reason why you get up in the morning.

Rather, she wants you to live your purpose, your values, and have your own life outside of hers. She wants to come along for the exciting adventure that is your life, not be the bedrock of your entire life. That dynamic puts all the weight on her shoulders to make you happy, which is what so many men slowly do over time. It slowly ruins the relationship.

A man with a strong social life is an attractive man, so here's an easy strategy to build such a life of like-minded people: Start with one to three friends or acquaintances and decide on a fun social activity that you can do consistently. It might be a game night, a BBQ, taco night, sushi night, a cocktail party, a pool party, or just something fun that you would enjoy.

Each guy needs to invite two other people, preferably two women but let them know they can bring a friend, too. The first event will be a laid-back test run for about five to ten people. Let everyone at the event know that you'll be doing the same thing or something similar next week, and that they are all invited. Instruct them to invite at least two more people for the next event.

Your second event should have around eight to twelve people, then rinse and repeat. Within a month, you'll have around ten to fifteen people regularly at your social outings each time.

Continue this pattern every week with a fun social event. It doesn't need to cost much if everyone pitches in and brings food and drinks. Over time, you'll be throwing events and social activities with higher-level people as you continue to grow as a man and meet new people.

What's great is this is a good way to meet women since you are the host of the party and are seen as man in a leadership role. People think you know everyone since you're hosting, but in reality, you're just getting to know everyone.

You just need to be more proactive about putting yourself out there, taking on a leadership role, and organizing events that will eventually turn into something much bigger in the future. You're not only meeting women, but you're doing something fun on a weekly basis which is healthy for your overall sense of well-being. If you were to do this for three months, how much fun would you have? Who would you meet? Imagine doing it for one year.

You know the answer, so get started and have some fun. At this point, you now have a broader and more accurate understanding of the dating landscape and the importance of developing the characteristics of the Grounded Man.

The success of this entire program is based on your ability to transition from an indecisive nice guy who settles in life and into a stronger Grounded Man who can boldly create the life he wants. If you want my help with this transformational shift then watch this presentation and learn more: knowledgeformen.com/live

Now our work has only just begun. Knowing about the Grounded Man and knowing how to be a Grounded Man are two completely different endeavors. Therefore, to succeed and fully embody the Grounded Man archetype, you must first optimize the one thing from which all of your results flow, a factor that is so often ignored when in pursuit of a higher quality dating life: Your mindset.

CHAPTER 2

THE INTERNAL MINDSET THAT WILL MAKE YOU IRRESISTIBLE TO WOMEN

"The trick is in what one emphasizes. We either make ourselves miserable, or we make ourselves happy. The amount of work is the same."

— CARLOS CASTANEDA

"Screw this!" "You're a fucking loser and you always will be!" It wasn't two people going at it fighting. Just me, by myself, shouting at my own reflection in the bathroom mirror like a lunatic. I was standing, hands pressed into the counter, glaring intensely at myself. I was fed up and frustrated with the man I saw. "You can't do this…"

If anyone had been there to see my one-sided yelling match, they'd have likely assumed I'd lost my mind. *Would they have been right?*

I was just a lonely, desperate guy who had lost his patience. It's been months after my breakup and, by day, sometimes I could trick myself into thinking I had finally achieved some sense of normalcy as I went through the motions of daily life. Once the moon came out, however, I transformed like a werewolf into an animal hell bent on raging against nothing else but myself. These screaming outbursts would inevitably end with me finding myself alone in bed at two in the morning, six drinks deep into the night, crying and pining over my lost love.

I had come across a photo on social media of her, already with her arms wrapped around another man. My imagination was hammering me with mental images of the incredible dates she was on with this tall, dark, and handsome man. Her darkened bedroom echoing with her cries of passion as she wrapped her legs around a man better than me. Was she sharing the same blankets with another man I bought her last Christmas?

I had been possessed by these demons for long enough, however. That particular night, I decided I was sick and tired of the one-man pity party I'd been throwing day after day, night after endless, sleepless night. Even in the throes of that inebriated rage, I was able to realize—no, to cling to the idea—that *nothing was going to change until I did.* I had a choice. I could either continue mourning my loss, my loneliness, and my increasingly depressing existence… or I could do something about it. Thankfully, I chose the latter.

Though still in mourning for that relationship, I was still relatively new to the dating game. I'd only experienced a small handful of women and only dated two of them seriously in my entire life.

So, I was going to do something about it, something big. Great, but *what?* Wracking my brain, I rubbed my hands and got to it. Researching my problem, the only way a heartbroken, drunk, twenty-something knows how at two o'clock in the morning, I went online and searched, "How to meet women."

As you probably know, the Internet is teeming with countless gurus, spilling their philosophies about how to meet and bed women. It's easy to take a deep dive down the rabbit hole of dating advice online. My search engine flooded with a litany of varying approaches. There were so many…

And I voraciously consumed every single one of them. Every page, post, and video that popped up before me. Eventually I was rudely interrupted by a San Diego sunrise beaming around the edges of my curtains. The morning birds chirping outside letting me know I had just pulled an all-nighter of dating advice. Was I losing my mind?

They made it sound simple, and I was committed to consuming every drop of content I could find, any source that made me think I knew *exactly* what women wanted and how to give it to them. It was easy: all I had to do was say a few lines just right, stand a little taller with my shoulders back, and wait until just the right time to go for the kiss until. From the sounds of it, I'd be back to dating a ridiculously attractive woman in no time!

By the time I finally shut off my computer and laid in bed I was trapped in a fantasy land I had built myself using their bricks. I imagined what my life would look like, how jealous my ex would be, how many exciting adventures I would soon be experiencing once I finally started using their techniques. The next day, I was ready to go out and practice everything I had learned. Truthfully, I was overwhelmed by the information I'd attempted to digest the night before, but I considered it a crash course. *What could go wrong?*

Once I got to a trendy bar, I stayed in my car and reviewed all of my notes. I had written down every step the gurus had taught as best I could, using every reference point and going over their routines and rules—word by word, step by step, do this, do that, I reviewed it all.

"Alright," I thought, "I've got this. Piece of cake!"

Except, I didn't. Not even close. That night, during the first thirty minutes inside, I was frozen in a corner nursing a beer. I'd see an attractive woman and do nothing, stuck in my head and unable to think of what to say. I stammered like a fool as I rehearsed what I should do, meanwhile, I'm still staring with a dumbfounded look. I must have allowed at least 7 attractive women to walk right past me. I was unnoticed, ineffective, invisible to these women.

The next two months of going out were just as much of a disaster. I was *terrible*. I'd see a woman standing by herself and think, "Here we go! This is it!" Then, upon my approach, I would stumble over my words and desperately try to remember all of the routines I'd learned online until I was rejected. Every. Damn. Time.

One night, I approached a group of exceptionally attractive women (a challenging feat in and of itself—it might have been liquid courage, but I'm proud I even made a move). Within minutes of my initial approach, I thought I was doing great. Then they started whispering to each other and—with no explanation—they literally *ran* away from me.

"WTF?!" I thought to myself, "Am I really that bad?"

A deep dread seeped in with that thought. If I was that bad with women, how was it that someone as beautiful as my ex had ever agreed to be with me? I started to worry that I had, in fact, lost not just the best woman I could ever be with, but the only woman.

I considered giving up. It was tempting to just resign myself to the single life of porn and living vicariously through my friends who were more successful with women. The following week, I was alone at a local mall with the intention of meeting women, but really just people watching. Hardly a place for an epiphany, but it happened. I was having some coffee and feeling, as usual, incredibly low. Then, in my isolated despair, I saw an old friend.

Enter Wayne: Charming, charismatic, and capable of making even the most anxious and uptight individuals feel completely at ease, Wayne was one of those guys that you couldn't help but like. And make no mistake, there *were* times when you didn't want to like him.

What set Wayne apart from most men is the effortless way in which he coupled his easygoing geniality with unfiltered self-expression. You never had to wonder what he was thinking—good or bad—because he told you...in no uncertain terms. Even if it hurt.

He spoke his mind completely and authentically and had no problem stepping on a few toes to share his truth. Yet somehow, he could make you feel respected and at ease...even if he happened to be letting you know what a total dumbass you were being.

And at that moment, Wayne was walking past me with someone who appeared to be his girlfriend. Their arms were draped around one another as they walked through the mall, laughing, smiling, having a great time. I watched enviously as Wayne grabbed her by the waist and pulled her in for a kiss before she walked away.

As soon as she was gone, I hastily walked over and surprised him. We hadn't seen each other in years. After a while catching up, I asked him how long he and his girlfriend had been dating. His response floored me: "Oh, her? Haha! We're not dating, I met her like fifteen minutes ago." I did a full double take. I couldn't believe it. The casual way in which he'd acted made it seem like they had been intimate for years. I was dying to be with a woman like that, and he could pull it off with a stranger at the mall?

"How did you do that?" I asked. His attention drifted to an attractive woman walking out of a store nearby and responded with a shrug, "It's not as hard as you might think. Here, let me show you"

What came next was nothing short of surreal. Without a moment of fear or hesitation, he walked right up to this beautiful woman and showered her with the *exact* same "lines" that I'd been using for the past two months. Not a word was different from those I had been poring over in my notes. At that moment, I remember thinking to myself, "Ouch. I'm about to see Wayne fail. Those lines never work. She's gonna reject him right before my eyes!"

Then, to my surprise, she responded with the biggest, most beautiful smile you've ever seen. Within moments of him introducing himself, she was laughing and touching him playfully like they were a couple. A few moments later, I couldn't believe it, they were exchanging phone numbers before she strutted away with a smile, obviously just as happy to meet him as he was her.

My jaw hit the floor. I was blown away. I'd never seen anyone do it in front of me other than videos online where I didn't fully believe if it was real or not. Wayne returned with aura of nonchalance. To him, this was just part of life. He had no idea he'd just performed art right before my eyes. The dumbstruck look adorning my face *must* have shown him how profoundly impressed I was, but his demeanor remained calm.

He simply walked back over and said, "What were we talking about again?" I proceeded to barrage him with endless questions about what I'd just witnessed, explaining that I said the exact same things but was constantly facing rejection.

His smile softened and he said, as concisely as he could, "Look Andrew, you might know *what* to do, but you clearly don't know how to do it *well*."

Damn. His words, although they felt like squeezing lemon juice into a paper cut, were undeniably true. He continued on, explaining that, although I knew what to say, it was coming from a place of outcome dependence, neediness, and approval-seeking behavior. I was giving away all of my power before I even opened my mouth, causing women to instantly lose attraction for me. Everything about that premise seemed to ring true. I needed him to explain further, "Okay. Okay, but what does that all mean?" Then he shared his most profound piece of wisdom:

"It's not what you say. It's the place it comes from that matters most."

Women can *feel* who you are and what you're about before you say a word. Techniques, tactics, and lines can help but you're missing the point entirely. You must become your own man, unlock your authentic self, and cultivate the right mindset to stand a chance with the highest quality women.

Watching Wayne confidently interact with such quality women in such a carefree and genuine way–holding nothing back, having no ulterior motives, and making them feel so safe and desired *they* wanted to flirt back too–showed me what was really possible if I continued this journey.

It was the spark to the ignition that began my never-ending quest to really understand what it means to interact with people, especially women from "the right place."

And this small shift precipitated a personal transformation in *my* dating life more powerful than any video, course or bootcamp I ever did. I transformed from a robotic, canned-lined guy with women into fully embodying the Grounded Man with whom women are happy to engage. Instead of being stuck in my head, searching for the perfect thing to say, I learned to go deeper and penetrate a woman's core with my presence alone—often while saying very little.

If common "pickup advice" was Level One Foundational Material, this is a Level Ten Master Class that has taken me nearly a decade to uncover. My life, relationships, and worldview have changed in ways I never could have expected. Beyond my relationships with women, this evolution of self has also created massive success in every other aspect of my life.

This is what I learned...

THE PSYCHOLOGY OF THE GROUNDED MAN

There's an old saying that goes something like this: "Success in anything is 80% psychology and only 20% mechanics." After almost a decade of both struggling and succeeding at the lowest and highest levels, I know this to be true. You can have all of the tools and strategies that you want. I could teach you the most advanced game techniques out there and give you everything that I've learned on my journey from shy and socially awkward to dating very high-quality women. But without the right internal mindset, it won't do you any good.

Unless you cultivate the right attitudes and thought patterns about women and dating, you'll stay stuck exactly where you regardless of the *strategies* and *tactics* that you learn. Other books will tell you that you should focus solely on the strategies and tactics. They'll instruct you to put on the "mask of pickup" and to try and manipulate your way into sleeping with a woman. Sometimes these tactics lead to results by sheer effort and numbers. But they aren't sustainable in the long run, healthy, or win-win for the woman. Because at the end of the day, true lasting attraction doesn't occur by manipulating a woman's psychology.

True attraction is the byproduct of authenticity, adding value, and sharing positive emotions with no expected outcome.

It occurs when you are able to fully express yourself and, as a result, turn people "on" and light up their day. To do this, you must share who you are with the world unapologetically, without shame or fear of judgment.

In the coming chapters, I'm going to teach you specific conversational and social techniques that you can use to create attraction. I know that you want to get to the "fun stuff" but I'll be the first to say it, what I'm going to share with you in chapters 4 and 5 *work*. The strategies are incredibly powerful and doable, and they *will* help you get results faster with the most attractive women than anything else out there. But those tactics aren't the main course, they're merely the side.

My goal is to help you cultivate such a powerful and grounded mindset that you no longer *need* any of the tactics I'll share with you later on. They are simply a stepping stone designed to help you gain momentum until you are able to open up your authentic self in every interaction.

Once you have your mind right, everything else will fall into place and you can create your own reality and decide what works best for you. Your goal is not to become me, it's to become the strongest version of *yourself*. This is where your journey will really begin...

THE KEYS TO THE KINGDOM

If you will take these lessons to heart and apply them on a consistent basis, you will experience a fundamental shift in the way that you view *everything* inside of your reality. I know that many of you are probably rolling your eyes and grunting in dissent, believing that the above statement is merely a steaming load of hyperbolic New Age bull shit. But it's the truth. I can say without hesitation that this *single lesson* was the driving force that allowed me to quit my job, build a successful business, create an abundant dating life, and build a high-quality social network. I hope I have your attention now. So what is this life-changing concept?

It's known as the "Growth Mindset," an idea as old as time itself but first officially posited by Dr. Carol Dweck in her groundbreaking book of the same title. As powerful as her research has been in shaping the way that we view success and achievement in the modern world, the Growth Mindset theory is actually incredibly simple.

Having a growth mindset means that you believe any skill, talent, or ability can be learned and improved upon.

A fixed mindset, on the other hand, is the belief that (as the name implies) your results, your potential, and your life is "fixed." For example, someone with a fixed mindset would say things like:

- I can't talk to women.
- I'm not a funny person.
- I'll never be a successful.
- I will always be single.

On the other hand, someone with a growth mindset would reframe these beliefs:

- I haven't developed the skill of talking to attractive women and don't have the results I want *yet*.
- I haven't learned how to effectively deliver humor or make people laugh *yet*, but I can learn how to.
- I haven't built a profitable business *yet*, but I can learn from my failures, and with enough experience and perseverance, I'll soon succeed.
- I haven't had a girlfriend *yet*, so I need to spend some time analyzing my habits, identifying my weaknesses, and strengthening my beliefs so that I can start improving.

Having a growth mindset doesn't mean that you deny the role that genetic predispositions and childhood advantages play in achieving success. But you know that anyone can become proficient at *any* skill given enough time, effort, and persistence.

With a fixed mindset, you define success as *winning*. Therefore, you can never be successful because to develop any skill and become proficient at any craft, you must first *fail*.

On the other hand, with a growth mindset, success is defined as *learning*. If you are improving, slowly getting better, and growing from mistakes, then you are succeeding. And with enough time and persistence, you will eventually reach bigger and bigger milestones, then eventually your ultimate goal. It doesn't matter whether you achieve the outcome you desire. What matters to someone with a growth mindset is that they are learning and improving, that they are 1% better at a particular skill than they were yesterday. And, for our purposes, you must accept one other premise:

Dating, relationships, and social dynamics are a skill set. And like any skill, they can be learned and improved upon with enough time, effort, and persistence.

I don't care if you are currently incapable of approaching and having small talk with attractive women or if you're used to getting results but not with the quality of women you really want. Where you are today does not define who you will be tomorrow. So long as you are willing to learn, put in the work, trust the process, and persist through the challenges, you can and will achieve goals you never thought possible in all areas of your life.

Imagine playing the guitar. Sure, some people start out with some sort of "natural" advantages. Maybe they have stronger fingers from doing manual labor, a talent for rhythm and song writing, and the ability to learn new songs by ear.

But anyone, no matter how genetically "ungifted" they might be, has the ability to learn a new instrument and become proficient. I didn't say "world class," but good enough to be able to play the guitar well and have fun doing it. Some of the most popular and highest-grossing songs of all time have the simplest guitar riffs that can be learned in an afternoon by any newbie guitarist.

What's great about dating, relationships and social dynamics is you don't need to become world class to get results, you just need the foundations. But to successfully internalize the growth mindset, you must first eradicate the limiting beliefs that you've allowed to govern your life.

- I'm not tall enough...
- I'm not handsome enough...
- I'm socially awkward...
- I'm not rich enough...
- I'm not the right ethnicity...
- I'm not funny enough...
- I'm too old...

These stories are nothing more than a fast track ticket to a life of mediocrity and victimhood. They serve as socially accepted and convenient scapegoats for your inaction, allowing you to waste years of your life, allowing your insecurities to be an excuse to ultimately avoid the hard work required to achieve your goals.

But you and I both know that these little stories you tell yourself are just that—stories. They might hold truth, but the interpretation and meaning attached to them are whatever you believe them to be.

You—yes, even *you*—know of at least one man who started off with fewer resources and talents than you have today and still achieved great success with the opposite sex.

The quality of women you date is in direct proportion to your level of adopting the growth mindset and treating the journey like a skill that can be learned and improved upon over time.

Every man has the capacity to develop himself into the type of person that women find attractive. Every man can become better than he is today and enjoy an abundant dating life, incredible sex, and a fulfilling relationship with the women he wants. I'll be the first to tell you that it won't happen overnight, but it can happen depending on your level of commitment to the journey.

If you develop yourself into a stronger Grounded Man, learn what women want, then deliver what they want to them, then you will be able to date the woman you want. It's the law of cause and effect. If you do the right actions from the right frame of mind, you'll get positive results. If you take no actions or come from the wrong frame of mind, you'll get negative results.

This sounds simple, I know. But if it's *this* simple, why is it that many men spend years failing to do anything that brings them closer to the women they want?

The simplest answer is fear. To achieve the results you want in *any* endeavor—be it with women, in business, or in the gym—you must accept that success is messy. It's not a "straight line" to the top and it isn't always going to be pretty. Your desire for perfection in the short term is the very thing that poisons your ability to get results in the long term.

Let's remove this issue holding you back now, shall we?

ELIMINATE PERFECTIONISM, RELINQUISH CONTROL, AND SET YOURSELF FREE

I'm about to tell you something that will permanently alter the way in which you view women and dating. That's a bold claim, I know, but one that I intend to prove.

Right now, in this very moment, you already possess many of the skills and attractive qualities required to succeed with women.

Maybe you aren't ready to date the *most* attractive, driven, and beautiful women in the world; if this is the first time you've genuinely taken this journey seriously, then you're probably not ready yet. But you *do* have what it takes to meet, attract, and keep a beautiful woman in your life. Just think back to the last time you were with a family member or close friend.

- Did you run out of things to say?
- Were you stuck in your head?
- Did you stumble over your words?
- Were you thinking about your body language?

Of course not, so it's clear that you know how to be social, have fun, and enjoy engaging conversations. Yet years of social conditioning have deeply embedded the psychological blocks and toxic behavior patterns.

It's made you incapable of fully expressing yourself and authentically sharing your value with the women you meet.

The very second that you see an attractive woman with whom you're interested in, your mind sets to work sabotaging and derailing your efforts, destroying any chance of success you may have had.

Why? Because you are entering into the interaction with two unacknowledged problems. The first is that you believe the lie that you are not "enough" to attract a beautiful woman. You just accept your own limiting beliefs, certain that you must say *just* the right thing, stand with *just* the right posture, and touch her at *just* the right time in order to create attraction.

This belief causes you to feel uneasy and insecure as you approach the women you desire. After all, you and your actions are *not* perfect, so you choke on your words, become stuck in your head, and find yourself utterly incapable of letting go and being the man that she wants to experience.

By trying to be perfect, you stifle your personality, thoughts, and actions, making attraction an impossibility instead of a foregone conclusion. In order to succeed with women, you must reframe the interaction in your head and realize that rejection is a natural part of any sexual interaction. Some women will like you, others won't. So what?

If you've just met a stranger at a bar, coffee shop, or even on the street, then why do you care what she thinks about you? Why does she sit on a throne with the power to make you feel better or worse? Reframe this by asking yourself if *you* like *her* more than worrying about whether or not *she* likes *you*.

But this problem extends beyond serving as a detriment to attraction. When you habitually engage in people-pleasing and validation-driven behaviors, you begin to compromise who you are and your sense of self-worth. The subtle manipulation that colors your interactions corrodes away at your very presence and energy as you find yourself thinking, speaking, and acting in a way that is totally incongruent with who you are, presenting a weaker version of yourself to women, where rejection is all but inevitable.

Your bullshit desire to please others at the expense of yourself leads you to be willing to castrate your soul or "thumos"—as the Greeks called it—and surrender the very parts of yourself that made you attractive in the first place. You *cannot* make everyone happy in your interactions. The very foundation of a free-thinking society mandate differences in political, religious, and philosophical views.

To put it simply, the thoughts and behaviors that will create attraction from one individual—*especially quality* women—are the exact thoughts and behaviors that will invite disdain from others. As such, the only thing you can do is be yourself and share who you are and what you value. If it sparks attraction, great; if it doesn't, you've saved yourself time and energy with the wrong woman. Also, great.

The lack or presence of attraction is not an indicator that there is something wrong or right with you, merely that there is congruence between yourself and another person. When you are true to yourself and you speak your mind without fear of reprisal or loss, you will naturally attract the right women into your life, find people who are aligned with your values and vision, and detract those who are not.

But authenticity is only the first step. To attract the women you want, you must address the second and more sinister saboteur of your results… your own expectations. What destroys success for most men—whether it's with women they crave or the goals they have for themselves—is their own hidden agendas and hard expectations.

The difference between a pickup artist and a Grounded Man is that pickup artists have a nebulous agenda to get laid and bring a woman home. It's about getting a specific result regardless of whether it's a win-win scenario for the woman.

A Grounded Man goes out to offer value, share positive emotions, and have fun interacting with all women without being attached to any specific outcome. He doesn't care if he "pulls" that night or not. He is going out simply for the sake of his own enjoyment. For a Grounded Man, the journey is truly the destination.

If sex happens, great! But sex doesn't need to happen for him to feel good about himself nor consider the night a success. More importantly, sex is not the barometer that determines if he is a worthy man. Ironically, this detachment from outcome is exactly what will attract most women and lead to a life of relational and sexual abundance.

When you let go of your need to experience a certain outcome, you allow yourself to be truly free and express yourself more openly. You can feel, say, and do whatever you want without fear of judgment or loss. You're no longer stuck in your head thinking, "Is this the right thing to say? Garrhh, I really hope she likes me!"

Screw that weak behavior, you simply flow more freely, have fun, and do the things that you want to do for no other reason than that you want to do them. Stop trying to force interactions to go a certain way. Honestly, it doesn't matter which moves you make, it just matters that you're making moves that are true and congruent to you.

A Grounded Man does not base his criteria for success on the reactions of other people. He bases his criteria for success on taking action, expressing himself fully, and living in alignment with his values.

Women that you meet for the first time are strangers and should be treated accordingly. She might have a beautiful face and a curvy body, but that does not mean she has a right to dictate or control your thoughts, emotions, or self-worth. She does not deserve your time, energy, attention, or resources simply because of her beauty. In the presence of an attractive woman always ask yourself, "What else is there?"

Until she has proven herself worthy of your attention and shared value with you, the fact is, she is simply another human in the crowd. As a Grounded Man, you must value yourself more than any stranger, regardless of sexual prowess.

When you internalize these two concepts, that you must eradicate perfectionism and discard any expectations or agendas, you become truly free. Rejection is no longer a fate to be feared, but rather a valuable asset that saves you time, money, and energy that would have otherwise been wasted with an incompatible partner.

Between the time that you decided to approach a woman and the time you were rejected; your life didn't change in any way. That's the beauty of living in the age we do today. Hundreds of years ago, there may have only been a handful of women in your immediate town you had access to, but today, the world is your oyster and there is an abundance of women to choose from, especially in the digital age.

As you improve yourself, your ability to attract higher-quality women will increase as well; in fact, it will become the new norm for you. You are the biggest variable that determines if you will attract the right women into your life or not. Trying to be everything to every woman, means you become nothing to every woman.

Value your own intentions and be the man you want to be without needing anyone's approval. Be attached to the actions you're taking and not her reaction or the outcome. That's what will boost your internal state and allow you to stand out, be more social, and feel more alive in your interactions.

That's how you set yourself free.

DEVELOPING CORE CONFIDENCE AND OVERCOMING THE "FAKE ALPHA SYNDROME"

If you've been mired in the world of trying to meet new women for any appreciable amount of time, then you have almost certainly been told to hide your deep insecurities and glaring flaws behind a faster car, edgier clothing, 15 lbs. of extra muscle, a few tattoos, and excessive spending at the club. And I'll be the first to admit it… this approach *does* get you more attention from women.

During the early stages of developing your social skills and becoming a more Grounded Man, there's nothing wrong with using every tool at your disposal to help you feel more confident from the *outside* in. However—much like pickup itself—this is not a viable long-term strategy for success with the highest-quality women. Your goal is not to use tricks, gimmicks, and flashy possessions to feel confident, rather your goal is to become the type of man who *is* confident.

Women can sense when a man is legitimately confident or when he's merely acting the part. No matter how tailored your suit, how great your table is at the club, how big your muscles, or how fast your car, a woman can sense when you're faking it and when you're the real deal. Fake confidence relies on external things like a leased luxury car, an oversized house that you can barely afford, a $500 pair of jeans, and a watch that costs more than an economy car. Without these external items, a man of fake confidence feels weak, afraid, and naked.

Conversely, a man with Core Confidence—confidence that permeates into his very being and is an inextricable part of *who* he is—feels and knows that he is fully capable, whether he's wearing a designer suit or an old pair of worn out jeans.

Core Confidence isn't something that you just "have." It's your identity. It's part of who you are. It means that you completely trust in *yourself*. You believe in your value as a man and your ability to do the hard things required to achieve your goals.

When you develop this core confidence in *yourself*, you trust that no matter how hard life might get, no matter what tragedy may befall you, no matter what shit storm life throws your way, you can figure it out and not point fingers at other people or social institutions.

A Grounded Man responds to deep adversity with the simple phrase, "I'll handle it."

Simply put, a man who embodies this type of confidence is attractive to women. They sense his innate capabilities—so long as his confidence is paired with character and integrity—and feel that they can trust him on a deeper level. Your confidence illustrates your capability for managing the chaos of life and overcoming the unexpected challenges humans are so often faced.

When a woman feels this level of certainty and security in your confidence and competence as a man, attraction is a natural byproduct. Unconsciously, she realizes that these positive traits suggest that you will be able to handle uncertainty and chaos, even in the most tumultuous of situations.

You don't *get* confidence externally. You *work on yourself*, overcome bigger challenges over time, and trust that you have the ability to learn, grow, and do whatever is required for success. But we're only at the tip of the iceberg with this conversation. To amplify your core confidence further there is one more mindset that you *must* embed into your psyche.

A mindset that society has fought tooth and nail to stop you from adopting. A mindset that frees you from the lies and bullshit of consumer culture, hyperbolic media, and scarcity driven marketing.

A mindset that will—once you adopt it—set you free.

THE THREE MOST IMPORTANT WORDS IN THE ENGLISH LANGUAGE

From the day you were born until this very second, forces far outside of your control have fabricated an artificial sense of scarcity and lack in your life. No, I'm not talking about the Illuminati or some other grand conspiracy. I'm referring to the seemingly innocuous influences all around us.

The marketing campaigns designed to make us feel inadequate without a new product or consumer good. The ads that tell us we aren't good enough unless we have a ripped physique or a luxury car. The movies and TV shows that either emasculate or vilify men, leading us to believe that there's something wrong with being a "man." All of these voices are telling us, "You are not enough." They're lies that undermine your ability to live a full life.

You *are* enough.

Right now, in this very moment, you have everything that you need to become the person you want to be and live the life that you want to live. You might not have the money, or the women, or the body, but you have something even more important: resourcefulness.

You have the resourcefulness to overcome your greatest obstacles, achieve your loftiest ambitions, and live a surreal life. Even better, you have the ability to start *today*. For those of you who don't believe me, allow me to share two examples, one in business and one with women. The first example comes from my own life when I decided to start the Knowledge for Men Podcast.

I had no experience recording audio, researching or interviewing guests, running the "behind-the-scenes" of a big show, or marketing my content to the right audiences. I literally knew *nothing* about podcasting—other than the fact that I wanted to share a message. And right there, I could have said, "I'm not enough. I don't know what I'm doing!"

Instead, I adopted a growth mindset, I knew I had what it takes to learn the skills I needed. Seven million downloads and a thriving business later, I'm glad I did.

The second scenario is likely why you invested into this book: wanting to approach and date a beautiful woman. Too many men allow their "I am NOT enough" mentality to sabotage them before they even begin. They concoct excuses like, "She's too beautiful", "She would never date a guy like me," or "She's probably got a boyfriend already." These are just stories we tell ourselves to dull the pain of our own inaction and ease the ache of our unfulfilled desires. The truth is you *are* enough right now and being a Grounded Man who shares positive emotions with no expected outcome is the *main* requirement to attract women.

Now, you might be thinking: "Well, if I'm enough, then why do I need to read books or even finish this book." It's simple, really…

You are only enough when you commit to a life of growth.

If you want to start an online business but don't know the first thing about entrepreneurship, you are not currently ready to succeed at a high level. However, you are currently enough to *commit* to the process and grow *into* any goal you set for yourself.

Michael Jordan, Kobe Bryant, and LeBron James, some of the greatest basketball players in the history of the NBA, still used a team of coaches dedicated to helping them improve. They were enough because they committed to growing and improving even when they were already considered the best of the best. If they stopped growing and gave up their commitment to their craft, their performance would suffer.

What makes you enough, what makes you great, is the fact that you've committed to constant and unending growth. The moment you stop, you're no longer enough and you will likely fail at anything you do in life. Commonly, I know some guys still feel like they aren't enough because they aren't having regular sex or getting the quality of women they want. They think, "If only I had a beautiful woman then

I could be enough." *The unhappiest people always place their self-worth on something outside of themselves.*

But they're missing the point. This attitude will kill any interaction. Women do not hold any power over you to determine if you are enough. When you place a woman on such a high pedestal, she can sense that you're trying to "get" something from her. Instead of going out there and meeting a woman with a hungry look of "I need you" on his face, the Grounded Man effortlessly connects with beautiful women by showing them that he's interested in all of her: her beauty, her personality, and her intellect.

He isn't there to take from her, he's there to give to her.

You need to stop fooling yourself into thinking if you just had sex with this "perfect" woman, your life would finally be complete, and you could be a happy man. We all love sex, but when you stop giving so much meaning to it, your interactions with women and sex comes with much less effort. Women will want to give it to you because you're not trying to "get" something from her; you're trying to build something with her.

Always remember that a Grounded Man is of immense value to women. You need to express yourself and share who you are with others because this is what you offer to the world: yourself. Girls will wonder, "Why isn't he trying to get me?" They'll ask, "What's this guy about?" Cut the game of "look at me, look at all my skills, I learned this new pickup move online aren't you impressed? Did you like that pickup line?"

High-quality women will be repelled by any sign of neediness and desire for validation, even if you say and do all of the right things. And if you aren't sharing yourself unapologetically, you aren't offering value.

But the "I am enough" attitude isn't something that you can simply "get" through external means. It's something that you consciously give to yourself. Here's the secret…

LOVE YOURSELF BEFORE YOU LOVE HER

You *are* the most important person in your life, and to live a full, happy life despite what you've been told by society and even religion, you must love yourself first and at times be very selfish. This is not to say that you should not have the ability to prioritize, care for, and love others *also*. Simply that *you* come first. Think about it like this: if you do not love and prioritize yourself *first* then you will constantly be in a state of need and scarcity. You'll be trying to get something from every woman you encounter in order to get love outside of yourself.

You cannot be attractive to women if you need their love to validate your self-worth. Instead, when you love yourself first and prioritize your own needs, you need nothing, making you freer and more attractive in the process. You aren't interacting with women to "take" something, you're interacting to give to them because you're already fulfilled.

The ugly, painful, and necessary truth is this: until you learn to love yourself fully, you cannot be loved by high-quality women.

This is not to say that you act selfishly and are not a caring or loving person. But you must first have the ability to take care of yourself and get your own needs met before attempting to care for or meet the needs of others. It's the same reason they tell you to put the oxygen mask on yourself first then help your loved ones in the event of a plane crash. You're no good to other people if you're dead – even spiritually.

When you apply this lesson to your life, you will have more energy, time, and attention to give to others. You'll be a happier person for loving and prioritizing yourself and, as a result, you'll be able to share more value with others. How can you start doing this? Anytime you have to make a decision or are faced with a challenging situation, ask yourself: *What would someone who loved themselves at a level 10/10 do?*

The truth will come to you immediately. Your logical mind may chime in seconds later and give you reasons why you shouldn't do this or that. Go with the first answer. When you love yourself, you'll take care of yourself, respect yourself, and not allow second-class behavior from others. This will help you develop your core confidence and become a man of true value, a man who adds more value than he takes.

Learn to love yourself as you are and for who you are while you work to transform yourself into the person you want to be.

Love yourself because you are on the journey, growing every day, committed to being a stronger more Grounded Man. Get excited about the process and the wonderful journey you're going to embark upon.

ALWAYS BE HAVING FUN & TURN YOUR LIFE INTO A GRAND ADVENTURE

The most memorable moments of the journey you're about to embark on won't be the random one-night encounters or even dating multiple attractive women. Sure, those are fun, but there is an even greater reward that many men miss out on.

The best moments of this journey will be the times that you made other people's lives better, more exciting, and more memorable. Everything that you do on this journey should be about one thing and one thing only: having a fucking blast. You are here to have the time of your life. And you'd better make sure that you do, because this is the only shot you get. One of the main benefits of this journey is to help you live a life so spectacular, adventurous, and exciting that you could die tomorrow without a regret in the world.

Every day when you wake up, ask yourself, "What can I do today so that, when I'm dying, I'll smile and laugh because I lived life the way I wanted to?" When having fun becomes the focus of every interaction, you no longer feel attached to any specific outcome. You're able to succeed in every encounter because it's about an amazing experience, not getting a woman to react positively to you. You're on the adventure of a lifetime and you're happy to share and laugh whether others accept your invitation or not. It's happening either way.

By learning to enjoy yourself, be amused, and find adventure in the mundane—regardless of who you're with, what you're doing, or where you are—you become the center of fun and excitement. Anyone who refuses your call to adventure is missing out on the opportunity to experience life to the fullest.

Don't believe me? Just sit and observe any social gathering and the people moping around like well-behaved robots, falling in line, looking around, hoping something happens that will suddenly make things interesting. Everyone is living their lives with such high levels of anxiety of fear of other people's opinions that they feel like they're stuck in a high stakes poker tournament or defusing a bomb—with only 30 seconds on the countdown timer.

There is no joy in life when you are trapped in an anxiety riddled shell and constantly living in fear of other people's thoughts and opinions.

Is your life so monotonous and boring that the only memorable moments are the occasional holiday and birthday? That isn't living, it's surviving and getting through life one day at a time.

By having the courage *to go first*, to lead the interaction, and to be the source of adventure, you can change your entire outlook. You create value just by being the person who takes that first step and leads the way. The more fun and adventure you can facilitate in your own life and for others, the happier your life will be, the happier their lives will be, and the more you will win in dating and in life.

But here's the "catch." Having fun is about making *yourself* feel good with your thoughts, words, and actions. It's about entertaining *yourself* and learning to smile and laugh because *you* want to, regardless of what others think and not because you're trying to become an entertainer for anyone.

And this is where most guys screw things up. They are only able to turn "on" and be fun when they are trying to get something from a woman. You cannot attract a woman by making her the source of fun, excitement, and adventure. You must first be the source and generate it from within to attract her.

But you also can't bullshit positive emotions and good energy. Women know when a man is truly alive, vibrant, and fun at his core and when he's only playing the part to try and get laid. The problem is that so many of us place ourselves in a mental and emotional prison, restricting our ability to have fun and experience positive emotions. We think: "Unless I...

- Am getting good reactions from attractive women
- Am on vacation in Hawaii
- Go to an amusement park in the summer
- Tell the funniest joke and everyone laughs
- Go skydiving or some other extreme sport

... then I can't possibly have fun.

But the truth is, there's no one holding you back from having more fun and making your life more enjoyable except for yourself.

And to experience the fun and joy that is freely available to all humans, we must reset our expectations for what we consider as fun. Learn to amuse yourself with the menial tasks of everyday life. Find the joy and pleasure in the most mundane tasks wherever you are and whoever you are with. Turn your life into a giant game where you are Player #1.

The moment you realize that life is a giant playground and that you have the power to engage in it is the moment you become truly alive and a pleasure to be around. Everything you do presents an opportunity to attract or repel someone. Don't wait for her or anyone else to entertain you. Take the lead, share your expressions, wit, and humor. I'm not concerned if she laughs at my humor because I am happy to be here, right now, having a good time with or without anyone.

"Hey, I don't like that guy. He's too much fun and makes me laugh all the time." – Said No One Ever

The big ah-ha moment in all of your interactions is when you realize that whatever you feel, she feels. If you're having fun, she's having fun. If you're feeling insecure and tense, she's feeling insecure and tense and therefore can't trust you. And without trust, there's no possibility of attraction. There is only a defensive wall or thoughts of how to escape, and rightfully so. So many guys start this journey of improving with women in order to validate themselves and fill a void in their souls instead of for the sheer pleasure and enjoyment of offering value to women.

In order to master the art of having fun, you *must* develop this next trait so you can create authentic, lasting attraction with the women you desire and earn respect from other men. It is a trait that will turn every single day into the most exciting day of your life, opening up new opportunities for success and growth.

THE #1 TRAIT THAT SEPARATES THE BOYS FROM THE GROUNDED MEN

One of the fundamental traits of all living beings is the ability to make decisions, even instinctive ones. As you climb up the evolutionary ladder, you'll notice that the more advanced a species is, the more evolved its decision-making ability becomes.

A flower instinctively "decides" to grow towards the sun, lose its petals in the winter, and spread its seeds to ensure procreation. Mammals, which have an even more evolved decision-making capacity, can decide to run from a predator or stay and fight. They can decide to risk going into a rival pack's territory to search for food or play it safe.

Finally, humans, the most evolved form of life on the planet, have the ability to make thousands, if not millions of micro decisions every day. The problem is that most men have slowly lost their ability to make important decisions that propel their life forward. As a result, they've lost the aliveness that lets them create an incredible life and attract the very women they want.

The bolder the decisions a man makes, the more alive he is. The more alive a man is, the more attractive he is to the world and the women around him.

When you look at weak men who are incapable of growing personally and professionally, you will always find that - beneath all of it - lies an indecisive nature that is subtly undermining their ability to live a fulfilling life. On the contrary, look at the strongest men you know; they possess the distinct ability and unshakable proclivity for making bold decisions.

They are willing to make imperfect decisions without having all of the information in front of them. Even if they make a bad decision, they are capable of handling the problem—an equally attractive attribute. As a result, they become more alive and start to experience more of the world, increasing their emotional and sexual value to women.

It starts small. They make the decision to overcome their crippling debt by building a side hustle, giving up TV, and devoting more of their free time to fixing their finances. This decision leads them to a place where they are debt free and able to quit their soul sucking job to pursue their passions full time. This decision leads to yet another outcome where they love the work they do, thus accomplishing more of it and mastering it faster than their competitors.

These decisions compound and cascade together into a life of success and invigoration as he becomes the man he always knew he could be and lives the life he always believed he deserved. When a man unlocks his natural decisiveness and becomes truly alive, you will find him smiling, laughing, and enjoying life more. Every day, he interacts with life from a position of aliveness, playfulness, and vibrancy instead of seriousness, stress and negativity.

A man who can be decisive will never feel like he's simply "getting through" life or "plugging along." He's always doing something fun and interesting to keep himself engaged with life, even if it's something simple.

If you are disengaged from life, you will never attract high-quality men and women into your life. The older a man gets, the harder it is for him to fully engage with life as he slowly stagnates and reduces his decision-making ability.

It is critical as you age that you make decisions instead of sitting in indecision for too long. The more decisions you make, the greater forward momentum you will have. You don't need to wait for someone to give you permission to come alive. You don't need to be rich to come alive. You simply need to make the decision that you are going to have fun and be fully engaged every day of your life.

This is the *fastest* way to make yourself more attractive to women, more enticing than even a multi-millionaire, celebrity, or male model. While other men run around blindly chasing success, fame, and money because they are victims of their own social conditioning, you show up engaged, present, and alive every day of your life.

I'll often find myself out at bars, clubs, or other venues surrounded by men who are richer, have more status, and are more attractive than I am. In fact, 90% of the time, I'm the poorest guy at a given social gathering or dinner. Yet, without fail, I'm also the man who has an abundant dating life full of high-quality women. Not because I'm better looking, richer, or more successful, simply because I'm more intentional about my dating life and view it as a priority. There's a special sparkle in my eye and a lust for life that you just can't buy at the store. The secret to the good life that I want to unveil is this...

Everyone is attempting to achieve a sense of aliveness and excitement by looking *outside* of themselves. They spend their entire lives chasing external validation in the form of sex, material goods, accomplishments, and praise, all in the futile pursuit of "feeling good" from the outside in.

But the *only* way to generate the positive emotional states and sense of acceptance you crave is from within. You can make yourself feel good right now because you have the power to create and cultivate the emotional states you desire. You can be the thermostat, setting the temperature and state of your life, instead of the thermometer, reacting to external influences.

And the best part? You have the ability to do this *right now* absolutely free. This is your unfair advantage, your edge, your secret weapon that so many people don't know. You are free, fully expressing yourself, enjoying your life, and *generating* happiness on demand. It causes you to be infinitely more attractive than the rest of the world. It's not over there, it's right here. It's not tomorrow, it's today. But, like everything else I've shared in this book, decisiveness isn't an inborn trait. It's a flex of a muscle, and like all other muscles, you must start lightly and gradually increase the load. Here's the thing...

- You will never have all of the information you need to make a perfect decision.
- You will never know *exactly* what to do in a given situation.
- You will never have true certainty in the outcome of any specific event.
- You will take risks that don't work out.
- You will fail many times in your life and fall flat on your face.

But failure is not fatal. A single wrong decision today will not prevent you from achieving success tomorrow. However, making no decision is the ultimate form of failure. You didn't give yourself a chance to win the game because you were too scared to play.

You must act independent of the perceived outcome and trust yourself to figure things out as you go along. You can't *know* whether moving to a new city, taking a new job, or getting into a new relationship is the perfect move for you to make. So just make the move that feels right and is most aligned with your values, then develop the self-confidence you need to overcome obstacles and challenges as they arise.

Now that we have addressed the important internal mindsets that you must cultivate about *yourself, we can now* shift gears and discuss the important mindsets that you must adopt about *women.*

Specifically, I want to begin this conversation by helping you reframe the way you view beauty in women. With this, you can remove women from the mind-made pedestal upon which you've mistakenly placed them…a position that they do not want to hold.

Here's why…

HOW TO END APPROVAL-SEEKING BEHAVIOR FROM ATTRACTIVE WOMEN

Since the day you were born, you've been conditioned to seek approval from everyone around you. Mom, dad, society, friends, family, coworkers, and *especially* attractive women. The reason is simple:

Our 200,000-year-old brains have yet to evolve to understand the times in which we live. We've been conditioned to seek validation because the disapproval of other individuals during our hunter-gatherer days could have meant ostracization from the tribe, resulting in starvation and death.

If you weren't "part of the group," it was likely that you would die at the hands of rival tribes or wild animals. Because of this genetic hardwiring, dealing with disapproval and rejection is one of the toughest feelings humans face. Most of us would move mountains just to be approved by others.

However, your ability to care less about the approval of others and more about the approval of yourself is the biggest turning point in your journey resulting in a quantum leap towards becoming a more Grounded Man.

All too often, men give women undeserved power and control over their lives simply because they are physically appealing. You must realize one simple truth that will reshape every interaction you have with women moving forward:

"Physical beauty is not enough!"

It's fleeting, skin deep, and reveals nothing of a woman's character, inner values or compatibility. Beauty is not enough to make a life changing decision. Beauty is not enough for you to act out of alignment with your values. Beauty is not enough for you to even *care* what a woman thinks or says about you. You must learn to see past the artificial exterior of a woman and see her for who she really is at her core.

Most men are willing to bend over backwards to capture the attention of a beautiful woman and, once captured, slowly and often unconsciously will spend the rest of their lives catering to and being dominated by a woman whose sole contribution is her physical appeal. It's a diminishing asset that does little for your overall life other than temporarily validate your self-worth as a man. Sure, it may impress others around you, but by doing so, you *guarantee* that you will lose her and fail to maintain her interest over the long term. Now, before we move on, I want to make something clear.

I am *not* claiming that *all* women are artificial, fake, or vain. There are countless women who are naturally beautiful, who focus on their character and living a life of substance, women who provide real value to those around them. These women are also *not* the exception, but they are also not the rule. A woman's outward appearance has very little bearing on her suitability as a life partner or true value as a potential mate. It says *nothing* about her character or who she is as a person. It is completely unrelated to who she is and whether or not she fits into the grand vision of your life.

I've seen many men completely ruined by physically attractive women who provided little value, acted disrespectfully, and—quite frankly—were *awful* human beings. But hey, they had a symmetrical face, fake tits, voluptuous lips, and a nice butt from all those squats!

When beauty is the sole arbiter of your romantic decisions, you surrender your power to women who haven't yet earned your time, attention, and resources. This approval-seeking behavior doesn't go away once she has sex with you, tells you she loves you, or when you enter a committed relationship. It follows you and tells her that she is in control, you are weak, and she can do what she wants and get away with second-class behavior because she is your source of validation.

Let me be clear: sex is not more valuable than what you offer as a Grounded Man to a woman.

A relationship—whether platonic or romantic—with a Grounded Man is priceless. It can quite literally change someone's life for the better. Meanwhile, sex—even incredible, earth-shaking sex is little more than a ten-minute naked wrestling match that feels good in the moment and temporarily validates your worth. Yet, the feeling dissipates, and you *need* it again.

Chasing approval leads you to do things that hurt you, to sell yourself out, to go against your core values, to enter relationships that you know are toxic. This is not to say that all beautiful women are bad for you. Not by a long shot! But a woman's physical beauty should not be the primary reason why you are with her. Instead, an attractive woman who also has those great inner qualities can add immense value to your life, just as you will add to hers.

When you encounter an attractive woman, you need to stay grounded and remind yourself, "Her physical beauty is not enough… what else does she have going for her?"

Without this attitude, you will never date the most attractive women who are also healthy, happy, and valuable long-term assets in your life. You need to ask yourself the right questions, namely, "Do I approve of her?" instead of, "Does she approve of me?"

Interestingly, a lot of men can remain Grounded with their close friends, family, and co-workers, yet completely abandon their values and power the second an attractive woman enters the room. They tolerate low caliber behavior, put the woman on a pedestal, and fail to act in alignment with their values. And for what? Nobody wins.

You want to attract the right partner who possesses both internal and external qualities that you are looking for in order to build an incredible life together. Anything less than this and you are devaluing yourself as a man and making yourself less attractive to women. Worse, you're treating her like an object of sexual conquest to feed a damaged ego or social construct instead of a human being with value.

But what if she doesn't feel the same attraction to you? That is her valid feeling but it's also her loss. Move on with your life because there are many women within a 25-mile radius who want what you have to offer.

The highest-quality women are not looking for men who need their validation to feel like a worthy man. They are attracted to the men who hold their own power and don't need anything from them. Instead, they want to share good emotions and add value from an abundant frame. Attractive women are just human beings who happen to have more physical symmetry than others, mostly due to genetics. So get her off that pedestal—where she never asked you to put her in the first place—and own your value and power as a man.

Now that you understand why you don't need validation and approval from a woman, you are free to offer pure value that will be openly received, making you the most desirable man in the room. Let's go even deeper into this concept…

BE A GIVER NOT A TAKER TO
OPEN PANDORA'S BOX

When you really consider the value that a beautiful woman brings into your life, you will have the realization that no woman—and indeed no *person*—can give you any form of positive emotion that you cannot first give to yourself.

Yes, she is beautiful. Yes, she has a captivating personality and breathtaking body. Yes, the allure of her eyes, the smell of her hair, and the titillating touch of her skin flood you with arousal and excitement. But how do these factors *really* affect you?

For most men it's something along the lines of:

1. They make you feel good.
2. They make you feel worthy as a man.
3. They make you feel validated and accepted.

But let me ask you, are any of these things exclusive to the realm of the feminine? Don't you have the power to give *all* of those things to yourself?

Of course, you can. That's what this entire chapter has been about, helping you reclaim your power as a man and effectively remove the one thing that women have been holding over you all of your life… their physical beauty.

From this frame you are free to enter into every interaction with only one thought: "What can I *give* to those around me?"

This does not come from a weak reciprocity driven frame—"I'll scratch your back, if you scratch mine and then spread your legs"—but rather from a place of abundance. Your thinking is: I am enough, I love myself, I am confident in myself, I have everything to give, and I'm open to receiving if she freely gives back to me.

The good feelings, worthiness, and validation that you want from a woman are all things that you can give yourself, which frees you to give pure value to a woman since you don't need anything from her.

Once you internalize this, you've opened Pandora's Box. The tides will have turned in your favor. She wants to unravel you. She's more engaged with you than you are with her and she's now chasing the grand prize... *you*.

But you cannot offer your value as a man if you're still stuck in a state of trying to take something from a woman. By its very nature, the act of *taking* value instead of *exchanging* value implies that you are incomplete. The second you believe the lie that she somehow possesses something you *need*, you resign control of your life. And the worst part? Women don't *want* this level of control and authority over your life! They want to be the recipient of your positive emotions.

Imagine if I challenged you to walk down the street and ask 10 people to give you $500 versus offering to give that money to 10 people:

- Which one creates tension?
- Which one feels good and painless?
- Which one seems like you could do it happily every day?
- Which one seems like you would give up after one week and hate every second of it?

Obviously, asking for $500 is taking value and offering $500 is giving value. One creates tension, the other elicits positive emotions and creates a virtuous cycle of fulfillment. The problem is that most men interact with women in a predominantly value *taking* way, without considering if they have given enough value first.

- Give me your attention because I asked.
- Give me your name because I asked.
- Give me your number because I asked.
- Kiss me because I want to kiss you.
- Go home with me because I want to take you home.

It's all about me, me, and me, like a whiny little boy. The boy attempts to take without offering equal or more value in return. It's win-lose, and the woman feels it. This single mental exercise is the *exact* reason why 99% of men fail to meet and attract the women they want.

Rejection, in its simplest form, is merely a signal that you did not offer enough value. It doesn't mean that there is anything inherently wrong with you as a man. Rather, it signifies that you were not offering enough value or you're failing to make that value readily observable.

But the world—thankfully—doesn't work that way. Instead, you must seek to make every interaction win-win. And so, you are probably thinking, "Okay Andrew, but what do I actually give her? Drinks? Dinner? Movie tickets?" No, no, and hell no!

The most powerful resource that you have to offer is to become the center of good emotions. You accomplish this through your unique personality, positive energy, and full presence in every interaction.

Your personality, engagement, and energy are figuratively equal to the five-hundred dollars you offer to strangers (in reality, they're worth so much more than that). Your energy and positivity radiate warmth and fun, lighting others up and unconsciously drawing them closer to you while giving them permission to fully enjoy themselves. Riches and physical appeal in men are valuable assets, but they are far outweighed by the energy, emotions, and presence a Grounded Man makes a woman *feel*.

Many men are so entitled and pretentious that they mistakenly assume they can skip past making others feel good and simply throw money at relationships in an attempt to make them better. But money is not a replacement for sharing positive emotions, being present, and having good energy.

This is not to denigrate other factors, such as financial success, personal growth, a strong social circle or physical appeal. Those are all important and they *do* have a strong impact on the longevity of a relationship. But make no mistake, positive emotions are the best gift that you can offer to a woman.

At this point, you're probably thinking, "Well, what do I need to say or do in order to convey good emotions in my interactions?" But you're missing one pivotal point. Positive emotions are rarely conveyed through words alone. They are conveyed with the energy behind those words.

HOW TO RADIATE
HIGH-STATUS ENERGY

The one factor that truly separates the most socially successful men from the ones who are stuck in mediocrity is the status of their energy. This is the unconscious language that communicates how you feel on the inside.

When you have low-status energy—in other words, the "energy" or mood of your interactions is colored by a victim mentality, scarcity, a desire to "get" something, or a sense that this journey is draining—you will attract low-status people and repel high-status people. When you bring negativity, a victim mindset, scarcity, and other toxic attitudes and behaviors into an interaction, you will repel high-quality women and attract women who are "broken", "toxic" and downright unhealthy.

People who operate from a low-status frame are actively taking value from whatever group they find themselves in, even without saying a word because their negative energy speaks louder than words. They are taking away the opportunity for people to experience positive emotions, which is why people will slowly exit and gravitate towards people with more positive energy.

When you operate from high-status energy, on the other hand, you will naturally attract more positive and successful people into your life increasing your success, happiness, and fulfillment. People with high-status energy operate from abundance. They are present, alive, and generally excited about life. They go out to share, have fun, and connect with other high-status people. They don't have a hidden agenda or ulterior motives to covertly bring others down, so they can rise up alone.

Can you think of an example of high-status vs. low-status people in your life? Think of people you admire; what level of energy do they give off? How do they make you feel versus the people you often avoid?

Low-status energy is immediately recognizable and nauseatingly palpable. The second you begin a conversation with a person who exudes low-status energy, you'll hear about how terrible their life is, how the government is out to get them, how their ex was a psycho, and a whole slew of other negative scripts.

Spending time in their presence is draining and toxic. You leave the interaction feeling *worse*, even if their words weren't directed at you and you make mental note to avoid interacting with this person again. When you're around someone with high-status energy, on the other hand, you can't help but feel naturally drawn to them. Not sexually, but rather that their presence is so positive and vibrant that you can't help but want to spend more time with them.

These are the men and women who are giving value constantly, who actively seek to lift up the people in their lives, who refuse to complain and be a victim, who lean towards the light vs darkness, who see the world through a beautiful lens.

Now let me ask you, which person are you now and which person do you want to be? If you want to attract high-quality women and have high levels of social success, you must actively cultivate high levels of high-status energy. And it's easier than you might think.

Never let anyone strip you of your right to experience more joy, happiness and aliveness. Refuse to complain, talk negatively about other people, or engage in fruitless conversations about hot-button topics like politics (unless you plan on actually doing something), religion, or other contentious conversations.

Spend thirty days going out with no agenda other than to make people around you feel good, more positive and uplift their moods. If you *really* want to spend some time building your high-status energy, go out for thirty days and *refuse* to ask for a girl's number or try to take her home. Ask for nothing, and only give. So right now, I want you to commit to eradicating *all* low-status energy from your life. Commit to becoming the type of man that makes other people feel *good*. You'll be surprised how this will make you feel, something that can encourage you to continue this cycle.

Right now, you probably feel like offering value and being a "giver" is too hard. You're probably saying to yourself, "Andrew, this sounds great in theory, but it's impossible to act this way when I'm so exhausted and drained by these interactions." I can relate. Plenty of men (my younger self included) find it difficult to internalize and effectively implement high-status energy and the "giver" mentality. It was always a challenge for me to consistently do this until I realized my interactions were being undermined by a sense of scarcity.

I'm going to show you how to eradicate any remaining scripts of scarcity from your life and adopt the most powerful mindset available to man.

WALK THE WORLD WITH PURE ABUNDANCE

The source of nearly *all* unhappiness in life is scarcity. Whether it's scarcity of money, resources, love, passion, or basic necessities, scarcity breeds one of the most dangerous human emotions: desperation. And while many are driven to escape their desperation, others try to find the fastest and easiest way out of it, likely repeating the very mistakes that put them there in the first place.

Good decisions are rarely made out of desperation. With regards to women especially, scarcity leads men to tolerate and accept behaviors, patterns, and habits from their partners they would *never* accept from a relative, friend, or colleague.

Men can slowly and subtly allow women to publicly berate them, treat them with disrespect, and knowingly cross their boundaries. When men operate from scarcity, they feel forced to tolerate low-class behavior and otherwise unacceptable actions. Both parties lose. From this weak frame, there is a loss of respect that undermines the relationship as she slowly pokes at the man, testing him and seeing how much she can get away with.

If you are unwilling to call her out when she disrespects you, goes against a strong value, or even leave the relationship, she *cannot* be attracted to you because you hide your truth and won't stand up for yourself out of fear of upsetting her. In short, she can't trust you. To attract the women you most desire, you *must* cultivate abundance. Without abundance, you'll lack the backbone necessary to attract the highest quality women and will find yourself endlessly settling in relationships that are "good enough.'

When you have no options, you settle by default. But by achieving abundance, you will reclaim your power, choosing the best women from a place of self-worth and self-confidence instead of being chosen from a place of scarcity and weakness.

A man of abundance walks the world with freedom and less attachment to anyone or anything. He is able to confidently walk away from people and situations that do not serve him. This attitude increases your value and will make you more respected and attractive to high-quality people.

Women don't *want* weak men whom they can easily control, walk over and manipulate. Instead, women *want* a man who has the strength and fortitude to stand up for himself, who is choosing to be with her and actively turning down other quality women.

Imagine the satisfaction and pride you would feel having an incredibly attractive woman reject another man—perhaps even a man who is wealthier or more handsome than you —because she wants to be with *you*. When you embody The Grounded Man and select a woman from a place of abundance, that is the *exact* feeling you are giving her. But there's a problem… all of this sounds great in theory, but achieving abundance is no simple feat. It's not something you can just "get" by reading a book. It's something you must experience firsthand.

And when you're just starting out, abundance can feel like an elusive and downright impossible goal. After all, you're the one approaching women, putting in all the work, and facing rejection. None of them are chasing or pursuing you (at least, not yet) until you learn how to effectively meet and invite women into your life with ease.

Because without fully adopting these core mindset shifts then the strategies and tactics prescribed throughout this program will always be an uphill battle. If you'd like my help upgrading your mindset around women, dating and relationships to allow your actions with women to flow more effortlessly and be received positively, then watch this presentation: knowledgeformen.com/live

And as scholars and psychologists have bemoaned for millennia, women are complex creatures. The question "What do women want?" is not always as straightforward as we would like—leaving most men to live forever in the realm of scarcity. However, after conducting many interviews with incredible women and spending the better part of a decade heavily invested in the dating game, I've discovered that there is an answer to the question. You'll know beyond a shadow of a doubt what women *actually* want.

And more importantly, you'll discover how *you* can give it to them in a way that makes you completely irresistible to the most beautiful women you've ever laid your eyes on.

CHAPTER 3

UNDERSTANDING WHAT WOMEN WANT

"What a strange thing man is, and what a stranger thing woman."

-LORD BYRON

Sunlight streamed across my face, awakening me in a daze. It took a few moments to remember where I was. This wasn't my bed. I smiled as it all came back to me.

I had travelled up to Los Angeles the day before and this was my hotel room, and a discounted room at that. Far more beautiful than the view from the window overlooking the city, however, was the gorgeous Brazilian woman still asleep resting on my chest. Although we'd known one another fewer than 12 hours, I felt as if I'd known her for years. How could I have not?

We'd laid awake the entire night, sharing our hopes and dreams, discussing our favorite philosophers (hers was Nietzsche, mine was Aurelius), and pondering the complete absurdity of life. She was different from most girls I'd met in Los Angeles, ambitious, driven–at the time she was studying pre law at UCLA–shared similar values and aspirations and was as smart as she was beautiful. The connection we shared, as shortly lived as it was, seemed to be something reserved for couples who had been together for years. I laid there in awe of not only her beauty but her intellect that could stimulate my own.

The morning light softly illuminated her smooth, olive skin and the perfect curves of her toned, athletic body. Her face, even without makeup—was refined and elegant. She was the very embodiment of beauty both inside and out. The soft white sheets of this king-sized bed fell loosely around her lower body. Her hand rested lightly on my chest. Half of me was very excited to wake her up, the other half wanted to bask in this angelic moment. I drifted my fingers along her naked back and lay quietly, watching her sleep. One amazed thought couldn't stop pinging in my mind:

"How did I get here?"

I started out the night before all alone. I'd braved the teeming nightlife of Los Angeles with only one lead as to how to have a good time—an old friend who worked at the hottest club in town.

When I got there, my heart sank as I drank in the seemingly endless swarm of people waiting in line to enter. The line was packed with well-dressed men escorting some of the most attractive women I'd ever laid eyes on, each of them sporting tight cocktail dresses, heels, and a slew of accessories. I'd never experienced anything like this before. Here I was, a random dude from San Diego. The length of the line—and the elite nature of the people in it—made me begin to lose hope that I would get in at all… until I saw my old friend at the front door, waving at me to come in. Jackpot!

I couldn't help putting a swagger into my step as I walked past these high-end types toward the front of the line. I was skipping the line because I was connected, but I had to ask my friend: "How is it possible that so many beautiful women are waiting outside as if they don't matter?"

He responded casually, "Because they DON'T, dude! Not to the club owners. Everyone in L.A. is hot. Your looks don't matter. Every hot chick here is just another face in a crowd. You have to have cash, celebrity status… or a friend like me." I thanked him as he walked me into the exclusive club—hell, I'm STILL thanking him today for what was to become an unforgettable night.

It started, however, as a very challenging evening. My friend hastily grabbed me a drink (saving me $26—another reason to thank him), then checked his walkie. He clapped my back, "Hey, I gotta jet, man. Duty calls. Have fun. You're on your own." I was indeed. As he disappeared into the crowd, the words of Jason Derulo came to mind: I was flying solo.

For the first half hour or so, my approaches were "unsuccessful." After a few moments of conversation, many of the women I approached suddenly needed to find their "missing" friends or go to the bathroom (from which they'd just returned).

Others, although interested in me (and none too shy about expressing it), lacked the character and qualities that I find attractive. They were beautiful, stunning even but our brief interactions made it abundantly clear they were lacking personality and depth to them. You're hot I get it, but I felt like I was talking to a wall and doing all the work. It seems as though many of these women feel they've already done their part by just looking good and being there.

I didn't care, however. I was just getting started and I knew that I was only one approach away from a great interaction. I laughed my way through maybe a dozen rejections and a few "bad fits' of women that I was uninterested in.

At one point, while talking with a beautiful blonde local, I ruined an otherwise perfect interaction because I glanced into the VIP section and became star struck by a big-time (read: Oscar winning) actor sitting in a private booth. He was surrounded by models, popping bottles, and partying like a regular dude. Well…Not *exactly* a regular dude.

My jaw hit the floor. I couldn't believe it. This fixated moment of "uncoolness" was just enough to make the woman I was talking to raise an eyebrow and leave me in the dust.

Growing frustrated, I began to contemplate going home early. After all, how could *I* compete with spoiled trust fund babies who had more money in their wallet than in my checking account and A-list celebrities whose faces were on billboards just outside the venue?

And then...I saw her.

Just one booth down from the Oscar-winner, surrounded by a pack of baby-faced rich kids wearing suits worth more than my car (illegally parked), was one of the most beautiful women I'd ever seen.

"Just keep walking, dude," I muttered to myself, convinced that the men she was sitting with were so far out of my league that any approach would be futile.

But I couldn't. She was mindlessly surfing on her phone while others talked around her. She was clearly bored. At first glance, I had considered her unattainable, but she actually looked like she was just waiting for someone to enliven her night. That's when it happened... she looked up! Our eyes met! What should I do?!

I was flustered, under pressure, not sure what to do. So, I winked at her. Then I WAVED! I broke out in a hot sweat as my body snapped into uncontrollable dorky instincts. *Damn it, Andrew! A wink!?! A fucking wave? You're horrible! Do something else, QUICK.*

I did the first thing that came to me. I started moving my shoulders in a playful dance that looked — I can only imagine — like the waddle of a half-crippled penguin. *Damn it, Andrew! This isn't better. Stop moving your damn shoulders and be bold!*

And then I remembered something... I didn't even know this woman! Her beauty, undeniably intoxicating as it might have been, was insufficient to take me out of my state. I didn't have millions in the bank or a designer suit, but I offered something even better. The ability to give her the most adventurous night of her life *or at least I thought that.*

Taking a deep breath, I flashed her a smile, slowed my dance, and signaled for her to come closer. It was a Hail Mary move, to say the least, but—to my surprise and elation—she gave me a playful smile...

... and started moving towards me!

She was entrenched behind an impenetrable fortress of velvet ropes and giant security guards (that likely didn't make the cut to become NFL linebackers) who glowered at me murderously. I did NOT belong in their VIP section. It was obvious (as was their desire to break my arms if I tried to enter).

Nevertheless, packing my fear way down, I extended my hand across the rope, "crossing the border" from the plebian dance floor to the exclusive VIP area. I was fully prepared to feel the bouncers start cracking my rib cage with their bare hands, but instead, I felt her soft fingers slide into my palm.

I pulled her closer and whispered into her ear, "You look like the perfect companion for my adventures tonight... come with." She laughed sweetly, attempting to let me down easy, "I can't, I'm with that group over there."

Pasting on an expression of mock incredulity, I looked at the suave men in her booth and responded playfully, "I know, that's why I'm here! Let me save you from them so you can actually enjoy your night." She feigned offense but was unable to hide her amusement. We both laughed at the same time, and I sealed the deal by grabbing her hand and holding onto eye contact as I guided her smoothly to the dance floor.

As we walked to the dance floor, she slipped coming down the stairs in her heels, dropping her small purse to the floor. I picked it up thinking it was full of makeup and I noticed inside revealed a small paperback copy *Beyond Good and Evil* by Friedrich Nietzsche.

"What's this?" I exclaimed playfully, picking the book out and holding it just out of her reach.

"What?" she responded with a twinge of embarrassment in her voice.

"It's awesome..." I fired back, "Don't get me wrong, this means you're a total nerd, but I think it's adorable." I smirked at her and slid the book back into her purse.

She playfully smacked my arm and then shot back, "Have you read it?"

"No," I responded honestly, "I prefer the Stoics, but you can give me the cliff notes later tonight...maybe over a glass of wine (or two) at my hotel."

She smirked at me, "Ooh I'd have so much to share on that...but let's go dance."

As we approached the dance floor, her hips started swaying to the music and I felt my heart fall straight out of my chest... I was awestruck by the perfectly round hips of her tight Brazilian body.

We danced, touched, teased and—when the DJ reached the hook of his track—I picked her up by her waist and spun her, both of us laughing as we heard a chorus of "screw yous" from the well-behaved couples dancing around us. As I set her down, she pulled me close and exclaimed in her adorable Portuguese accent I was quickly learning to love, "You're so crazy! Who are you?"

I answered back fast, "I'm the man who saved you from the worst night of your life." She leaned in close, resting her head on my shoulder, "I'm glad you did."

I teasingly whispered into her ear, "My job isn't easy, ya' know… tips are always appreciated." Laughing, she slapped me playfully on the chest and responded flirtatiously, "I don't have cash… but maybe there's another way I can repay you…"

Inhaling deeply, blood pulsing at her connotation but not knowing how to respond to her provocative words, I pushed myself to be bold and take a risk, "You're onto something. This place isn't us. I want to show you the epic views back at my place and discuss philosophy over wine." I stood and extended my arm, then led her confidently out of the venue. She was probably the only woman in Los Angeles where using the word "philosophy" would excite her to want to leave a high end night club.

That next morning as the sun rose, it excited me to think about all that had happened the night before with this beauty. I was excited for her to wake up, however, I wanted to let her get more rest—

—which was suddenly interrupted by a loud knock on the door! A thick Spanish accent came barreling through the room, "Excuse me! Housekeeping!"

My lover shot up in bed, blurting out, "No, thank you! Please come back—whoa!" She suddenly realized that she was bare naked, almost showing her exposed breasts to the cleaning lady. She quickly fell back to the bed and I covered her in the thin white sheets, embracing her in my arms and laughing together as the cleaning lady shut the door behind her. She came back to bed and laid her head on my chest. I asked her, "I see your stance on 19th century philosophy, but what is it that you want in a man?"

She quickly responded, "Oh, that's easy!" she responded confidently, "I want him to be rich, drive a Ferrari, and live in a big house in the Hollywood Hills." I laughed and looked at her playfully, "Then why are you in bed with *me*? I'm sure at least one of those guys you were with last night has a Ferrari and a big house. I on other hand, made you *feel* something you haven't felt in years."

She laughed, got up and threw a pillow at me not once but twice, but let's think about what she said there for a moment…

Women have been conditioned to think that they want a certain type of man. Chick flicks and romance novels have given them this idea about who their ideal partner is and what they want, or at least what they think they want.

More often than not, the man women actually respond to is someone completely different from the man they claim to desire.

This is why women will friend zone "Nice Guys" and sleep with "Bad Boys," even though they *claim* they want a nice guy. It's why they will cheat on partners who have all of the qualities they've been told they should want—fidelity, stability, love, kindness, a good job—all to leap into the forbidden embrace of another man who possesses the character traits to which they actually respond.

This is why men struggle to attract the women they want, despite doing everything that those same women are telling them to do. This ambiguous messaging has led to an epidemic. Men all over the world are following false societal scripts trying to attract women without realizing they are actively repelling the women they wish to attract.

It's not entirely our fault. If you're like I was, back when I was on my quest to figure all of this out, you've tried to understand women for many years. You've asked your friends, read articles, watched videos online. Heck, you've even asked the women in your life what they want in a man.

Yet time and time again, you have been fed well-intentioned but ultimately hollow advice that simply does not work. Every time you've acted on it, it's pushed you further and further away from becoming the type of man women actually want. Therefore, let's begin answering the old adage question: "What do women want?"

To find out, we first must start by excising the toxic lessons and ineffective patterns we've already learned. Only then can we replace them with the traits to which women *actually* respond.

THE WORST DATING ADVICE YOU'LL EVER HEAR

Most dating advice does not come from a healthy place of wholeness and a desire for genuine help. Instead, as well intentioned as it might be, it is delivered through the lens of other people's past trauma and emotional wounds. They are sharing advice that would have kept them safe from the pain and heartbreak they experienced in the past.

They'll make claims like:

- Women just want a nice guy!
- Just be yourself!
- Only date a man who will commit to you quickly!

While these platitudes sound great in theory, they rarely deliver the results that women actually respond to, nor is it what they really want. What's worse, many of these stories are so ingrained in our subconscious minds that we never even *consider* the possibility of their inaccuracy. To help you achieve the results that you want in your romantic life and attract the women you most desire, you must remove these toxic social beliefs from your psyche and replace them with the only thing that works... the *truth*. Let's dive in…

1. Just Be Yourself and The Right Woman Will Come Along

Since early childhood, you've been errantly taught that success—with women and in life—is nothing more than a byproduct of "being yourself." Your friends, parents, and likely the women in your life—*especially* the ones who have friend zoned you in the past—repeat this tired phrase over and over again, but they never provide any practical advice for implementing it and rarely, if ever, can explain what they really mean.

As a result, men will blindly run with this advice and then think to themselves, "Well, I went out to a venue, sat with a friend drinking in a corner, and didn't have a conversation with anyone else... and no women showed any interest in me. This is who I am and what I honestly wanted to do that night, so I guess being yourself doesn't work!"

But they're missing the point entirely. Men often assume that being themselves somehow gives them permission to stagnate, do less, and slip into unproductive patterns and behaviors. They believe that women will find them attractive *even if* they lack social skills, have soul-sucking jobs (and lives), and spend all of their free time fantasizing about their future living in "someday land," cycling through a never-ending stream of ways to escape life: porn, the latest TV shows, video games or engaged in ego driven workaholism.

After all, they are indeed being themselves since that is what they genuinely want to do and what feels most *comfortable* to them. But nothing could be further from the truth.

Women aren't attracted to weak and purposeless men simply because they are "being themselves." They want men who are committed to becoming their best selves.

The right woman won't want you to change who you are at your core or pursue goals and ambitions that are incongruent with your values. But she'll expect you to have your life together, be moving forward, and know how to lead your life. They don't want a man who puts on a mask and pretends to be someone he's not. They want a man who is unapologetic about who he is and what he wants in the world, a man who isn't afraid to express his desires.

For example, let's say that you're currently overweight, working a so-so job to pay the bills, and generally unsure of who you are or what you want as a man. You aren't a goofball, party animal, or jock. In fact, you're a bit of an average guy and prefer to spend your evenings watching TV or hanging with friends over a few beers. Becoming your best self wouldn't require you to relinquish your TV, ditch your friends, get tables at the club, or become a wildly extroverted party animal.

Being your best self would mean optimizing your life to become closer to the man that you aspire to be. For instance, hitting the gym and losing the love handles, quitting your awful job in favor of a career that you love (even if it pays less), traveling alone for a while to develop core confidence in yourself as a man, starting a business that you'd always wanted to launch, or building a more powerful social network of men and women that you've always wanted to surround yourself with.

When you go out, instead of trying to make things work at a loud club or social venue, opt for a quiet location where you can engage in the deep conversations that you naturally enjoy. You don't need to become someone that you aren't! But you must maximize who you are and develop the attractive traits you already possess. It's about putting yourself in environments that you will naturally thrive in. Because here's the hard reality...

If who you are today was sufficient to attract the woman of your dreams, you would already have her. You cannot "be yourself" and expect women to flock to you. It is only by becoming your *best self* that you will achieve the results you desire.

2. Just be a "Nice Guy" and Women Will Love You

First and foremost, they do *not* mean they want a man who will:

- Bend over backwards to meet her every need and desire at the expense of his own well-being.
- Refuse to call her out when she acts inappropriately or sit by quietly when she is acting disrespectfully.
- Supplicate to her every whim and need her approval.

These are unattractive, weak behaviors that actively repel high-quality women and showcase to everyone in your vicinity that you are a man who lacks backbone and self-worth. In short, that's *not* what women want!

> **What women really mean when they say they want a "nice guy" is they still want a strong, masculine man with backbone yet who treats her and others with respect and kindness.**

No woman wants to be with a man who will lie to her, cheat on her, degrade her, or act like an arrogant asshole. But neither do they want a weak, approval-seeking man they can easily walk over and who cannot stand up for himself. Instead, women want a strong, assertive man who can be both dominant and kind, someone who marries the best parts of the nice guy *and* the bad boy. They want a man who is free, self-reliant, and powerful in his own domains but also has the capability of being loving, tender, and generous both to her and others around him. But here's the catch that most men miss...

Before she can view your nice and caring side as attractive and not weakness, she must first *feel* the masculine side. Women don't want you to only have the soft characteristics of the "nice guy." They want a man who is strong, emotionally resilient, and self-reliant but who can *also* be kind, caring, and compassionate.

There's nothing wrong with being nice, vulnerable, and emotional to others. These are universally good human traits across many different cultures. But relying exclusively on the nice guy archetype to create attraction is a zero-sum game that you will lose to more dominant men.

3. Women Want a Man Who Will Commit Quickly

The third and final lie is that women want commitment right away. The most bewildering part of this statement is that it is both true *and* false. Yes, women want a man who is willing to commit, be faithful, and whom they can trust. But women don't want commitment from every man that they meet and if they do like you, then they certainly don't want commitment right away.

When you commit to a woman too early and too fervently, she won't see your commitment as the sign of loyalty and integrity that you intend it to be. Instead, she will view your commitment as a sign of scarcity and desperation. It's not commitment, but rather an indicator that you are not Grounded; you are quickly willing to sacrifice so much of your time, energy, and resources for someone that you barely know. They want commitment from the right man at the right time *after strong* levels of attraction have been established.

They want commitment from a man *they* are actively pursuing and chasing, not from any man who meets their bare minimum requirements and is ready to get on a knee within a few months of knowing them. Commitment is most attractive when a woman feels like she is being selected by a man who could also be with other women, but he actively chooses her.

If you don't have other options, aren't dating other women, and she is the number one source of your happiness, guess what? It's not attractive, and you're stuck in a needy and validation-seeking frame. You have little to offer her and she will reject your commitment with a common phrase: "You're really nice, but I think we should be friends."

Commitment is more valued when it comes from a place of abundance. Selecting one woman from a pool of many and making the decision to say "no" to your other good options to say "yes" to her.

Otherwise, your commitment carries much less weight, if any at all. While these three lies have proliferated our society for years, there are two final lies that are even more sinister and widespread than these. If you believe them, they will ruin your chances of succeeding with women and cause you to spend *years* of your life chasing the wrong things.

Let's prevent that from happening now.

DON'T I NEED TO BE A RICH, JACKED, MALE MODEL TO DATE MY DREAM GIRL?

If you pulled 100 random men from any city in the United States and asked them the question, "What do women want?" at least 90% of them would respond with something along the lines of: *"Women want a tall, good-looking, rich man with six-pack abs."*

Now, I won't bullshit you and claim that you can live in your parent's basement until you're 40 years old, demand regular meals of meatloaf from your "Ma," flip burgers for minimum wage, and still date high-quality women.

Money and physical looks *do* indeed matter—and anyone who claims otherwise is either lying or selling you something—but they don't matter nearly as much as you might think. Money is a strong indicator of diligence, persistence, and intelligence; good looks are simply a sign of good genes and that a man respects himself and cares about presenting his best self to the world. That's it.

Both of these factors demonstrate the results of character traits indicating that a man can provide value and safety for a woman. However, there are plenty of very successful men out there who are lonely, settling for subpar (in some cases toxic) relationships, or simply the most unhappy and miserable people you've ever met.

Money matters. But in and of itself, it is insufficient to attract a woman of quality and real substance. In fact, the most attractive women I've ever encountered were not dating men who were famous, wealthy, or had a stellar physique. They were with Grounded Men who knew how to elicit positive emotions, high status energy, and were socially competent.

On the other hand, I've encountered countless good-looking men who were wealthy beyond most people's wildest dreams, yet they couldn't get a date with an attractive woman to save their lives. These guys that supposedly have everything that women want are constantly settling for low-quality women.

When we talk about relationships, it's always the same. *"I'm not ready for the woman of my dreams yet. She won't want to be with me until I'm making more."* Or, *"I'm ready for the woman of my dreams, but I don't have time because I'm so focused on my work."*

Seriously? So many men miss out on the opportunity to share their life with the woman of their dreams because they falsely believe they need to hit a certain financial milestone before a high-quality woman will want to date them. And because they have erroneously correlated money with success and desirability (e.g. "more money means higher-quality women will want me") they forego the best years of their romantic lives to increase their bank accounts.

Most women don't care about your bank account as much as they do the quality of your character and the behaviors that you exude. Rich men are out there, but Grounded Men who are happy and vibrant are scarce in society, which makes them highly-valued and admired by both men and women.

A man making $50,000 a year, living below his means, and full of vibrancy, aliveness, and positive emotions is infinitely more attractive than a man making $250,000 a year who wastes his money on status symbols. High quality women do not want a man who's emotionally dead and drained by the 80-hour work weeks to which he voluntarily subjects himself.

You are capable of dating very high-quality women the moment that you step into and embody the Grounded Man, regardless of your financial status or physical appeal. She will come with you on the journey and share in the experience *as* you rise through the ranks, not once you've arrived at the pinnacle in old age. And if she doesn't want to be with you because you aren't earning above a certain threshold, then why would you want to be with *her*?

Besides, how much more fulfilling is it to date the woman of your dreams *now* and bring her along for the journey to success? More importantly, how much more would you trust each other? How much deeper would your intimate connection be if you knew beyond a shadow of a doubt that she would be with you even if you lost everything?

The reason quality women are attracted to men with financial resources is rarely the money itself. It's the character traits and qualities that allowed a man to make that money.

If you already have those qualities and are working diligently towards your biggest goals, the right woman will have no problem joining you on your journey while you achieve the success you desire. Now, does this mean that you shouldn't go after big goals in your career or try and accumulate wealth and financial abundance? Of course not! You absolutely should, but do it for *yourself* and your own reasons, not because you think it will make women flock to you.

What most men fail to realize is that, after a certain point in a relationship, women cease to "see" their partner on a physical level. Instead, they "feel" them. And if the right character traits and behaviors are not there, they feel nothing, regardless of the size of your bank account. This is a hard concept for men to internalize because men are so visually stimulated by the opposite sex. Overtime women care far more about the way a man makes her feel and less about the way he physically looks. What's missing for both the handsome and rich single men are the Grounded Man attributes and the right internal mindset.

Fortunately, you now have *both* of these, and in the coming pages you'll unlock the third and final piece to the "inner game" puzzle…

THE #1 WAY TO INSTANTLY KILL ATTRACTION WITH BEAUTIFUL WOMEN

How would you feel if I walked up to you on the street tomorrow and handed you an Olympic gold medal? Do you think you would feel satisfied? Would you feel like you'd actually *achieved* something? Sure, it might be a cool token or something you could sell for quick cash, but would you value that medal the way you would if you'd actually *earned* it? Would you treat it the same way as someone who had sweat, bled, and worked hard daily for most of their lives?

Of course not. The reason is simple. Human beings are hardwired to value things that are hard to attain more than they value the things that come easily. And this applies to *you* as well as a gold medal. Women aren't drawn to a man who is easy to "attain" or who is an easy catch.

They don't want to feel like they have you wrapped around their finger or like their beauty is enough for them to walk all over you, especially so soon after meeting. They want to know that they *earned* your love, attention, and affection by being the best person for you. They want to feel like they had to work hard to get something worth having and were able to beat the competition of other high-quality women.

The problem is that most men are too easy and available. They'll open up their entire lives and their resources to a woman after just a few dates and good sex. When you allow a woman into your life without any sort of challenge or filtration process (which we will cover in detail in chapter 6), she won't value you the way she would if she'd worked to *earn* a place in your life. And make no mistake, she *should* have to earn it, just as you must become a Grounded Man and bring value in order to earn her time and attention.

No woman, no matter how beautiful she might be, immediately deserves a long-term place in your life solely because of her physical appearance. You should have such high standards for yourself regarding the character of the women you date that you will turn down anyone who isn't aligned with who you are, what you value, or how you want to live.

It's impossible for every attractive woman that you meet to be a good match for you. The more a woman invests in securing you as a partner, the more she will *value* and respect you and your relationship moving forward. Women want a man who is worthy of their time and energy. They *want* someone who is a challenge, which is the irony of all of this.

If you are too easy and overly available, then you are depriving women of the fun, excitement, and emotional stimulation of earning and returning the love, attention, and affection of a Grounded Man.

Stop being so damn easy, with women you want to date or with anyone else. Demand that the people in your life *deserve* to be there and refuse to settle for second-class behavior from anyone. When you establish your values, the woman in your life will respond differently to you than to other men because she knows that her looks alone aren't enough. She will prove herself to you by showing you respect, being responsive, and enjoying the dating process much more with you.

Now, this doesn't mean you should be too uninterested or that you can be so hard to get that you expect women to approach you. You must still take initiative and make the first move to do this effectively, you must show up in your most powerful state and bring high levels of energy and aliveness into your interactions.

Here's a simple framework you can use to consistently do this…

GETTING INTO YOUR MOST
POWERFUL "STATE" EVERYDAY

State, in its simplest form, is simply the energy and presence that you carry with you and bring into any interaction. If you're feeling happy, motivated, and excited to go out and be social, then you're in a positive state. If you're feeling anxious, nervous, or lethargic, you're in a negative state.

You may have experienced a time when you were out with friends and firing on all cylinders. Every word that left your mouth elicited hysterical laughter, you felt confident and bold, you pushed your interactions as far as they could go and had a blast. What if you could command your body and mind into this level of state and high-status energy every day? How would this affect your interactions?

Well, you can. The trick is to understand the power of your "default." Your default state is the day-to-day state that you live in the majority of the time. If you regularly feel depressed, anxious, and nervous and your physical state reflects the mood of your emotions, this will become your default state. If you normally feel positive, energized, and excited about making the most of the day, this will become your default state.

The good news is that you have the power to change your state in the moment, which will change your default state overtime. If you want to achieve more results with women and in your dating life, then changing your "default" state to include more positive energy, being social, and having more fun will do wonders for your dating life. And it's actually a lot easier than it sounds.

Most guys will operate in a low-status energy state all day long then attempt to shock themselves out of this boring and unexcited state moments before going out to meet women. But to achieve the best and most consistent results, you must focus on cultivating a positive state the moment you wake up till the moment you go to sleep, *whether or not you are going out that night or have attractive women in your life.*

Say "hello" to the people in the elevator. Flirt and make small talk with the barista when you get your coffee in the morning. Chat with strangers in line at the grocery store. Smile more as you go about your day. Spend a few extra minutes with people versus quickly exiting conversations.

The more social you can be in your day-to-day life and the more you can create a default state of fun, higher-energy, and sociability, the easier it will be to have effortless interactions with women.

If you don't talk to anyone other than your dog and can't have small talk with a middle-aged cashier at the grocery store, then how on earth do you think you'll be able to suddenly flip the switch and get into a good state with an attractive woman? The guys who can effectively create abundant dating lives with quality women are the guys who live in more positive states and have higher levels of social skills. But there's another element to state: momentum.

Let's say you've been working on the computer all day on work projects and have had little social interactions throughout your day. Obviously, you're out of state at first when you get into a social situation. You need time to adjust from work mode to social mode, as much as an hour to come alive, get present, and be more social.

As a side note: when you're eating right, exercising regularly, sleeping well, doing things outdoors, having a fun social life, then tapping into a positive state will come a lot naturally and easier to you. When you're healthy, your base level of state is an unhealthy person's highest level of state. The goal is to constantly raise the bar of your base level so you're producing consistent results every day and you're not relying on things like excessive amounts of alcohol just so you can start and enjoy conversations with strangers and have fun.

All in all, to reach your state, you must take more action, lower the time between interactions with men and women as you go about your daily life, and know that you have massive value to offer as a Grounded Man. When you can tap into this unrestricted sociability, you will increase your level of attractiveness.

Here's why…

THE POWER OF SOCIAL PROOF
AND DESIRABILITY

I'm going to be incredibly blunt here. You might not like what I have to say and it most certainly won't be easy to hear. You ready? Here it is: People are attracted to that which is attractive to others. People desire that which is desired by others. And most men lead unattractive and undesirable lives.

It's important to note that this tendency is not new. It's driven by millions of years of evolution. Human beings are hardwired to "follow the crowd" and desire, fear, and believe the same things as those around them. It's kind of like an evolutionary shortcut. Instead of having to constantly vet, filter, and weigh different options, we simply pay attention to social cues, using them to quickly determine which things are valuable and which ones aren't.

When it comes to women and dating, this principle plays out in a profoundly simple manner. Instead of trying to meet, talk to, and filter every man they see, women look for men who have existing indicators of social value, and vice versa. When a man is surrounded by beautiful women and admired by other successful men, his social value increases.

Being social signifies that you are a healthy male with high self-esteem. When a woman sees that you have a strong social circle filled with other attractive women and successful men, it implies that you have a history of social success and are more likely to be worth her time.

The approval of others serves as a "pre-approval" for her. It unconsciously increases your perceived social value, making her view you as a higher value man. The problem is that most men struggle to build this social proof into their lives. They lack the requisite social skills to garner the respect and attention of others around them and, as a result, they are immediately seen as low-value men.

Their lack of social proof serves as a warning to women that these men may be emotionally unhealthy, lacking self-esteem, and plagued by a myriad of other interpersonal issues. Even though they might be interesting, down to earth, and emotionally stable men, women will see these weak social signals. It will prevent the interaction from getting to the point where they uncover the good qualities you possess. When you lack obvious social value, you will always struggle to attract the highest-quality women. The fix is quite simple, though. Slowly increase your sociability and extroversion in everyday life.

You've heard of introverts and extroverts. Introverts tend to go deeper with fewer individuals in conversations, while extroverts go wide, establishing surface-level rapport with the masses. Both approaches and personalities can lead to great results socially, so you cannot use "I'm not an extrovert" as an excuse to avoid being more social. You absolutely *can* be an introverted person who still makes a habit of connecting and building rapport with more people every day.

Make it a priority to introduce yourself to new people and share more positive emotions with others wherever you are. Conversations and interactions in everyday life are the best activity to improve your sociability and practice being more engaged and alive. The more easily you can connect with strangers on a bus, in a plane, and people waiting in line with you at the store, the more easily you will be able to connect with the women you desire.

After all, human beings are wired to connect. It's in our DNA and it's one of the reasons that we became the dominant species on the planet. For millions of years, we lived and died by our ability to socialize and cultivate relationships with other humans. Yet as we've become more technologically advanced, we've arrived at a point in our evolutionary journey where we no longer need to rely on other humans for safety and survival. We've become isolated and often socially incompetent as we share, post, and hashtag our way through life.

This isn't just counterproductive for your success with women and in relationships, but for your health and success in life. Dr. Douglas Nemecek, MD, Chief Medical Officer for Behavioral Health at Cigna, claims that loneliness is worse for your health than smoking a pack of cigarettes a day. You are not saving energy and time or getting ahead by not socializing with people. You are damaging your mental health and reducing your social value.

The easiest way to increase your social health is to set a series of increasingly difficult challenges for yourself that stretch you out of your comfort zone and teach you how to engage with others in more exciting ways. To get started, simply commit to making small talk with a few strangers each day. Once this becomes easy, you can push yourself to complete more and more intimidating challenges.

Start watching stand-up comedy and then challenge yourself to share a funny story or difficult-to-pull-off joke to someone that you just met. Take improv classes, join speaking clubs and attend local meetups to make socializing a regular part of your life. Find an area of interest and join a group or class. Stop being afraid of the people around you and realize that they are just like you. They are *waiting* for someone to come along and give them permission to have more fun, be more alive, and enjoy life too.

But the question still remains: beyond surface level socializing and fun conversations, how do you break through the noise in your interactions and create a deeper level of attraction and connection with women? It happens by learning to transform the *language* in which you communicate.

Here's how you do it...

EMOTIONS VS. LOGIC BASED ATTRACTION

Attraction is an emotional reaction, not a logical one. You can't reason a woman into your bed, on a date, or into a relationship, no matter how much sense your logical argument makes. Women are either instinctively attracted to you or not.

In the same way, a woman cannot logically convince you to feel attraction for her. Either the woman you are talking with is physically attractive and intellectually engaging enough for you to feel attraction, or she isn't. Consider the phenomenon of dating apps. Studies have shown that men will swipe—that is, decide whether or not they are attracted to a woman—three times faster than a woman will. Men are instinctively attracted to a woman's appearance, whereas women are instinctively attracted to the way a man makes her feel. They need more time to read the bio to gauge a man's personality before feeling anything.

You either feel attraction for her or you don't. She either feels attraction for you or she doesn't. There's no amount of logic or reason that can force either one of you to feel attraction.

Some guys will try to logically work their way into their relationships and then spend the rest of their lives frustrated that quality women don't respond well to them, but to other men who may not be as credible or successful logically speaking. So let's clear this up once and for all.

A woman does *not* tally up all of your assets, pore over your tax returns like the IRS, and look at your credit score, then think, "Okay, take me home." The only thing that will determine whether or not she will enter into any kind of relationship with a man is the quality of the emotions that the man makes her feel. This is why you'll often hear women who have one-night stands say things like:

- It just *felt* so right, and one thing led to another.
- We were having so much *fun* and then "it" just happened.
- He just made me *feel* so alive, I couldn't control myself around him.

How many times have you heard a woman say, "Yeah, I know he was really boring, lacked a personality, and the conversation was like talking to a wall but hey! It was so exciting to discover that he has an 825-credit score and a condo with a two-car garage, so I couldn't keep my hands off of him!" It just doesn't happen. I have to be honest with you. There will be strategies and recommendations made in this book that you might find at first immature, eccentric, and downright silly. But when you feel the resistance, pause and ask yourself whether you're filtering that thought through a logical or an emotional headspace.

Are you speaking the overly-serious and often restrictive language of "logic" or the free flowing, exciting, and stimulating language of "emotion"? You must learn to speak the language that moves women by getting out of your head and sharing positive emotions.

Logic and reason are important assets for accumulating wealth, ascending your chosen career ladder, and making wise decisions, but can sometimes be the death of attraction in the world of the feminine. You will *never* win a woman over with cold hard logic. The only thing you'll win is a new female friend, and that's great if that's all you wanted. Just think about the last time you were in a room with a bunch of male friends—talking about serious topics like politics, business, or world affairs—and a woman suddenly walked in.

What happened? The energy of the room completely shifted and every man in the circle started to let loose, have more fun, and tap into their playful side. Women, more specifically feminine women, are great at getting men out of their head and into the present moment. They offer so much emotional connection, fun, and playfulness that they allow men to briefly escape their logical headspace and truly come alive. Rather than fighting against this in frustration, join them.

Female attraction is an emotional, unconscious reaction to the energy, emotions, and behavior that you present to her; it is not a calculated decision.

The characteristics that you present to women are honest signs of whether or not you present the qualities of a good partner. Women have to make quick decisions about whether or not you're a viable potential partner since there are many men to choose from. She wants to select the *best* one... as do you.

Women are evolutionarily programmed to identify traits in a man such as strength, power, assertiveness, caring, and kindness, which they see as beneficial to them for survival or a reproductive advantage for child raising. This is sexual selection. Women choose a mate—often unconsciously—based on the traits the man possesses. The evolutionary goal is for those traits to be passed onto their children. They are a honest sign of her own and her children's survival. If you were a woman and you had to recreate a society, would you pick a weak man? Or the strongest, most reliable male leader who also cares for you and the tribe as a whole?

Why does this help you? When you understand attraction is an emotional, unconscious decision for many women, then the thought that you need to be incredibly good looking or make a lot of money carries much less weight. Women are doing the right thing for themselves, and you're no different. You unconsciously try to find the most beautiful women with healthy skin, glowing hair, large breasts, and good hip-to-weight ratio because this is an unconscious biological sign of a healthy, fertile woman who can bear healthy children.

Female mating preferences are designed to choose men who are best for their survival and reproduction. Male mating preferences are designed to choose women who are best for giving birth and raising children. This means women aren't rejecting you as a person, they are rejecting how you present yourself to them. And what's great is this can all be fixed so you can start attracting the women you want.

However, there is a difference between understanding that emotion-based attraction is important and actually having the ability to leverage it in your interactions with women. The lesson you're about to learn—if you will take the time to apply it—will drastically alter the interactions that you have with the women. You'll wonder how you ever showed up to women in any other way...

DANCING WITH THE FEMININE

The hallmark of the Grounded Man is that he is a lover of the *feminine,* the feminine essence that makes women so intoxicating to men. They don't only see her breasts, butt, and legs. They notice the way she walks, the subtle smell of her perfume, the way that she laughs, her voice, and the way she brushes the hair out of her face when she gets nervous.

Most men are only able to experience surface layer attraction because they are still trapped in a validation-driven and needy frame. Grounded Men go beyond artificial exterior beauty and see women for who they truly are, not just *what* they are. That alone is one of the many failures of men today, to not have the ability to see the inner beauty of a woman and only see her physical beauty.

When you are the rare breed of man who can see a woman for who she is on a deeper level and connect with her inner beauty, attraction is the only natural conclusion.

But so many men are only able to see a woman's surface level beauty. They see her as something to be conquered, as a prize to possess, or as a toy for their entertainment to show off to other men.

They don't see her for who she is and what makes her unique amongst all women. This superficial and egotistical attitude causes women to embrace their masculine edge and become more cold, distant, and defensive towards men. They constantly have a shield up because they can sense that the man wants something from her and is not trying to connect *with* her. Too often, they simply want to experience a woman's physical assets instead of experiencing *all* of her—both her physical beauty and inner beauty.

When a woman is forced into her masculine, it creates friction between her and the men in her life, leading to unhealthy games and psychological tricks where there should be balance, harmony, and cooperation. The masculine and feminine are a dance, but it only works if both parties are moving together in unison instead of trying to fight against each other. A Grounded Man embraces all of the craziness and quirkiness that make her unique and doesn't attempt to change her into his version of a woman with logic or reason.

He creates a safe environment for her to feel more like herself, which makes her feel even more deeply connected to this type of man. Let me be clear, there is a big difference between a man who *pretends* to be a lover of the feminine and uses the facade to get laid, and a man who truly understands and embodies this feeling at his core.

To truly fall in love with the feminine, you must learn to appreciate the feminine for all that it is, even the "bad" parts that drives most men crazy. You often hear men complain endlessly about women spending too long on their makeup, freaking out about small challenges in life, and getting overly moody about silly crimes like leaving the toothpaste cap off.

To a Grounded Man, this is merely a part of her beauty. Not only is he unfazed by such trivial concerns, he chuckles and is *aroused* by them. He has learned to enjoy the chaos of the feminine, to stand strong and to appreciate it even when it's at its worst.

When you do this, a woman is free to fall completely into her feminine without fear of shame or judgement. Then, she will feel completely safe and seen when she's with you, a rare gift that most women never experience in their lives: true connection and love. And, at the end of the day, women want to be loved for who they are, not for what they physically have to offer (a fleeting asset). However, with this attitude a man can subconsciously strip himself of his power and unwittingly adopt the "nice guy" habits and tendencies while trying to support a woman's feminine. That only pushes women away all over again.

To remedy this challenge, you must work just as diligently to tap into the more primal side of your masculinity to embrace the dance of the feminine in unison.

ON BEING DOMINANT IN A HEALTHY WAY

Highly-attractive women are conditioned to be attracted to powerful, dominant, and masculine men. Despite what pop culture and mainstream media might tell you, they don't want a weak, emasculated, or effeminate man.

Yet most men are stepping so deeply into their feminine and putting women on such a high pedestal—an "honor" they neither want nor appreciate—that they instantly turn women off. #Friendzone, anyone? Women want to be with men who have a high sense of self-worth and confidence, and who demonstrate the dominant and commanding masculine energy women find most attractive.

Dominance makes women feel like you can protect them and their offspring. This is not to say that there is anything wrong with being connected to your feminine side, like caring about your appearance, developing skills like art or dance, or being vulnerable and in touch with your emotions (all attractive qualities). It's to say that you cannot exclusively *live* there and not have the ability to be dominant when necessary.

Most women view the man of their dreams as someone who is the leader of his own life, who takes her hand and guides her on his adventure. The weak, timid man who can't approach her or talk to her and isn't clear in his intentions because he's scared of rejection repels women.

Grounded men must be the path, the way, and the light to lead those they care about into a better life.

It's important to note that there is a fundamental (but not obvious) difference between aggressiveness and assertiveness. An aggressive man is relying on unhealthy dominance and *imposes* what he wants on others without any consideration for how it will impact them. He has no problem using verbal assault or even violence to get what he wants.

An assertive man is using healthy dominance and does not use violence simply to get his way. He's capable of violence if the need should arise, but it's not for self-serving reasons. It's the difference between the type of man who would physically harm a woman for talking negatively about him and the kind of man who would firmly stand up for himself verbally, set a clear boundary, and make it clear that he will walk away should any more disrespectful, second-class behavior occur.

If a woman only wanted someone who was capable of being sweet and loving, they'd start dating their best girlfriend. They want a powerful Grounded Man who can provide a broad range of both. You must be unapologetic and able to own your desire. Be okay with the fact you want things, especially women. You don't simply want to be her friend. She already has plenty of friends. You want to be *with* her, so you must be clear in your intentions. Men are respected more if they act on what they want in the world. A man who hides his true intentions is less respected and less trusted by others. Women want a man of honest action who can make bold moves in the face of fear and go after what he wants fervently.

Now in being dominant, men often assume they are "taking" from a woman and this is something that women do not equally want, which is why men resort to being a nice guy. I'm quite happy to report that couldn't be further from the truth.

WOMEN ARE INNATELY SEXUAL BEINGS

I'm going to share something that many of you might not believe: women love sex just as much as men. By being clear in your intentions and expressing your sexual desires, you are not taking from a woman since it is something she too wants. The highest selling book genre is romance/erotica purchased by yours truly: women. This is not to say that women are sluts. I personally believe we need to quit vilifying women who are confident in their sexuality, rather we must understand that women equally have a strong biological *desire* for sex just as men do. They simply have more self-preservation regarding their sexuality because there is infinitely more at stake for them than there is for men. Think about it: everywhere and everyday women get offered sex.

By the time the average woman is 20 years old, she's declined more sex than you will ever have in your entire life. The problem is, it's being offered by men who are not Grounded, who don't see her for who she really is, and who provide little value for their lives. As such, they have no choice but to decline. Thanks to the double standard from society, women are worried about being labeled as sluts and ostracized from their peer groups. In many instances, they may desperately want to have sex with a man but resist because of fear of the social and physical consequences.

Many women think of sex every day and would *have* sex every day if the conditions were right. The difference between men and women, however, is that men are aware of whether or not they want to have sex within minutes of meeting a woman, and women typically go through a stricter "vetting" process before deciding to risk any social repercussions, pregnancy and disease, and even physical harm.

It takes longer for a woman to screen a man's personality than it does for a man to screen her appearance. Remember, men get turned on like a light switch, women get turned on like a volume knob. Women must first feel comfortable, secure, and safe with a man before sex is even a thought in her mind. But they must also feel arousal, attraction, and excitement. As such, there are two roles women put men in: the "lover" who is fun, exciting, and typically short-term material, versus the "provider" who is more reliable, trustworthy, and long-term relationship material. Most men are one or the other—but very rarely will you meet a man who embodies both. The Grounded Man does...

Enter the relationship as a lover, experience her, and see if she fits your value system. If so, slowly introduce elements of the provider role and begin testing the waters of a more serious relationship. Intimacy is the fastest way to get into a relationship. If a woman is sexually intimate with you, then you have passed many of her tests and met those qualifications. She's invested massively in experiencing more of you and will respond better to a man she's already slept with than a man who just messages her on social media.

The lover gets her attention and spikes her emotions, and the provider shows her there is the possibility of a sustainable future. It's the perfect combination that leads to being sexually intimate quickly and leaves the door open for a possible relationship if she meets your criteria over time. However, you cannot lead with the provider. Unless she feels desire and sexual chemistry, she will struggle to crave a more intimate, serious relationship with you. She must become emotionally invested and sexually interested in you before she will be willing to enter into a serious long-term relationship with you.

Leading with the provider role signifies to her that you are coming from a place of scarcity and lack. It's leading with your resources instead of your behavior and personality and relying on what you have instead of who you are.

Women don't read erotic novels about Jerry the accountant with a maxed out 401(k) and a nice sedan that gets great gas mileage. Women crave having the lover archetype in their life. They read and fantasize about men who are dominant, masculine, polarizing, and capable of spiking their emotions, men who are exciting, adventurous, and unreadable.

Men who pull them out of their daily lives and inject aliveness and uncertainty into their day, but this is not to say that women *only* crave the lover. Rather, they respond better when you *lead* with the lover archetype. However, if you rely solely on the lover archetype, you will struggle to *stay* in long-term relationships and will be prone to short-term relationships. Women want excitement and adventure yes, but they also crave stability and trust. They want a man with whom they can rely on, a man who will support them, stay faithful once committed, and care about them.

Therefore, you must learn to couple the lover *and* provider archetypes. You should always *lead* with the lover archetype, but once sex is happening regularly and you begin engaging in a conventional dating relationship, you must balance both character types. When you forego the lover archetype the relationship becomes stale and mundane.

However, one of the problems many men encounter is believing—quite falsely—that women are disinterested in sex, that they are somehow taking something from a woman when she sleeps with them. Not only is this belief counterproductive to your goals, it's total bullshit. Why do you think it is that women invest hours of their day into finding the right outfit, perfecting their makeup, fixing their hair in *just* the right way, and ensuring that their clothes reveal just enough sex appeal? It's because she is *trying* to attract a Grounded Man on some level.

The women you see when you go out to bars, clubs, and other venues are actively attempting to attract the right partner, they simply don't know you well enough to target you... yet. When you realize this, you can shift from gawking at and putting women on a pedestal to appreciating them for their beauty and feminine energy and entering the interaction with curiosity instead of neediness. You no longer feel like you are trying to win or take something from a woman. Instead, you realize that women want to meet a strong Grounded Man just as much as you want to meet a beautiful, fun, and intelligent woman.

Your job is simply to make the introduction, share good energy and positive emotions, and invite her into your life. Then you can decide if she's the right fit for you after a few dates. You are not supposed to drop your entire life, go against your core values, or change your entire identity for a woman. You are simply supposed to appreciate the value that women provide and see if there is a mutual connection to build something further. She wants you as much as you want her. She just doesn't know it until you allow her to experience you as a Grounded Man.

And until you find and settle down with the woman you want, this is the mindset from which you must approach women. If you're still struggling to believe this, then I challenge you to flip the script in your head.

- Don't *you* want a beautiful, fun, and intelligent woman with whom you can share your life?
- Don't *you* want someone who gives you positive emotions and makes you feel happier and more alive around them?
- Don't *you* want someone who challenges you to be your best self, stands strong in their convictions, and acts in integrity with their core values?

Everything that *you* desire in a woman (other than the exclusively sexual factors), *she* wants in a man. You are not taking anything from her by approaching and interacting with her any more than she would be taking something from you by approaching or interacting with you.

Now that you know what women want—a man who is dominant, of higher social status, embraces the feminine, and leads with the lover frame—we must now ask an important question. It's a question that, if ignored, will lead you aimlessly from relationship to relationship without ever making real progress or finding true happiness in life…

GET CLARITY ON WHAT YOU WANT TO RECLAIM YOUR POWER

The way to significantly reduce painful break ups is to not settle with any attractive woman you meet, but to select a woman you genuinely enjoy spending time with, have a deep connection with, and love inside and out.

Sex should be an amplifier of an already great relationship, not the main reason why you're together. If after sex you can't wait for her to leave and you're not at all interested in conversing with her, then you're settling, and this relationship will end in a break up eventually. I often hear guys say things like, "We fight all the time and we're just not working, so I think I need to break up with her. But damn, the sex is just too good to walk away from."

"Just one more time" can last for a decade.

This relationship will eventually end—and it will end horribly—because the man has lost his power, putting sex above his own values, needs, and desires. When sex is the sole factor upon which you predicate the existence of a relationship, the woman is always in a position of power *over* you instead of holding equal power *with* you.

She has something that you desperately want and knows that you will tolerate any amount of second-class behavior to obtain it. It's a vicious downward cycle. The more she can get away with, the more power you lose. The more power you lose, the less respect she has for you. When you surrender your power for sex, you create a lose-lose scenario where neither of you are happy in the relationship.

> **You must remove all traces of scarcity from your mind. You don't have to choose between an attractive woman who offers great sex but nothing else, and an unattractive woman who shares your values and you connect with. As a Grounded Man building an abundant dating life, you can have both.**

If you have put in the work to develop yourself as a man, then you *deserve* to have the full package—a physically attractive woman who has all or the majority of the internal qualities that you desire for a long-term partner—and never settle.

The great irony of the dating game is that most men fail to realize women actually *want* to be selected by a Grounded Man. They want a man who is interested not only in their physical beauty, but their inner qualities, character, and those little nuances that make all women unique. In order to know what you want in a woman, you need to define your dating goals and the character traits that you desire in a partner. But most men never take the time to do this. Remember, you can't blame her for not meeting your standards if you never shared with her in some way what those standards are.

Men are often clear about what they want in their physical health, their career, and their bank account, yet they remain ambiguous about what they want in a potential life partner. Why? That is arguably the most important decision of your life! So to prevent an emotional storm, you must ask yourself: what do I want in a woman? Not what society or my friends and family want, but what do *I* want?

If you don't know, then you'll never be happy and you're aimlessly chasing women without a clear purpose other than to get laid and have someone to eat and watch movies with. If you don't know what you want, then you're picking women at random based off their physical looks—or worse, their sheer proximity to you—and overlooking other negative aspects. In my own life, what I desire and require in a partner has evolved over the years. So will your desires. Take some time *right now* to write down the answer to these questions:

- What type of woman do you want?
- What are the traits you want in her?
- What type of relationship do you want?
- What are the deal breakers that you will not allow?
- What level of commitment do you want in a relationship?
- How involved will you be in her family's and friends' events?
- Is she close with her family?
- Does religion matter?
- Is she a career-oriented type or is she a stay at home with passionate hobbies type?

Being aimless in your desires will lead to aimless results. Instead, know what you want so that you can find it with precision. You will now have clear expectations so you can avoid any signals that will tell you if a woman isn't worth your time. It gives you the power to walk away from women who do not fit the majority of your criteria. When you find this woman, you will have more conviction and drive to go after her; she can feel attraction by your certainty in her.

But to do this, you must get out of your head and into the real world. You must step out of the game of theory and into the game of action. At this point in your journey, you understand the importance of being a Grounded Man, you've set to work developing the right internal mindset, and now you understand what women want and how you can give it to them.

Now, it's time to meet, approach, seduce, and date the women you've always dreamed of. You'll create an abundant dating life filled with women you once believed were out of your league. You can *finally* step out into the world with the confidence and certainty you need to attract the women you desire in your life.

And best of all, you will look at and see yourself as a new man, a confident, powerful, Grounded Man. You will know that you are capable of achieving anything to which you set your mind.

Let the show begin.

THE MISSION TO IMPACT 1 MILLION MEN

I am on a mission to impact the lives of 1,000,000 men with this book and give them the knowledge, skills and tools they need to become their strongest selves and develop themselves into strong Grounded Men—but I need your help to make this happen.

If you've found this content helpful in any way so far, please pay it forward by leaving me a helpful review on Amazon to ensure we can get this book into the hands of as many men as possible.

The more reviews this book has, the more men it can impact, and the greater dent we can leave in the world together; ending the pain, suffering, and loneliness with which so many men are faced today...one man at a time.

And with that...we enter into the next stage of your journey.

CHAPTER 4

HOW TO MEET AND ATTRACT HIGH-QUALITY WOMEN

"Everyone sees what you appear to be, few experience what you really are."

– NICCOLO MACHIAVELLI

Twenty minutes had passed. Looking down at my watch, my heart began to race. "Where was she?" I thought to myself, anxiety slowly starting to creep in as my mental monologue continued. "We agreed to meet almost half an hour ago. Is she flaking on me?"

And then... I saw her. Although dozens of people swarmed the busy boardwalk of San Diego's Mission Beach, it was as if the crowd intentionally separated so I could see her. Her long, blond hair fluttered gracefully in the summer breeze. Her white shorts were just short enough to reveal slender legs with a perfectly tan glow. Her shirt was cut to showcase her smooth, perfect waist and clearly hard-earned physique. Her gaze lifted to meet mine, deep blue eyes piercing straight into the very fabric of my being. It was the kind of look that makes your heart stop.

She flashed a quick smile and raised a hand to greet me. "I was just texting you!" she exclaimed as she walked over and hugged me. "Glad you could make it," I responded.

"Me too." She smiled as she pushed a stray strand of hair behind her ear. "Sorry I'm so late," she continued with a hint of guilt in her voice, "my best friend is going through a really hard breakup and I was helping her work through everything." I smiled, "No need to apologize. Sounds like she's lucky to have a supportive friend like you."

Despite the anxiety I'd felt as I'd stood by the beach, staring at the second-hand tick on my watch, I couldn't help but appreciate her adherence and empathy for her friend. I would have done the same. After my own insecurities led me to spend years struggling through shallow and toxic relationships, it was refreshing to spend time with a woman focused on someone other than herself.

Our rendezvous had been planned a few days earlier when we'd run into each other at a local farmer's market. I hadn't seen her since college Art 101 class when I'd first developed a crush on her. She wasn't only beautiful, but everything she created in that class was marvelous.

And it wasn't hard to see why. She was beautiful, yes. But there's was so much more to her than that. She possessed an easy grace and kindness that is rare in our ego-driven society, especially for a woman as beautiful as she. When we first met, however, I fell into the dreaded friend zone. And I couldn't blame her. During my college years, I lacked the backbone and grounded behavior to attract and keep a woman of her caliber. Instead, she'd chosen to pursue a more popular (and, I'll begrudgingly admit) more social guy.

But he was now long out of the picture. So, after reconnecting, I invited her out to the beach just a few hundred feet from my embarrassingly small apartment, yet perfect location. As we walked the boardwalk, I asked her about her goals and aspirations, attempting to break through her exterior beauty and get to know the real her. She responded, much as I expected, with surface-layer answers about her career that she clearly wasn't excited about, fitness goals that sounded more like a chore, and material aims that were, shall we say, "uninspiring."

Trying to dig deeper, I continued prying. "What would you do if money weren't an object? If you were totally free to do and be anything you wanted, how would you spend your time?"

"Well," she responded timidly, "I've always loved dancing, it's just not realistic, as my parents keep telling me." It was an intriguing answer. I pushed further, "Why dancing? What about it makes you come alive?"

She shrugged. I could tell she wasn't used to guys asking her intentional questions to get to know the real her. "I guess I've always loved expressing how I feel inside through my body. It's one of the most authentic ways to share myself with the world. I can express myself in ways words can't communicate."

I lifted my eyebrows, impressed and slightly aroused, "Damn… that's real," I responded, "Most of the pretty girls I know are too concerned with how they look and how many followers they have on social media to even consider something like that."

She gave me a smile and fired back, "Most of the guys I know are too busy thinking about getting in my pants to ever ask me that kind of question!"

I smirked. "Well, I have to make sure you're more than a pretty face before you can touch me. I'm not that easy." She laughed and smacked my arm playfully.

We arrived at the boardwalk directly down the court from my apartment. Instead of taking her to my place just a hundred feet away, I walked her down to the sand and pulled a frisbee—an absolutely essential item for any outdoor date—from my bag. As we began passing it back and forth, she flipped the script and began asking me about *my* goals and desires.

"What about you?" she asked. "What would *you* do if money were no object?"

"Honestly?" I responded. "Exactly what I'm doing right now."

She looked at me more interested. "What's that?"

"I run a podcast, a YouTube channel and create courses to help men overcome their biggest challenges and live a better life."

"Really?" she shot back. "What do you enjoy so much about it?"

Pausing with the frisbee in my hand, I looked at her and responded, "I get to wake up every day and help people grow into the life they want. I mean, the money is okay, but I love having the opportunity to make a real difference in the lives of others."

She looked me up and down and then smiled. "I really respect that. Most guys just want the fast cars and fancy houses. It's cool that you *actually* care about what you do." "Thanks," I said with a grin, "I'll have to show you one of the projects I'm working on later. But first...think fast."

I threw the frisbee in her direction and she goofily dove after it, falling into the sand and laughing before she playfully yelled, "Asshole! I was just starting to like you." I laughed with her and grinned, "I'm pretty sure you still do." Rolling her eyes, she threw the frisbee back in my direction, missing me by half a mile and sending it flying off into the receding tide, almost hitting people passing by.

I smiled to myself—the perfect opportunity—and jogged down the beach to retrieve it, motioning for her to come over to me. I instructed her on proper frisbee-throwing technique. It was all an excuse to touch her, of course. We both knew that, and I loved that she was just as into it. I stood behind her, one hand resting on her lower back, the other guiding her arm. I felt her press her body against mine, both of us doing the dance, the rise and fall of her breath crashing over me like the waves of our little strand of paradise. The tension between us was subtly increasing and we both knew it. I could feel my breathing growing.

It made her grow playful. She smirked at me and tried to pull the frisbee from my hand. We were caught in a brief tug of war. I teased her as she tugged harder. "Give it back!" A hint of desire colored her tone. I pulled harder. "Earn it."

Her big eyes lit up with the challenge, "Don't be rude! Just so you know, this is *not* a turn on." *Though we both knew it was.*

I yanked the frisbee behind my back, smiling at her and holding eye contact. "I don't give away things so easy, you're going to have to … come on, you just might get it from me *this* time." She lunged forward, reaching behind my back while looking up at me with a mischievous grin. "That's it, Andrew," I thought to myself, "Time to move things forward."

My free hand reached out to grab her lower back, pulling her close, looking her straight in the eye. I leaned my head forward until our lips were almost touching. She closed her eyes and prepared for a kiss…

… and I teasingly pushed her away, responding, "You're definitely going to be trouble for me, aren't you?"

Looking me up and down with a suggestive gaze, she purred, "You seem to be able to bring out that side of me, don't you?" I casually tucked the frisbee into my bag. "Let's go. I live just down the court. I'm working on this exciting project for work I'd like to share with you. Come with."

I draped my arm around her, and she slid hers around my waist, replying, "Sure, okay." As we walked through the shared courtyard of my apartment complex, my neighbor spotted me walking back with my new lady and raised his drink in the air, giving me a small cheer and a nod. I smiled, giving him a nod back, unlocking my apartment as I invited her into my place.

She casually followed me into my bedroom as I was putting things away and of all the books laying around, she picked up my journal and started playfully reading out loud the first line in all caps, "If your vision can be achieved in one lifetime, it's too small."

"Wow, that's so cool, Andrew. I respect that so much."

"Thank you, I like to write out my thoughts over tea every evening," I responded. "Girls I've dated before weren't ever into my journaling which is my thoughts, fears and dreams."

"Well…I'm not like most girls."

What is happening? I thought to myself. *To think this was the same intoxicating woman who'd friend zoned me only a few years ago. Yet here she was, standing in my bedroom flirting with me.*

My chest beat rapidly as I stepped over to her, put my hands on her waist, and led her to my bed. She surrendered to me, falling into the sheets—even in the somewhat darkened room, I saw the innocent look in her eyes dissipate, replaced with one of desire, waiting for my next move.

Climbing on top of her, I ran my hands gently over her forearms, slowly making my way up to her shoulders. I ran my fingers through her hair and touched her jawline to turn her head until our lips were almost touching. I playfully pulled away as she tried to kiss me, rubbing my cheek against hers and drifting my hands along her lower back. I let the tension build while rubbing my hands over her soft body and bringing my lips close to—but never quite touching—hers. Then…

… she quickly pulled away to sit up, resting herself against my headboard. "Oh no," I thought, "what did I do wrong?"

Then, settling my nerves in an instant, she reached out and grabbed the back of my neck with both hands, pulling me in until her lips were kissing at my ear.

"I want you right now," she whispered softly, biting my ear and pushing me back with an innocent, yet seductive look—I had unleashed a wildcat in her as she took my lip in her teeth. Reaching for a condom in times like these still always made me think, "I can't believe I learned how to do this."

Hours later, after a very stimulating afternoon to say the least, I walked her out through the courtyard and kissed her goodbye. As she left, she said, "Let's hang out soon, yeah?"

I was thinking, "OMG yes, any time!" But I gave her a confident playful response, "If you stay on your best behavior… just maybe." She smacked my arm and sauntered away, leaving me to watch her lovely legs in short white shorts walk off into the distance.

I'd known she was beautiful before our date, but after spending an afternoon with her, I realized she was so much more. Funny. Confident. Caring. Creative. Wildly playful and spontaneous. She was the type of woman you could see a future with. Yet there she was, walking away from *my* apartment after one of the most memorable afternoons in years.

Before she rounded a corner out of sight, she turned around and flashed me a big smile with a little giggle and a wave. I felt like I'd just been hit in the face by a 10ft wave of awe and gratitude. Laughing to myself and shaking my head, still unable to believe what had just happened, I headed back to my apartment before being greeted, once again, by my neighbor.

"Andrew!" my neighbor shouted, waving at me across the courtyard, "Well done! When you first moved in here, I thought you were just this guy reading books and glued to a computer all the time, but you're dating girls like *that!*" He flailed his arms wildly in the direction of my recently departed date.

I responded, "Thanks, but these women mean much more than *that* to me. I really enjoy getting to know them and of course being playful with them too." It was amazing to think of how far I'd come, but I didn't think about the fact that he had no idea what I was talking about.

"I'm serious." He needed answers bad, adamantly blocking my path, "I don't get it. No offense or anything, but you're an average looking guy living in a normal apartment and driving a beat-up old car. What am I missing?"

"Well," I responded, sensing his sincerity and desire to learn, "I realized long ago that most women don't care about those things as much as you might think."

"Right..." he continued, "But what do you do when you see an attractive woman that you want to talk to? How do you actually go up to her, get her phone number and get her out on a date?"

I was eager to go back to my place and catch the sunset and relax, but I felt sympathy for the guy. Not long ago I was asking those same questions, all before I started to do something about it. Not realizing what a door I was opening for this guy, I mentioned, "It's just all in my notes I've taken."

The second I said that, I knew I was going to miss the sunset. His eyes widened like a ten-year-old kid on Christmas morning, "Notes?! What do you mean notes?!"

I was caught off guard by the almost-primal look of hunger on his face. He was ravenous for the kind of lessons that I had spent a long-time learning. I tried to limit his expectations. "I've been journaling about my interactions with women for years, jotting down what works and what doesn't. It's really powerful stuff but you have to really focus, have an open mind and put the time in."

Without a moment of hesitation, he fired back, "Fine. Time in. Sure. Just tell me how much?" I froze where I stood. Was he suggesting...

"I'm sorry, what?" He instantly pulled his wallet out. I couldn't believe it, "I'm not waiting, how much for the notes?"

It was in that moment that I realized just how far this journey of mine was going to go. My work up until this point was solely focused on personal development for men and did not include dating at all. I was doing this for my own self-betterment, but in that moment, I realized that I wasn't the only guy who struggles with women, dating, all of this, even if on the surface it doesn't appear that way.

Many men, even the one right in front of me that day, on the surface look like there would be no problem with women but yearn to improve in this area of their lives silently, but lack a real plan. There must be countless guys out there like him—like I used to be—whose lives could be transformed by being able to see the work I had done, the progress I had made. *Why keep it all to myself?*

My journey and my records of it didn't *just* have the ability to help me. They had the vast potential to help legions of other men around the world overcome the very same obstacles and challenges that I desperately struggled with.

Before beginning my journey, I hadn't begun to imagine how far my lessons would spread. All of those illegibly written shorthand and long-winded ramblings on napkins, loose papers, and journals I'd written down about my experiences and lessons with women became a guide to help men remove their insecurities around women, reclaim their power and embark on the most epic, fun, and adventurous dating experiences they'd ever had.

My work has been able to lead others to become Grounded Men, to free themselves socially, to help them come alive by waking them up from the boring mundane monotony of life.

I had written a "playbook," if you will, that would help men meet and attract the highest-quality women wherever they are and wherever they go. It became clear to me that this journey would become much bigger than myself. I felt it was my duty to help the men that were just like me before. The following are my notes…

CREATING YOUR PERSONALIZED 90-DAY GAME PLAN TO BRING HIGH QUALITY WOMEN INTO YOUR LIFE

When I first entered the world of dating and social dynamics, I became a master of game *theory*. I read every book, attended countless seminars, and even hired several dating coaches to help me gain the knowledge I needed as quickly as possible.

My goal was to learn *everything* that I could about dating and seduction so that I could mitigate or completely eliminate any potential mistakes during my interactions. And it worked... sort of. Within eight weeks, I logically knew exactly what, how, and when to say certain things to achieve my desired results. But, as is often the case, the abundance of information in my head didn't translate into real world success when I was out and interacting with women.

Even though I'd memorized all of the lines, knew the specific postures and physical gestures to use, and had every interaction mapped out from start to finish in my head, when it came time to actually *apply* my newfound knowledge, I'd freeze up and sputter through my words with women, utterly incapable of taking action and getting any substantial results in my dating life.

This pattern continued for months as I'd read more content, attend more seminars, and then half-heartedly apply what I'd learned thinking all the while that more information was the answer to my incompetence. I'd go out, see an attractive woman, start walking over to her, and then walk right past her telling myself, *"I just need to review xyz article or re-watch this video so that I'll feel ready next time. She probably had a boyfriend anyway."* And this is exactly what happens to most men.

The average guy becomes so mired in theory that he's unable to make real progress because he's missing one of the most important components of success in any endeavor: taking action in the real world. When you take action, you get feedback which tells you exactly what you need to work on so you can get better results next time. Therein lies the secret to getting results with women (and in any other area of your life). Have a plan that works for you, take massive action consistently, and follow advice from people who have the results that you want.

Your results will always be a direct reflection of the amount of action that you've taken and the amount of effort that you put into refining your skills overtime. Although you cannot succeed at the highest levels without first embodying the Grounded Man, cultivating the right internal mindset, and understanding what women want, these factors aren't worth anything if you aren't going out, taking action, meeting women, and allowing them to experience what you have to offer.

If you believe you are a great product, then it is your duty to market that product as hard as you can to all the people who would love that product. Having the right mindset, knowledge, and attitude *is* important and it will dramatically shorten your learning curve, but without a commitment to consistent action, you'll never get the women you want or achieve anything worthwhile in life.

So fall in love with the process. Treat it like a journey (because that's what it is) and learn to enjoy the interactions, the flirting, the rejections, the mistakes, *and* the successes. If you can commit to taking consistent action while having a ton of fun, you will one day look back on this time and remember them as the best years of your life. You'll look back on the things you did and laugh to yourself, "I can't believe I really did that!"

However, if you want to achieve your desired results as quickly as possible, you'll need a plan that is custom made for *you*. While most pickup guys will tell you, "Go to bars and clubs five nights a week," that would be all but impossible with your busy schedule. Your journey would end right there.

As such, you'll want to create a strategy that fits into *your* life and is built around *your* interests, a strategy that allows you to simultaneously gain as much experience as possible while actively meeting women at the locations you'd naturally enjoy on your own. Here's what this strategy will look like:

1. Day-to-Day Activities

The first part of your strategy will include things you do on a regular basis where there is the potential to meet attractive women. That might include going to the gym, attending yoga, CrossFit, or kickboxing classes, going to the farmers' market, or checking out popular parks, malls, lunch spots, or coffee shops in your area.

2. Leverage Your Social Circle

The second prong of your strategy is to leverage your existing social circle and continue going out and having fun with friends while keeping an eye out for any woman who captures your attention. If you see a woman you're interested in, take the initiative and go meet her.

The social proof you'll possess by being out with friends and already having fun will make this far easier than going out alone and "cold approaching" solo.

A few ideas to help you capitalize on this are hosting your own social events (like those BBQs, pool parties, game nights, or movie nights I mentioned before), going out to popular bars, lounges, speakeasies and nightclubs, or heading to a wine tasting, art gallery, karaoke, or local sporting events.

3. Go to More Social Events

The third aspect of your strategy is to use your favorite social events to meet women who will be more aligned with your ambitions and lifestyle than the women you might meet at bars and clubs.

For example, if you enjoy charity or volunteer events, galas, concerts, comedy clubs or open mics, these are all great locations to meet like-minded women you can invite into your life. Other examples are meetup events, dance classes, adult co-ed sports, and self-help events like business or personal growth-related activities.

4. Online Dating and Social Apps

The fourth component of your strategy is to use online dating and social apps to meet women in your area that you otherwise would not meet in person.

Let me be clear, the focus of this book is meeting women in the *real* world and refining your social skills by learning how to invite women into your life in person. You must be careful not to allow these apps to become an excuse to not go out and meet new women in person, as this will stunt your growth and prevent you from fully developing yourself as a Grounded Man.

However, assuming that you are taking action on a consistent basis and going out to meet women at different venues, using dating and social apps is a great way to supplement your other activities and bring new women into your life. The best apps that I've found are Tinder, Hinge, and Instagram... *mostly* Instagram. (If you want a primer on how to best use dating and social apps to maximize your success with women, remember to download your free dating toolkit at: knowledgeformen. com/dating-toolkit

5. Referrals

The final component of your traffic strategy is to get referrals from your social circle to "shortcut" the attraction process and gain instant social proof.

People inside of your network *might* know the woman that you want to meet, so ask. By getting "referred" to an attractive woman, you begin the interaction with more credibility and typically get extra time and attention from her. There's no "cold approach," no trying to figure out what to say, no wondering whether she feels safe. There are several different sources from which you can gain referrals depending on where you are in your social game. Let's take a look at a few of my favorites.

Friend Zone Referrals:

On this journey, you will inevitably meet women who, as beautiful and fun as they might be, aren't a good fit for your life. Whether they friend zone you or you friend zone them (a much more common occurrence as you make progress), it's important that you don't *end* the relationship simply because the two of you are not romantically compatible but do connect well together.

Instead, foster a friendship. Share that you will be on the lookout for someone who would fit well in her life and ask that she does the same.

You're introducing each other to your friends in a mutual exchange where you both win. It's important to note that this strategy will rarely work with women whom you dated over six months and then friend zoned. It's only effective with women who you quickly decided were not the right fit for you romantically, or vice versa.

Network Referrals:
Another source of referrals is your existing social network. Be open and honest with your friends, acquaintances, and business colleagues. Tell them that you're single, interested in meeting a certain type of woman, and would appreciate any introductions that they can make.

If they're single, offer to do the same thing for them. If they're in a relationship, find other ways that you can exchange value. Is there a business connection you could make? What skill do you have that you could offer to them for free?

If your friend is in a relationship, don't be afraid to go out and third wheel with your friend and his girlfriend to have fun, share your value, and show them your unique personality. More often than not, his girlfriend will ask if you're dating anyone, giving you an easy opportunity to ask if she has single friends, she could introduce you to.

The bottom line is that you can't be afraid to ask people within your network who they might know. Your dream woman could be only one introduction away.

Socialite Referrals:
The final referral strategy—one that admittedly might not be available to everyone right away—is to befriend major socialites in your community. Socialites are the connectors, the master networkers, the charismatic extroverts who know *everyone* in your community. They might work at or own a popular bar, lounge, or club. They could be a well-connected businessman in the community. They may be someone who serves on the board of a specific cause or charity that you also care about. They might just be that gregarious guy or girl who is constantly arranging fun events and bringing together large groups of people. Find individuals in positions of leadership at venues or events where your ideal woman

frequents. They likely have more women in their network than you'll befriend in a lifetime. Now, why would they help you?

The key to making these types of relationships work is to find unique ways of offering value. It might take some creativity, but *everyone* has problems in their lives that they want solved. Gain their trust, identify those problems, genuinely help solve them, and then ask them to introduce you to your ideal woman. Heck, if you have the financial means, you can even *pay* these people to make introductions and help shortcut the introduction process. It's not the only way to add value, but it is one way.

While this referral strategy requires thinking outside of the box, you'd be surprised what effect having a consistent stream of regular referrals will have on your dating life. People want to help you if you are equally returning value back to them. Individuals who introduce you to a long-term partner are uniquely fulfilled and grateful for the opportunity. Imagine how it would feel to attend a friend's wedding and know that *you* were the man who introduced him to his wife-to-be. As a Grounded Man with good intentions, you are not doing anyone a disservice by asking them if they know someone who would fit well into your romantic life.

Now, it's important to note that you don't need to do *everything* that I've just shared with you about your traffic strategy. I'm giving you a multitude of options to choose from. You can achieve high levels of success by selecting and devoting 80% of your time to three to five different activities and venues.

Overtime, you'll want to find your unique niche that yields you the most results where you have the most fun. Some guys do better with cold approaching at their favorite venues, others with social circle and others with dating and social apps. I like to combine them to diversify where and how I can meet women. What's most important is that you have a consistent strategy for bringing new women into your life. If you execute this strategy consistently, you will easily be able to meet your goal of having two high-quality interactions with women per week during a 90 day sprint.

Write down and clearly outline what your "traffic strategy" will be and how frequently you will do it to meet women, otherwise nothing is going to happen.

For example:

1. Day to day: Monday through Thursday, I will go to the gym or yoga class, check email and read at trendy coffee shops, then go to a local farmer's market every Saturday.
2. Social circle: Every other Thursday evening, I will host dinner parties, and every Friday and Saturday evening, I will frequent trendy bars and lounges with friends for at least two hours.
3. Social events: Twice per month I will attend a comedy club and once per month a local concert with a friend or potential date.
4. Dating and Social apps: Sunday through Wednesday, I will spend 15 minutes on dating and socials apps in the evening making connections, following up with women I know and inviting women out to something fun.
5. Referrals: I will reach out to someone in my network once per month, communicate what I'm looking for in a woman, and ask if they can make any introductions. I will equally look for ways to reciprocate the value to ensure this relationship is win-win.

Now, you can quickly see how easy it is to have just two high-quality interactions with women per week when you have a crystal-clear strategy laid out. Again, your goal is to design your dating life around activities that you would naturally enjoy *whether attractive women were there or not.*

The purpose of this strategy is not to add *more* work and stress to your busy schedule, but rather to help you consciously craft a livelier social life that helps you attract high-quality women (which should be one of the highlights of your week, not a chore).

For most men, being single is merely a symptom of an inconsistent social life. Once you commit to leading a more adventurous life and meeting women on a regular basis, you'll be able to select your ideal woman from a pool of many.

As simple as this prognosis may sound, most men will never implement the strategies that have been laid out. Instead, they'll ignore their romantic lives, devoting most of their time and attention to their careers and businesses without ever acknowledging the fact one of the reasons they're working so hard in the first place is because on a deeper level they want to attract high-quality women. But working longer hours, closing that next deal, or expanding operations will not fix the major problem which most single men face: that your ideal woman doesn't know that you exist.

Women aren't sitting atop a high tower, peering down at you through a pair of binoculars and waiting for you to hit some arbitrary financial milestone before they suddenly reveal themselves to you at your doorstep. If you are single and not standing in front of attractive women on a consistent basis you will likely remain single or settle out of scarcity.

Bottomline: If you want more connection, intimacy, love, and sex in your life, then you need a strategy to achieve it. Your dream woman isn't likely to fall into your life by happenstance. And if she does? Good luck keeping her around without the invaluable lessons, growth, and maturity gained from this journey.

And for those of you who are formulating excuses in your head about why you "don't have the time" for this, let's cut the bullshit. If you are single, what are you doing from the hours of 7pm-10pm that is so damn important?

This is the time to be social, have fun and meet new women, at least a few evenings per week. If you work night shifts, then there are still a few days per week that you have off where you can spend a few hours out to be more intentional about your social and dating life. Having the ability to date the women of your dreams and enjoy a life of sexual and romantic abundance is one of *the* most important journeys that any man can embark on and should not be viewed as stressful or tedious.

Men are so quick to want to settle in their romantic lives, check the box and get on with life, but what if this was the best part of life and you were missing it all along?

Brother, there's *no* shame in planting a flag and saying, "This is it. I'm going to do everything in my power to attract the right woman so I can experience more joy, love, and connection." There is nothing more masculine and badass than embarking on a journey to discover yourself, experience more women, and ultimately find the love of your life. This journey is uncommon, which means you'll get negative feedback from the masses. Yet, in the near future, you'll be the one with the uncommon results that make other men envious of you.

Commit to this goal now. Write down your traffic strategy. Act on it daily. Have no shame or self-judgement about owning your desires as a masculine man on his path in life. Go after what you want and, eventually, you will get what you want if you stay the course, be patient, and follow the strategies and action steps laid out before you. Here's your step-by-step guide to meeting new women.

THE 5 GOLDEN RULES OF APPROACHING

1. Shift Your Anxiety into Excitement

If you feel anxious about approaching an attractive woman, congratulations! You are a healthy functioning human being, and nothing is wrong with you. However, what you do with that feeling is entirely up to you. You can use it to serve you or allow it to deter you.

> **The moment you see a woman you want to talk to and feel that "anxiety," that is the moment to get excited and come alive. You now have an opportunity to do something fun and positive that can improve both of your lives.**

In our modern times, you must understand *no one is going to hurt you* for approaching a woman. If she has a boyfriend, he won't do anything but put his arm around her and walk away. Her friends aren't going to attack you like a pack of female MMA fighters. So long as you're providing value, they will likely *welcome* you and encourage the interaction.

The worst thing that can happen to you is the conversation will end and the woman will make a random excuse to leave the interaction. You will have lost nothing, and your life will not have changed in any way. So take decisive action without hesitation and that feeling of approach anxiety will quickly become a moment that excites you and turns you on to make something beautiful happen.

2. There is No Perfect Thing to Say Except What You Want to Say

When most guys are talking with women, they are stuck in their heads. They are constantly trying to think of the *perfect* line or phrase that will spark instant attraction.

As such, rule #2 is simple. Relax! Fall into the present moment. Listen to her intently and then share whatever comes to you, trusting that what you're saying is important because *you* are the one who is saying it. The more freely you express yourself, the more polarizing you will be. Some people will love what you have to say, and others will hate it, yet both can still find you attractive. Because the simple act of expressing yourself freely and without reservation is a reflection of your inner status. It's an "unfakeable" social signal that you are a Grounded Man. True freedom of self-expression illustrates that you have high levels of confidence and self-esteem and women will be attracted to these qualities *even if* they don't agree with the words coming out of your mouth. Again, it's not the words, it's the place it comes from that matters. This isn't about being perfect. It's about being *real*.

3. Embrace Your Masculine Desires

One of the most common reasons that men fail to achieve results with women is because they are afraid to be masculine and show their desires. Too many men enter into interactions with women in a way that is disingenuous and screams "I'm friend zone material." Escalation—both physical and emotional—is all but impossible if you hide your masculine desires. She will rarely lead the charge and flirt first.

By simply taking social risks with witty comments and being flirtatious, you will help her realize that the encounter is sexual not just friendly, and she can respond according to how she feels.

For example (in a confident and playful nature):

"You look like trouble… I hope I know what I'm getting myself into."

"You and I probably aren't going to get along."

"There's a part of me that likes you and a part of me that can't trust you."

"You're pretty cute, but I'm worried you might be too (sassy, innocent, wild) for me."

If she teases you back: "Oh, that was adorable. Keep it up and you and I are going to wrestle in the backroom."

Most men will shy away from these risky statements or think these are silly, thinking, "I can't *really* say that, can I? Won't she be offended?" For most women, the answer is, "No." Being playful is a dance that women respond well to and separates you from the masses of overly serious, logical men.

Whatever it is that you think you shouldn't say is likely the very thing you must say to create tension, be polarizing, and keep her engaged.

The more emotions you stir in a fun, playful and challenging way, the more time and interest you will have with her. She must be aware that you are a masculine man with sexual desires, and the longer you talk to her without making it clear that you are interested in her *as a woman,* the more likely it is that she will begin to view you as a friend instead of a viable sexual partner.

Women know when they're being "hit on" but can still enjoy the process, just like a great salesman can be pitching you and you can still enjoy it. Own your desires and be clear in your intentions from the beginning. You're a man who's interested in her as a woman. You're not someone who's just looking for a new friend in a conversation to nowhere.

Maintain strong eye contact, use deep vocal tonality, and engage in light physical touch throughout your interactions. Lean towards wit and playfulness. Tell her she's cute, adorable, that she looks like trouble. You're not expressing your undying love to her, but you are making it clear that you are interested without being completely sold so easily.

4. Imagine She's an Old Friend

Imagine that you're walking down a street in your hometown and you see one of your oldest childhood friends. Would you feel nervous, afraid, or anxious about walking up to him and starting a conversation? Or asking to exchange phone numbers to connect later? Or giving him a friendly hug out of joy?

Of course not! You'd be excited, alive, and fully confident that you're going to get a good reaction from this person. And because you expect this sort of reaction, you often get it. This same level of energy and enthusiasm is important in your interactions with women. Don't sit there stuck in your head, wondering whether you can approach or what you should say. Just go over and approach her with the same energy you'd approach an old friend and see where the conversation goes.

With this attitude, you will expect positive things to happen. You won't judge yourself. You won't slip into self-critical thinking. You'll simply be *you*. Engaged. Alive. Free. And from this place, the interaction can escalate *much* faster. You won't worry about asking for her number. You'll simply do it. You won't second-guess whether you can high-five her or hug her or put your arm around her.

You'll simply flow and escalate as the interaction unfolds because it's what you want to do. This level of energy and freedom can make your approaches effortless and spark instant attraction.

5. Make Her Feel Alive and Beautiful

Women, just like men, are bored of the mundane and banal conditions in which they find themselves on a daily basis. From jobs they don't like to conflict with family to crazy exes to financial problems, women are dealing with the same issues you are and *hoping* that it changes. And *that* is where you come in.

The goal of your approaches is to add value to her life, to inject adventure and aliveness into her otherwise dull day. And more importantly, it's to make her feel beautiful and unlock her feminine, playful nature. When you can interact with a woman authentically and see her for who she is, deeply penetrating past the surface layer that most men see and peering into the nuances of her femininity, she will feel beautiful and alive. It leads to a place where attraction stems.

I will teach you different conversational techniques that you can use to accomplish this goal later in the chapter, but for now, simply have the goal in mind. Leave every woman you meet feeling more alive, beautiful, and appreciated than she did before she met you.

When you get turned on by turning women on and making them feel alive, anxiety and fear will dissipate, giving you the ability to interact more freely without hesitation or fear.

When you walk away from an interaction, whether it was successful or not, the woman that you approached should feel that energy. She should feel beautiful. She should have the same feeling as if you'd just handed her a priceless gift (because you did). She should miss you when you leave (even if she has a boyfriend or couldn't continue the interaction), not because *you* are so alive but because you made *her* feel so alive.

But now you might be thinking, "Ok Andrew, I get this... But what am I actually supposed to say when I'm out approaching a woman this sounds like a lot of theory?"

Well, now that you have a better understanding of the thoughts that should be going through your mind when you're meeting new women, let's take a look at the actions and conversational tools that you can use to take your interactions to the next level.

HOW TO APPROACH AND START ENGAGING CONVERSATIONS WITH NEW WOMEN

The opening lines that you use to start a conversation with a woman are not the deciding factor if she will be attracted to you or not. It's how you act *after* opening her that matters more.

The first few words are only designed to shift her attention from her previous activities to you. You want to get past the opener as soon as possible and start the interaction where the real work is done. There is no perfect opener that makes her want to fall madly in love with you.

Guys get so caught up on thinking of the perfect opener that it prevents them from taking action.

The goal of the opener is to get past the opener as quickly as possible and into an engaging conversation.

Just like the purpose of your car key is to simply start the car. It does nothing else but get the car started so you can go somewhere. You still have to drive the car to its destination. Here are a few easy openers you can use that worked well for me and will—if delivered with confidence and positive energy—work well for you, too.

1. **Basic Verbal Opener:**
   "Hi, I'm (insert name)."
   "Hi, who are you?"
   "Hey, you're cute I'd like to meet you."
   "Hey I saw you, I'm (Insert name). Who are you?"
   "Hi, I don't think we've met yet. I'm (insert name)."

2. **The High Five Opener**
Confidently smile, make and hold eye contact, raise your hand up like you're giving a high five, let her hand meet your hand, then close hands firmly. Hold the hands closed for a few seconds then let go. You must be Grounded here, or this can be very awkward.

   Don't be too aggressive or this will scare her and do not squeeze her hand too hard. But commit and own it if you try this. If she doesn't follow through, then revert to the verbal opener and keep going. If you get upset that she didn't comply with you, it's over. The benefit if she complies with this is that it's very clear that you like her and are a fun guy.

3. **The "Reach" Opener**
Extend your arm and hand out and reach to take her hand. She has to participate and meet you halfway. You extend your arm and she either follows through or not.

   You don't forcefully grab her ever! Let her come to you. She either accepts or not when you extend your arm. If she does accept, then you have some compliance from her which usually makes for a more physical interaction from the start, which is really arousing for both of you.

4. The Moving Opener

If she's walking, then you'll have to catch up to her with a brisk walk then be slightly in front of her and say confidently "Hi, excuse me... (pause and wait for her to give you her attention) I saw you walking, and I wanted to come by and introduce myself real quick."

That's it. Be sure that you approach from the front or side—never from behind as it will immediately make her feel unsafe and defensive— and don't be afraid to walk with her to continue the conversation if she keeps walking, which is usually the case.

Most men will see an attractive woman walking down the street and immediately reject the approach, thinking, "She's probably got somewhere important to go, I don't want to stop her." But this self-defeating attitude will cause you to leave countless amazing interactions and connections on the table—or in the street, as it were. Just ask yourself... Would you get upset if an attractive woman stopped you to talk to you?

Of course not! It would make your day. And, as a Grounded Man, your approach—if done correctly—will make her day, too. In time, you'll develop your own "approaches" and learn how to confidently introduce yourself to new women, regardless of the scenario.

However, if you're just getting started, I recommend these options as they tend to yield great results. At this point, you may still be stuck in your head, worrying about what to say and when to say it. To help you escape that mental prison, get into the real world, and begin taking action, I'm going to breakdown the fundamental "rules" or guidelines that will help you bring attractive women into your life with ease.

If she doesn't see the value in what you're offering, this means one of two things:

1. She was not the right fit for you and you're better off moving on to the next woman, which is perfectly normal.
2. You made a mistake in your approach and she misread your signals, assuming that you weren't being a Grounded Man.

The former is unavoidable and should actually be seen as a good thing—remember, she's saving *you* from the pain of a mismatched relationship—and the latter can be avoided if you understand how and why most approaches go wrong.

Let's talk about that now...

REASONS WHY YOUR APPROACH CAN GO WRONG

Most failed approaches have NOTHING to do with you as a man, but everything do with how you *present* yourself to the woman.

You can be the most amazing guy in the world: financially and professionally successful, emotionally mature, highly social, physically dominant, and attractive. But if the sub-communications like body language, vocal tonality, and eye contact don't reflect who you are internally, your interactions will be in jeopardy and she'll be waiting for an excuse to leave. The interaction won't get to the point where she'll discover those great things about you.

When you approach a woman, what you say matters far less than how you say it. Be sure that your shoulders are back and your chest upright. When you speak, ensure that your voice is deep and resonant but filled with inflection, energy, and aliveness.

Let yourself be heard. You're a Grounded Man. What you have to say is valuable, and your tonality and volume should reflect who you are and all your past success. Keep your composure throughout the approach. Don't fidget, don't touch your face, don't shake your legs or nervously tap your foot. Instead, remain calm, cool, and collected.

Finally, the level of aliveness and engagement is all in the eyes. When a man has the confidence to approach a complete stranger, look her in the eyes, and speak his truth without flinching or wavering, it is *extremely* attractive and arousing for a woman. She will feel something for you even if she is unwilling or unable to escalate the interaction.

You must go out, stand in front a woman, express yourself, have fun, be clear in your intent, and okay with the fact that she may not like you or be available.

And if the approach is ever socially out of context, then acknowledge the weirdness.

"I've never done this before."

"I know this is weird, but..."

"I'm really shy and new to this, but I wanted to say..."

It's okay to say the truth, and in many ways it's appreciated. What most women won't tell you is that they *want* you to succeed. They want their search to be over, too. They want a confident, fun, Grounded Man to introduce themselves to her. You're not taking anything away from her and, you're likely saving her from meeting an arrogant jerk who was going to approach her if you didn't or from having a boring monotonous day. You're bringing more excitement, a spark of energy, and aliveness into her day.

But more than *any* of these factors, the number one reason why most approaches go wrong is that they *never happen in the first place.* If you see the woman you want to meet but do nothing, then that feeling is a deep masculine-rooted pain. Not introducing yourself, not talking to the girl, not getting her phone number, not asking her out, not physically escalating must be unacceptable in your life from this point forward. Associate more pain with not doing the approach than with any possible negative outcome of the approach.

Missing out on time spent with a high-quality woman should haunt you more than fear of approaching and making advances. From this point forward, rejecting yourself is no longer an option. Go plant your feet in front of her and express yourself.

Make it a personal code to never reject yourself again. It must be forbidden if you are truly committed to a life of growth.

You can go through life having rejections, but you cannot go through life not having ever tried. Remove the need for validation and fuel your ego with action instead of expected outcomes. Courage isn't the absence of fear, it's feeling the fear and taking action anyway. You must love yourself enough to stop rejecting yourself.

If this is a struggle for you, download the 30-Day Challenge to Social Freedom Guide that I've created for you here: knowledgeformen.com/dating-toolkit.

Focus on developing your social skills before diving into meeting women. Having a basic understanding of social dynamics is essential to get the full benefit of this program. You've got to build your social muscle so you can learn to get out of your own way, have more fun, and fully accept yourself.

After you've invested some time into developing your basic social skills or you are already socially competent, you'll be able to enter into one of the most exciting parts of the interaction with women.

HOW TO HOOK ANY GIRL'S INTEREST SO SHE'S CHASING YOU

Men are attracted very easily to a woman. When a man sees a physically attractive woman, he is typically "hooked" within seconds. Let's be honest, male attraction isn't exactly complicated.

Women, on the other hand, need to experience a man's personality, character, and energy before their attraction can be established.

Here's how you can accomplish this: Following a strong opener—meaning that your energy, body language, and tonality were strong instead of worrying that your first words were perfect—you'll want to make an observation about her: notice what she's wearing, ask where she's from, notice what she's doing. Be genuinely *curious* about her and what she's about.

Examples of what to say after the initial approach:

"You look like a ___ (good, bad, playful, spiritual, artistic, dancer, up to no good) girl."

"I see you're a ___ (very outgoing, positive, enthusiastic) type of person."

"You must be from ___ (a small town, large city, urban town) because you seem ___?"

Once you've started the conversation and captured her interest, it's important that you verbally escalate the interaction to make it clear that you're interested in her. You're not a nice guy, you're a Grounded Man who is interested in her as a woman and you're not ashamed of it. Now it's up to her whether she wants to stay or not.

To establish this frame, *you* must dictate the rhythm of the interaction. Don't go in and wait for the woman to lead the conversation, because after all, you're the one who approached her. You must lead the interaction and clearly set the tone. Be confident, playful, and fun with this escalation.

Examples:

"Okay I like you so far, but I think we should take things slow from here."

"I thought I loved you until you said…"

"Stop it! You're so hitting on me."

"I can tell we're not going to get along."

"You're adorable but seem like trouble."

"You're not so bad. I kind of like you."

"You remind me of my ex, this could be dangerous."

"Hey, I'm not that easy! I have standards."

If she rejects the invitation into a flirtatious conversation, then calmly revert back to a social conversation. If she is still chatting with you, then relax, you may have escalated the interaction too quickly or caught her by surprise, but she has some interest in you since she's still talking to you. In this instance, take her rejection as a "Not yet" instead of a "No." It doesn't mean that she doesn't like you, simply try again after more rapport is established.

She needs to accept your advances before moving on otherwise she is still viewing you as a friend and is unclear about what this interaction is about. You'll know she's accepted your flirting if immediately after applying social pressure, she is laughing, agreeing, saying something witty or being playful with you. Pay attention to her sub-communications and body language for other signs of interest (playing with hair, licking her lips, touching you, blushes, body is squared up to yours) too.

Remember, women feel attraction on an emotional level, not a logical one. If there are no emotions, then there is no possibility of creating attraction. This form of emotional escalation works well because attractive women are used to having sexual power over men.

When you show her that she holds no power over you by being more free, firing off flirtatious and witty comments, and taking a lead role in the interaction, it provokes her to flirt back, which unconsciously suggests that you have equal or greater social value.

It shows that you're not overawed by her physical beauty the way that most men are. It clearly illustrates that you are willing to take social risks and be disliked so that you can speak your truth.

Treating women like normal human beings and taking them off a pedestal indicates that you are a high-value man who has had success with women of her caliber before.

You're polarizing the interaction by taking a social risk and separating yourself from other men. Most guys keep it very platonic, friendly and safe creating a very boring emotionless interaction. It might seem counterintuitive, but the only way to successfully escalate a conversation is by being bold, speaking your truth, and making your intentions clear. Bold moves spike emotions which create the possibility of attraction; ordinary moves get you friend zoned.

Being an overly nice, agreeable, ass kisser does nothing to spark attraction especially with higher quality women. Few women will take the lead and make flirtatious advances until you have first opened the door and led the way. And you do this by applying social pressure with flirty and risky comments throughout the interaction.

If you stay in the normal conversationalist zone for too long without applying any pressure she will by default leave with the infamous, "It was nice meeting you, I have to go now." And if you managed to get her number, it may not lead to any further contact, so establish this tone early in the interaction. Either way it's a risk, so you minus well take the risk that leads to the outcome you want – her flirting back with you.

It needs to be clear within minutes what this conversation is going to be about—that you like her, but you're not sure until she proves herself to you.

This gives her a choice to either play and flirt back or not. When she does flirt back, she's investing more into the interaction, signifying that she's interested in you. And just because you've flirted once does not mean that you stop doing that and she's now head over heels for you. It's important to continue to take occasional social risks to maintain tension between both of you throughout the interaction. This will keep her emotions engaged while having a genuine conversation. (I'll explain more on how to avoid playing "20 Questions" and have more stimulating and meaningful conversation in a later section.)

Now that you've hooked her, you can increase your value in her eyes by doing less and allowing her to pursue *you*. Most guys will start nervously talking at lightning speed and sharing everything about themselves the minute they meet an attractive woman, clearly displaying that they are easy to be had.

If she knows she can have you, then you are not the prize. Give her the opportunity to chase you by doing your part then shutting up and letting her chase.

It's kind of like when a sales guy is selling non-stop and not allowing you to participate in the conversation. Bad sales is the sales guy doing most of the talking and convincing, whereas good sales is the prospect is doing most of the talking and convincing themselves that they want the product.

After the hook point, relax. Slow down your gestures and more importantly, your speech. Allow her to invest into the interaction with you and begin to chase.

It comes down to being comfortable, leaving gaps in the conversation, and trusting she'll fill in and do her part. When she invests more of herself into an interaction after she has been "hooked," it unconsciously suggests she values you more.

Now once you have her attention and she's hooked, she's naturally going to throw in some tests to see if you're the real deal or if you're just like every other guy who approaches her. How you handle her tests will make or break the entire interaction and any chance of a future with her.

HOW TO HANDLE HER
TESTS WITHOUT FAIL

Women naturally test you to ensure that your outward actions are a congruent reflection of who you are on the inside. While most men view tests as a negative thing, like she's being mean or as a subtle indicator that they are not good enough, nothing could be further from the truth. When a woman tests a man, it's a *good* thing. She's interested and simply wants to determine whether you're truly Grounded or not.

She's thinking, "Is he really that confident and witty, or is he faking it?"

If you pass her test, you're moving forward with her. If you stumble, it can be difficult (if not impossible) to recover. This is where most men get stuck, spelling the death of their interaction. View her tests as an opportunity for you to create more interest and increase your value. When you pass, you instantly become more attractive to her and she'll want to spend more time with you. The basis is to remain emotionally unreactive without flinching, nervousness, and fidgety body language. You're grounded, self-reliant, and you don't need her approval because you are enough with or without her. If she gives you a test, for example, "You're too old for me." Then you can do one of four things:

1. **Ignore it and move on.**
    "So, what are you doing here?"

2. **Answer it straightforwardly and move on.**
    "Yeah true, so what are you doing here?"

3. **Misinterpret it as her being too forward.**
    "Too old for what… we just met?"

4. **Accept it, exaggerate, and challenge her back.**
    "Yeah, I'm way older than you. Feel all my wrinkles! And are you even old enough to be here? That's it, I'm calling security!"
    Or try a lighter version:
    "I was thinking the same thing, but the real question is are you mature enough to keep up with me?"

In sum, if you own her test and respond to it with confidence, you are deepening her attraction for you and demonstrating that you are a Grounded Man. If you let it get you down, show any physical flinches or change in your state, she realizes that she has the power. It's not because you're actually older; it's because you were not a Grounded Man who draws his state from within and can handle himself in ambiguous situations.

A test is a dance of whose frame and reality is stronger. In other words, you pass her tests by staying grounded.

Higher-quality women typically throw more tests to filter out weak men because they know their worth and won't tolerate any fake behavior. When the tests come, just relax and don't make it a big deal. It's not you versus the woman, it's you two creating an interaction together and dancing with the masculine and feminine. It's a fun game. You've just got to know how to play!

Also, be aware that these tests don't only happen when you first meet a girl. They occur throughout the entire interaction and even in the relationship in various forms. Women want to know deep down what type of man you are. If you're only managing an impression, then you will fail at the tests she throws at you. She needs to know if she is with a Grounded Man she can trust and ultimately feel safe with, otherwise you can expect more tests.

But you're not the only one who gets to play this game. Once you've passed her test, she's showing even more interest in you, so now it's your turn to play... and play you will.

REGAINING YOUR POWER AND TESTING HER

Once she is hooked and you have passed some of her tests, you need to reestablish your power. Just as she is evaluating you to determine if you're the right fit for her, you must be evaluating her to determine if she's the right fit for you.

If you haven't evaluated her in some way and she hasn't qualified herself to you, it doesn't make sense to escalate, ask for a phone number, or try and setup a date. You must assess her value and figure out if she is even worth your time. Approaching women is not about trying to win them over and you doing all of the work. After you've approached, hooked her, and passed her tests, it's now her turn to prove herself to you.

Most guys fail to do this or are completely unaware of this, which is one of the leading reasons for flakes and a lack of follow up from her, even when the interaction supposedly went well. After all, you're a Grounded Man who has immense value to offer, so it would make sense that she has to first earn your time, attention, and energy, right?

People value what is harder to obtain, not what is easily and widely available. You need to figure out if she is special, worthy, or different in some way other than her pretty face. If not, then why are you sold on her so quickly?

The woman must feel like she won you over in order to value you as a man. She wants to feel special in some way, not that you are just "flirting with her" because she is physically attractive.

Assessing her sets the right frame for the interaction and implies that you are of high-value. It says that she needs to meet you at your level of value.

So how do you set this up correctly so she's qualifying herself to you when you just met? First, you must have demonstrated enough value and dominance that she feels the *desire* to qualify herself to you.

Women rarely experience these types of polarizing interactions from men, giving you an unfair advantage over the competition. Men don't think to do this because they're afraid it will push them away, when in fact, it will increase their desire for you. After she has qualified herself your success rate with any further escalation will increase, like leaving the venue together, getting her phone number, her responding quickly when you call or text, and showing up to dates in a timely way. Here are some examples of tests that you can use to deepen her investment in you and increase your value.

1. "Beauty Isn't Enough For Me"

This is a powerful assessment that will show her that you are more interested in her character than her physical beauty, and this is a powerful turn on for women. Her response to this is an obvious qualification of her personal character, values, and other life goals.

However, it's important that you deliver this test with a playful smile in a good-natured tone. If you sound too serious or like you're putting her down when you say it, she'll assume that you're being a jerk and refuse to try and pass your assessment. Make it clear that you're being flirtatious and have fun.

"You're adorable, but what else do you have going for you that's exciting?"

"You're cute and fun, but what else do you have going for you?"

"You're just too cute. There's no way you were gifted with a fun personality and interesting hobbies/goals/passions, too."

2. The Tease and Challenge

Teasing is a powerful way to spark a woman's emotions and put her in a position of validating herself to you. Again, it's important that you keep this playful, not insulting or demeaning in any way.

A lot of this will be in your sub-communication: your body language, energy, and vocal tonality. A well-timed and delivered tease or challenge can spark instant attraction, but a poorly delivered tease or challenge will make you seem like an arrogant jerk.

"You're embarrassing me, are you always like this in public?"

"That was adorable, but are you always like this with guys you just met?"

"I see what you're up to and I'm not that easy!"

3. The "Values Test"

Share something that you value and impose your values onto her, then assume that she naturally values the same things by stating, "I love/do this. You love/do it also, right?" This makes her follow your lead and qualify herself to you even more.

"I love going to the gym, it's so good for you. What kind of exercise do you do?

"I love yoga, it's so relaxing and feels great. What yoga studios have you been to?"

"I love entrepreneurship, it's so exciting. What kind of crazy business ideas have you thought of?"

"I've been journaling a lot about my goals for the rest of the year, what do you like to journal about?"

Of all of the assessments, the journal one is my favorite since it really shows her character. You learn more about who she really is at her core. I use these a lot and learn so much about her, which tells me where she'll fit in my life if and even if she'll fit at all.

4. The "Why" Test

This is the simplest assessment you can use in conversation. Anytime she shares something about herself, especially if it's something personal, respond with a confused, "Why?" and she will explain herself to you. When someone explains themselves to you, it suggests that the listener (you) is important enough for them to justify their actions/logic.

Her: "I'm in law school."

You: "Why do you want to be a lawyer?" or "Why would you do that to yourself?"

Her: "I want to travel to New York City after I graduate"

You: "Really a concrete jungle?" or "What made you pick *that* city?"

Her: "I love xyz movie"

You: "You're kidding me, right?" or "Okay I'm not going to judge, but you have three minutes to change my mind about that movie."

She's instantly put in a position where she feels like she has to justify herself and her decisions to you, which suggests that she finds you important and of value when she responds. You don't justify yourself to people you don't value.

5. The "Disagreeing" Test

There is a lot of value in disagreeing with a woman. Low-status men would not dare to disagree with attractive women out of fear they won't like them and, ironically, this is a powerful attraction amplifier.

By simply smiling and agreeing with everything she says, especially if it's something you genuinely disagree with, you will come off as a soft Nice Guy and be unconsciously placed in the friend zone. You need to respectfully assert your opinions, challenge, and disqualify. If you genuinely disagree with something shared, refuse her a positive response when she is used to everyone giving her praise and putting her on a pedestal.

Do not confuse this with putting her down and being an arrogant jerk by any means. You can disagree in a respectful and fun way by simply smiling while you assert your opinion. Disqualification encourages qualification on her part, so occasionally disqualify rather than easily being won over by anything she says.

Be careful not to take this one too far by disagreeing with too much of what she says. If it's just for the sake of testing her, you can push her away because it's becoming too much work to have a conversation with you. You don't want to overdo it, just show that you have the ability to disagree when necessary. Sprinkle it in, especially when you genuinely disagree with something she says.

6. The Light Push Test

Most men are so scared of pushing women away for fear that they won't come back. In reality, when a man pushes a woman away through verbal disqualifications, she will feel the need to prove and validate herself that much more. This will deepen her investment in the interaction and showcase that you are a challenge that is not easily won over by beauty.

"I'm going to pretend you didn't say that."

"I love the answer until you said…"

"Okay I'm leaving now."

"Wow, really I'm subtracting 5 points."

"Now why did you have to say that, I was really starting to like you."

The best forms of qualification are more subtle and very casual, not coming from a weak, arrogant frame or trying to one up her and bring her down. It's not a checkmate scenario where she loses, it's challenging her, stimulating her emotions, and giving her an opportunity to qualify herself in a flirtatious, good-natured way that benefits both of you. When she qualifies herself, you'll have avoided putting her on a pedestal while making her view you as a high-value man worth more of her time and energy.

At this point, she is interested in you and the interaction can now be successfully escalated from here. If a woman has not qualified herself to you in any way, then she will be hesitant about any form of escalation.

You do not have to copy what I've shared word for word as long as you understand the underlying meaning behind each assessment test. You can take any of the above examples and work to create your own. The main idea is that you do assess her in a way that is congruent to you because again, you should never be so easily sold on *any* attractive woman.

Now, a lot of guys get frustrated and find it difficult to have a real conversation with a woman they just met. Often, that's because she did not see him as a high-value male who is worth her time and energy.

But now that she has qualified herself to you, the doors are open to go *deeper* and really get to know *her*.

HOW TO HAVE STIMULATING CONVERSATIONS WHILE AVOIDING THE TRAP OF 20 QUESTIONS

Much of what you're about to read or parts of what you have read so far might *seem* silly, over the top, or immature. But I challenge you to analyze the lens through which you're judging these tactics. If you believe that these strategies are too silly or immature, you're judging them from a logical headspace. And if you're reading this book, then I'm going to assume logic-based attraction has led to a lot of frustration in your dating life.

Most men are too logical and fail to realize that logic alone—although important in your career and life—is not enough to spike a woman's emotions or elicit her more flirtatious and feminine side. You *must* be bold and engage her emotions to create attraction. Even if it seems silly or over the top to *you*, the suggestions I'm about to share with you aren't for you. They're for the woman you wish to attract.

So, it's important to remember that after approaching, hooking her, passing her tests, and getting her to qualify herself to you, the responsibility still falls on you to keep her engaged in a stimulating conversation. This conversation pushes the interaction forward and allows the two of you to connect and share in a lively experience.

Your goal is not to find common ground or "shoot the shit" about surface-layer topics like any other random guy at that bar, a discussion which reveals nothing about either of you. High-quality women have neither the time nor patience for this sort of dribble and as a Grounded Man, neither do you.

Your goal is to create an adventure with her and keep her emotions engaged through the words you speak and the behaviors that you present.

But most men are so focused on what *they* are going to say next that they don't even listen to anything the woman is saying. Instead, they fire off a barrage of lines thinking in their head, "Oh, that just bought me at least ten to twenty more seconds with her. Now I'll think of what to say next." This is a completely backwards way of doing things. You don't talk non-stop like this when you're with your friends do you? Of course not, so it doesn't make sense to do it with women either. When you initially approach a woman, your conversation will likely go like this:

1. 80/20 first 2 minutes (you are talking the majority of the time)
2. 50/50 after 2 minutes (balances out)
3. 20/80 after 5 minutes (she's talking the majority of the time)

Then bounce between 50/50 and 20/80, like a dance. You do your part and she does her part; otherwise you might as well be talking to a wall. Men need to shut up and allow the woman to invest more in the conversation. The more she invests, the more engaged she becomes while talking with you. Unconsciously, this says, "I value this person."

This will strengthen your connection and increase her desire for you to escalate and ask for her number, suggest going to another venue, or even decide to go back to your place. It's important to realize that approaches often throw women off because they are rarely approached in a genuine way. No matter how wonderful you might be, the first few minutes of your interaction will always fill her head with the overriding question, "Am I safe?"

Once she becomes comfortable with you and realizes that the answer is "yes," she'll begin to invest, open up, and become more involved in the interaction. But at this point, you may still be wondering what you should say when interacting with women. Don't worry, I've got you covered.

Remember, you are the Grounded Man with the internal mindset, so whatever you have to say has value becomes it's coming from you. It doesn't matter so much if other people find it interesting at first; it matters more that you find it interesting and then it will become interesting to everyone else.

For instance, have you ever watched Jim Carrey's old stand-up comedy? The content he's saying really isn't that funny if you pay attention to the words, but it's the way he says it that makes it funny. If you believe it's funny, then others will believe it is, as well.

You must lower your standards of how good you think what you're going to say needs to be because it's not what you say, it's the energy behind how you say it.

I'm going to give you a few things to play with in your interactions. Always remember, you can use these for fun but DO NOT THINK THESE ARE THE ONLY THINGS THAT WORK. I really want you to be more free-flowing in your conversations and have your own material. These are merely suggestions to get started so you don't have the infamous excuse of saying "I don't know what to say" with women ever again.

*All of these are said in a playful, fun and witty way coming from a place of offering positive emotions never an arrogant or rude way.

Role Playing: Fun ways to create a sense of adventure and togetherness.
> You are my… (partner in crime, wife to be, girlfriend for the rest of the night).
> Imagine that… (you won the lottery, you saw your favorite celebrity, you can go anywhere in the world)?

What if we... (ran away together, robbed a bank, jumped on a plane to Vegas)?

Push: These are negative emotional statements that you can carefully use to create a challenging vibe. Remember, the light laughter and playful phrasing are essential to avoid being a jerk.

You are so... (much trouble, stressed out, confused).

Are you seriously... (immature, boring, socially awkward, and insecure about that)?

I never thought someone would actually do... (something dorky/quirky/funny she did).

How does it feel to know that you're... (a horrible dancer, kisser, drinker)?

No, you didn't.

I'm not sure we'll get along.

I'm not going home with you tonight.

I'm out of your league.

You don't have to try so hard, I like you.

I doubt it.

Pull: These are positive emotions to show your interest in the person. It's good to balance out the negative with these positive emotions, a yin and the yang type of thing.

I like your... (outfit, hair, smile, eyes, energy, laugh, free spirited nature).

You have the most beautiful... (way of thinking, style, heart, soul, vibe).

You really come alive when you... (talked about your passions, talked about your pets).

You have this great energy about you... (that makes others feel alive, that spreads across the room).

Disagreeing:

I don't believe you.

I don't agree with you.

I can't believe you would say that.

You are not telling the truth.

Disagreeing with a woman, especially very attractive woman, is very powerful. Many men agree with anything a beautiful woman says because they don't want to upset her. Disagreeing is not only very genuine, it's also very polarizing and separates you from the crowd. If you genuinely disagree on something and can support it, then mention it in a respectful way. This is not permission to be a jerk.

Go-to phrases when talking to a group:
It's important that you immediately inject yourself into the group rather than standing off to the side as an outsider. If you say nothing you will be slowly outcasted by the friends.

Great, introduce me to your friends.
How do you all know each other?
Who are the inseparable best friends?
What are you guys celebrating?
You girls out picking up guys tonight?
How many numbers have you gotten so far?
Who's the troublemaker between the two of you?
Who would win in a fight?

Statements of empathy to show you understand what she's feeling:
Admitting that what you're doing isn't normal is okay. It's good for connecting, developing rapport, and establishing trust when you're doing something out of social norms.

I know it's... (awkward, weird, strange, or unusual).
Let me know if I am being too... (forward, touchy, talking too much).
This rarely ever happens this fast too.
I don't normally stay out this late either.
I've been working a lot lately so I'm really out of it.

If she's being rude:
When a man does nothing and accepts rude behavior, he instantly loses value, but when you challenge her back in a playful way your value increases.

That's cute. Do it again, but I want fifteen percent more this time.

You remind me of my friend, she does that, too.
You're kind of like my dorky little cousin.
You keep this up, I'm calling security.
You seem cranky, have you eaten yet?
This is exactly why you're single (if you know she's single).

You want an emotional investment to increase her desire in you:

"You can go if you want."

"I like you, but the door is always open."

"You're too cute, you should leave."

"I can tell we're going to break up six months from now anyway, just leave now and save us both the heartbreak."

She'll respond to emotional investments with statements like, "No, I'm having fun here." And she'll be thinking, "Why is he willing to let go of me? No guy does that." When she affirms that she wants to stay it reinforces to her that she likes you and increases your value.

Now, you're probably asking, "Where am I deriving all of this content from?" I want to teach you how you can create your own content that can be just as effective if not more. Here's how you can do this:

"You?" Interview Questions:

Where are you from?

Do you live around here?

How old are you?

What are you studying?

Where do you work?

Use these logical based questions sparingly to learn more about her. When relied on too aggressively, these interview-style questions will make a woman feel as if she's being interrogated instead of being heard. The number one frustration women have with men is they are not listening to them, they wonder why they should talk when he's just waiting for her to stop so he can say something ridiculous next. Women often feel like, "What's the point of talking to this guy?" Be present. Be interested in her instead of trying to be interesting. Here's how to do it.

After she's done talking say:

"Really?"

"That's so cool!"

"No way!"

Repeat the last sentence she said, showing interest and with an engaged facial expression. Don't be too cool to express yourself fully in a conversation. I'm talking about your energy, facial expression, the physical space you take up, and vocal tonality. Don't be fake; but be aware that being too cool comes off as if you don't care about her, which we know you do.

When you do ask questions, stay on the same topic. However, when you're asking a question from left field and another one that isn't even related to the conversation, then it will seem as if you're all over the place, which suggests you're overly nervous about the situation.

Think of each topic as a tree that has unlimited branches. There is always something you can take from the topic she's on and expand on it, branching out to extend the conversation on the same topic.

Each question opens up another set of branches you can choose. Women are always showing you what they want to talk about. She just told you something, so that's all you need. Whatever topic you have in front of you is the best part of the conversation. Don't look anywhere else outside of the material she's giving you. Refrain from searching sporadically for something you like or have in common.

If you're talking about where she went to college, follow up with something relevant to her college experience, like the town it was in, sports, studying abroad, organizations, parties on campus, if she's still in touch with her college friends, and why she left or stayed in the same city after college. Instead of going from, "Where did you go to college?" then jumping to the next topic with "Oh cool, what do you do for work?" expand on the topic at hand. It just doesn't make sense and it feels like a painful interrogation that you want to escape from.

When you're asking questions, keep it all relevant and dig deeper into each topic (we'll discuss more on how to have meaningful conversations later inside this chapter). Here's how to keep the conversation going in a positive and engaging way...

"You" Statements

You seem to be really adventurous.

You really came alive when you talked about XYZ.

You have this really good energy about you.

You have a beautiful smile.

You seem very ambitious in life.

People love hearing about themselves, so if you notice even something small about someone that's positive then share it on the spot.

"I" Statements

I'm from San Diego.

I like to salsa dance.

I like to surf in the mornings.

I like to do yoga.

I went to the University of ___.

These are good because you're sharing a bit about yourself which prompts her to do the same. Always have the courage to go first and trust she will follow or simply ask.

"We" Adventures

It helps to seed potential dates with the "we" statements in the conversation to make getting the number and date in her head. If she agrees to the "date" in a playful story, then she'll likely agree to doing that in real life.

"We should get yogurt with unlimited toppings."

"We should try a salsa class and have tacos."

"We should get drinks and watch the game from the sky bar."

You're not actually going to do it right now. It's really a good-natured joke, but potentially, in the future, you're planting the idea of you two doing something fun together at a later time, which insinuates a perpetuating relationship. Now, you can bounce between these in an interaction and never really run out of things to say.

Just to recap the conversations with women: Really focus on slowing it down. Don't react so quickly to everything. Just relax, have fun and be present. You're not a clown, a comedian, an entertainer, or a dancing monkey. Slow down and be more present to prevent this from happening. Speak up and have strong vocal tonality: talk "down" like a king with authority, not "up" like a mouse asking for permission.

Don't confuse these interactions with being rude, arrogant, or lacking empathy, but don't sound like a dead zombie who has no energy and inflection in their voice. The sub-communication of your vocal tonality, facial gestures and body language is more important than the actual words you say. Be more alive, elicit good emotions, and radiate positive energy to others through your voice and body language, but do these things because it feels good for you and you want to do them, not to get a reaction from her.

Now that you've learned how to keep the conversations fun and engaging, you might be wondering, how can I take these playful conversations deeper and establish stronger connections? Here's how to connect with a woman's core to be so memorable that she forgets about everyone else in the room...

HOW TO HAVE MORE MEANINGFUL CONVERSATIONS FOR DEEPER CONNECTIONS

Once you have hooked a woman through fun and flirtatious conversations, tests, and qualifications, you can slowly shift into deeper and more meaningful conversations. It's important to note that you should not rush into deep conversations without first establishing rapport and creating a fun vibe. For the most part, deep conversations should serve as the epilogue of your interactions, not the introduction.

After you have engaged a woman's emotions and established a playful man to woman vibe, you can begin to fully tap into the core of who she is and add more value in a meaningful way. You do this by simply going deeper in your answers and questions to penetrate the core of what makes her, *her*.

When you accomplish this, she will begin to feel seen. You will likely be one of the rare men in her life who has been able to look past her beautiful exterior and appreciate her femininity and inner beauty. This will cause her to feel safe and freer when she's around you. Her guard will slowly come down and she will think to herself, "There's something different about this guy, he gets *me*." She will begin to no longer "see" you on a physical level. Rather she will "feel" you on a deeper emotional and psychological level, allowing her to remove the defensive mask she wears and reveal her true self to you.

When you see an attractive woman with a downright unattractive man it's because she no longer sees that man on a surface level, but rather feels him, trusts him and feels safe with him which is more important. The secret that beautiful women don't want you to know is that they are just as weird, quirky, confused, and lost as everyone else in the world. They are confused as to why so many men put them on a pedestal and treat them so differently. If you want to tap into her core femininity and develop a higher level of attraction, then you must go deeper than the basic interactions in which most men engage.

If a woman asks, "What's your favorite movie?"

A normal guy would maybe state, "*Star Wars*, of course!"

That would be a surface layer answer. Instead say, "*Star Wars* because it's about the hero's journey of a common man who rises to the call to adventure, overcomes extreme challenges, and transforms into someone who saves the world from evil. I can relate to this story because I'm in a similar place in my life where the odds are stacked up against me, but I'm working really hard to get to where I want to be in life." Do you feel the difference?

Let's try this again now, "What's your favorite music?"

A guy would maybe state, "I like Thirty Seconds to Mars."

A deeper answer would state, "Thirty Seconds to Mars because their songs are about doing the impossible and going after your dreams. They remind me of my childhood where I was always trying to challenge myself in a new environment. I wanted to be a football player, but I was the smallest player on the team."

Do you see how much more you are revealing about yourself? It gives her an opportunity to experience more of you and connect with you on a deeper level. What she responds with afterwards will be genuine curiosity rather than a forced comment. Now, let's say you're asking the questions and you want to get deeper with her.

If you ask, "What's your favorite movie?"

She might say, "I really like *50 First Dates*."

Instead of ignoring the gold right in front of you, stay on that topic and learn more about what this *really* means about her.

You can add, "What is it about *50 First Dates* that you like?" She might say, "It's about having to recreate love every day instead of just going through life in such a boring mundane routine." You can keep going by stating, "I see, and what is it about recreating love that gets to you?"

She might say, "Well, my last relationship was very boring, and we stopped growing together after the first few years. I wish more men were willing to recreate love every day. It would show me that men still care about building a relationship after the excitement has burned out."

And in these moments, when the woman in front of you finally lifts the veil and reveals her truth to you, look her in the eyes and confidently respond, "I get you." Be silent, hold eye contact, and relax into the moment together. No more words need to be said. Now, do you see the impact you're getting out of just asking for her favorite movie?

The more she reveals about herself and opens up with you, the more she is investing into the interaction which suggests she values you. You are worth her time and are important to her. Stop asking surface layer questions to nowhere and start penetrating deeper into what her response really says about *her* life, past, and worldview.

We often go from question to question desperately looking for something in common to talk about. It's really about asking basic questions then going deeper to understand what that says about her and who she really is as a person.

At the same time, if she is asking you questions, you should be prepared for these traditional questions and add more intrigue to your answers, so you can reveal more about yourself to her. For instance, what do you do? You might say: "I'm a real estate investor"

Most people don't know what that really means, so the conversation ends awkwardly. It sounds like you might do something with properties, but it doesn't reveal what you do, how you spend your time, or anything about yourself. A more intriguing response: "I make this city beautiful by taking old dilapidated buildings and turning them into modern works of art for the local community to enjoy."

You might be thinking that was too easy, what if I'm a boring software engineer? Well, then say: "I build apps like the one you're on right now to share ideas and connect the world together."

Or how about if you're a student studying something dull like classical history? Try: "I study how the world works and how we got here today so we can push the human race forward."

Do you *feel* the difference? Any profession can sound more intriguing if you spend time thinking about it and get a little creative. This leaves room for her to ask more questions and be more engaged in what you do. At the same time, it reveals more about yourself, which prompts her to do the same. Boring responses breed boring conversations whereas intriguing responses breed intriguing conversations. If you want to have better conversations, simply lead the way.

When each of you get vulnerable and share more about yourself, you are investing more into the interaction. This creates a deeper, more meaningful connection.

When you get emotionally naked and vulnerable, you open the doors for her to be exposed and reveal her true self, too. It's this level of conversation where the two of you can have real conversation about topics that each of you care about and make it feel like you're long lost friends.

This combination of having fun, flirting, stimulating conversations first combined with meaningful exchanges will make you more memorable. It's really about having that balance of both stimulating and meaningful conversations. Lead with fun, stimulating conversation to spike emotions and garner attraction then pepper in meaningful conversations to display you're not only someone fun, interesting, and engaging, but also a man of substance who cares about who she really is.

We've covered a ton of content here. I made socializing with women a big priority because so many guys struggle with having fun, flirtatious conversations without being needy. At this point you've learned a *lot* of new concepts that you can use the next time you approach women. However, at some point, it's inevitable that your interactions won't always go as you'd like. You'll come across as needy or rude, she's just not into it, or you're simply having a bad day or night.

How you handle this dilemma internally will dictate whether you fail or succeed at creating an abundant dating life.

HOW TO USE REJECTION TO PROPEL YOURSELF FORWARD

You *will* get rejected on this journey and no matter how much you improve, it will always happen. It's kind of like training in mixed martial arts: no matter how good you get, you can always expect that you will still get punched in the face. But do you get back up or do you give up?

After a certain amount of time on this journey, some men will have very little results and they will indeed give up. But I have uncovered this little trick: if we change what rejection means to you and your internal dialogue, then your chances of staying on the journey increase tenfold.

You must shift rejection from something negative into a learning experience.

Failure is only telling you what not to do and what you need to work on. Therefore, the more action you take, the more feedback you get, which improves your skills and leads to better results. You cannot eliminate rejection, you can only change the meaning you give it. Does it empower you or disempower you?

The harder you are on yourself, the harder it becomes to take action tomorrow. The negative self-talk is something you are doing to yourself. The rejection may have occurred weeks or months ago, but the negative story is still playing in your mind and stifling your results.

An experienced Grounded Man will learn from negative feedback. He'll become better and not bury himself in self-defeating talk. You must learn to differentiate between the two types of rejection. The first type occurs whenever *you* mess something up. Maybe you didn't speak confidently, got choked up, were boring, or simply being incongruent.

These rejections should be treated as learning opportunities. You made a mistake and now you have a chance to learn from it, so it doesn't happen again. The second type of rejection occurs whenever you meet a woman, authentically express yourself, and she doesn't reciprocate. This is not your fault. It's simply a sign that the two of you have mismatched core values or it's the wrong time.

If you do get rejected and the interaction is clearly over, end on your own terms. Don't wait for her to leave. Say, "I've got to run," or "I've got to get back to my friends. The night is young." Never degrade women if they're not responding well to you, or if you get flat out rejected. Simply bow out gracefully and move on to the next interaction with your dignity intact. You've lost nothing and your life has not changed in any way.

These rejections are actually a *great* thing because her rejection saved you time, energy, and resources that would have been wasted on an unfulfilling and unsatisfying relationship. That rejection gave you plenty of time for another woman who would fulfill you, not to mention time with your friends, your family, and your goals, too.

Guys often build up rejection to be something so much bigger than it really is. She doesn't know you well enough to reject you as a man. She doesn't know your background, history, and life experiences. It's easy to assume that she knows this and when she walks away, you take it very personally, as if she rejected everything about your life. Until she hears you, sees you, and experiences your reality over time, you haven't even given her the opportunity to meet you, let alone reject you.

Accept that rejection is supposed to happen and it's a part of the journey. If there's a day that you stop getting rejected, you're likely trying way too hard, being fake or manipulative, or you're compromising who you are as a man. Your goal is not to become the ultimate people-pleaser and get everyone to like you in every situation to avoid rejection.

You should be screening women as much as they are screening you.

We'll dive into this topic more deeply in chapter six, but it's impossible for every woman you approach to be a good fit in your life. Some of them simply aren't meant to be with you and honestly SHOULD NOT BE WITH YOU, so the interaction is supposed to not work out. It's better to be single than to be in a relationship with the wrong woman.

Learn how to differentiate these types of rejections. Learn from Type 1 rejections and celebrate Type 2 rejections. The former is an opportunity for growth and improvement. The latter saved you from a potentially life-altering mistake. Either way you're winning. The day will come when you have an incredible woman at your side; will those past rejections really matter to you years from now?

You are enough right now, in this moment, to get started making progress. The more you go out, the more you learn, the better you become at meeting new women and inviting them into your life.

I understand approaching and interacting with attractive women can be a daunting experience for any man regardless if he's successful financially, good looking or an average joe. If you'd like my help to master this process so you can effortlessly approach any woman and have her responding positively to you with lots of laughter, then watch this presentation and discover how I can support you further for those that need it: knowledgeformen.com/live

And now things really get exciting. It's time to learn how to escalate your interactions, from the first interaction to being more physical to getting her phone number to taking it to the bedroom, the first date, and beyond.

In the next chapter, I'm going to teach you the proven strategies that I've used for years to effortlessly escalate my interactions, get physical, and create high levels of sexual tension with the most attractive women, so she wants whatever happens "next" to happen.

This is exactly what you've been waiting for, so get ready. It's about to get *really* fun...

CHAPTER 5

ESCALATING THE INTERACTION TO CREATE THE MOST ADVENTUROUS DAYS & NIGHTS OF YOUR LIFE

"Is this not the true romantic feeling; not to desire to escape life, but to prevent life from escaping you."

– THOMAS WOLFE

"What the *fuck* is happening?"

The words almost failed to register in my brain. Whether I simply didn't hear them because of the inescapable "thum thum thum" of the nightclub's blaring music or because of the fact I was lost in thought, imagining I was somewhere else, I can't remember. But I *do* remember the one thought running through my head as I processed the scene playing out before me.

Sitting next to me in a tight black dress, clearly tipsy from multiple vodka martinis, was arguably one of *the* most attractive women I'd ever laid eyes on. She wasn't just "attractive." She possessed the sort of beauty typically reserved for the Hollywood elite. Her blonde hair up, neatly showcasing her cute neck and shoulders, her skin was smooth and tan, without a visible blemish in sight. Her makeup perfectly done to accentuate the contours of her unnaturally symmetrical face. Her body fit and shaped like the perfect hourglass. And her eyes, pupils as large as they now were, were captivating.

And here she was, sitting next to me in a Las Vegas nightclub booth, her tight body pressing up against mine. She snorted lines of cocaine off her wrist before cleaning her nose and taking a stream of selfies—with but mostly without me—seemingly ad infinitum.

I can't remember how much cocaine she did, what she said to me, or how many ridiculous faces she made while looking into her phone. All I remember is wishing I was somewhere else...with *someone* else. Thinking back to the beginning of my night, I remembered who I *really* wanted sitting next to me.

A few hours earlier, I'd walked by a wedding chapel inside the hotel. "Damn," I'd thought, "they aren't kidding about those things." But my train of thought was cut off when I saw *her.*

Standing at the entrance of the chapel was a brunette with long, slender legs, clear skin, toned body, a natural physical beauty who was perfectly accentuated by just a light touch of makeup. But there was something more to her. She carried herself with an unmistakable sort of grace and carefreeness. Even at a distance, you could *feel* it.

I had to say something, but the night had just begun, and I was caught off guard. *You always see the best ones when you're unprepared.*

My heart cringed. "I can't do this," I thought to myself. "I just woke up from a nap after a long day at a business conference, I'm just going to…" My thoughts were cut short. As I walked past her, waging an internal debate and trying to summon the courage to say hello, she looked at me. And before my anxiety could catch up with my thoughts, my instincts kicked in and I smiled at her. "Hey," I said, barely believing the words were leaving my mouth, "are you waiting for the groom?"

She laughed and brushed a strand of hair behind her ear. "No! Just my friend," she answered in a soft voice. I shrugged and smiled a little wider, extending my hand and responding, "Let's get married while you wait."

To my surprise (and delight), she playfully agreed, and exclaimed, "Only if it's a small wedding. I can't stand being the center of attention."

"Done," I said, spinning her around playfully while she laughed.

She asked, "What about our honeymoon? Rome or Paris?"

"Rome, obviously!" I said. "I've always wanted to see the Coliseum."

She responded enthusiastically, "Oh good idea, *Gladiator* was one of my favorites." Oh my gosh, I'm drawn to her.

"Also, we're living in San Diego, it's my favorite city. It's where we're going to have more fun adventures."

"Not a problem at all," she casually responded, "I actually want to go to grad school there to become a physical therapist."

"No way!" I responded, "Why's that?"

She looked at me for a moment, pausing to gather her thoughts, "Well, I used to struggle with chronic back pain after a car accident as a kid and my physical therapist helped me heal after doctors had given up on me. I want to help people be pain free, after all, a pain free body is the greatest gift, you know."

I respected that she wants to help others for a living. She's not only attractive, but fun and has depth to her. I'm drawn to her even more.

"That's ama—" But my compliment was cut short by the return of her friend, who rushed over frantically, interrupting us and making it abundantly clear she did *not* appreciate how close we were conversing.

My heart sank, but I didn't show it. "So, is this one of our bridesmaids?" I asked, trying to make light of the situation.

"Haha, of course!" my soon-to-be wife responded. "This is my friend Lacey." Lacey flashed me a despicable look that could have killed a small puppy with her eyesight alone.

"And I'm Averi," she said as Lacey pulled her away, yelling that their ride that was apparently late. Blowing me a kiss and smile, she added, "It was so nice to meet you!" Those dreaded words made me face the reality of the situation.

"Great to meet you too, I'm Andrewwww!" I yelled through the crowd, but it was too late. Lacey wasn't having it as she pulled Averi with her like a hostage rescue operator. In and out, never to be seen again.

I hesitated. I should have followed her and gotten her number at the very least, or even gone with them and paid for whatever shared ride or taxi fare they had. The interaction, short as it had been, was intoxicating.

Upset with myself, I made my way to the trendy club and sauntered to the bar where I was meeting my friend Jameson. He had already ordered me a bourbon, neat. Moments after sitting down, he tapped my shoulder and whispered, "Those girls over there are gorgeous and there's no one talking to them. Let's go see what they're about."

Attempting to cheer myself up and shake the thoughts of Averi from my head, I stood up and raised my glass, exclaiming, "Let the night begin!"

Within seconds of walking over, Jameson had all four women laughing so hard that mascara was beginning to run down one of their faces. His conversation flowed effortlessly. His jokes landed perfectly. His teasing struck a balance between gentlemanly wit and comedic aloofness. I was very impressed and glad I'm out with him.

As Jameson continued to chat and laugh, my attention drifted to the most attractive woman—not just in the group, but in the entire club.

Smiling, I reached out my hand to her, but she didn't move. She's glued to her phone, the validation toy where the world approves of her every whim. Instead of feeling rejected, I sat down next to her and started making faces in her phone while she's taking selfies and put my arm around her. She plays with me, expecting a simple ordinary conversation, but then let out an adorable giggle as I stood her up and spun her away from the group to engage her.

"Okay, so you are dangerously cute," I said with a smirk, "but what else do you have going for you?" She shrugged her shoulders with a touch of arrogant nonchalance. "What else do you need?" It wasn't playful, she was serious.

I knew girls like this. Beautiful. Untouchable. On top of the world. Able to get what they want, when they want, and always the center of attention and recipient of adoration. *I'll give her a chance*, I thought to myself. I continued, unphased by her overconfidence, "So tell me a little bit about yourself. You know, things you do with your life outside of getting thousands of likes."

I looked at her straightforwardly and she continued, "Well, I dropped out of ASU, school is so boring, but I model here and there...."

The internal battle ensued. She was *exactly* the opposite of everything I wanted in a woman. Conceited. Self-centered. Narcissistic. Focused solely on herself, failing to realize that she was focusing all her time and attention on a fleeting asset. Her intellect, personality, and skills were nowhere to be seen. Her growth was stunted by her over-obsession with her captivating, jaw-dropping appearance.

I sighed again. *When in Vegas*, I thought to myself, resigning myself to my ironic misfortune. "Do you want some blow?" she happily offered out of nowhere, seemingly in her own world.

Her words jolted me back into the present moment. I fell into the booth where I witnessed my companion take yet another messy line from her wrist before snapping *yet another* duck lip selfie, although undeniably sexy. *This is exactly why the war on drugs failed*, I thought to myself. I rolled my eyes and looked over my shoulder. And that's when I saw her. Averi. I couldn't believe it. The women I'd met not two hours before was standing across the bar.

I should go talk to her, I thought to myself, but she was with another man. *Was it her boyfriend?*

The woman I was with was clearly interested in me but is more or less a shit show. A stunning one at that, but I had such great chemistry with Averi and—my thoughts were once again cut short.

"Are you gonna do a fucking bump or not!" the selfie queen shouted impatiently in my direction, making my decision clear to me.

"I'm good," I replied. "Enjoy the rest of your night, there's someone else I've gotta go explore."

"Wait? You're fucking leaving!" she exclaimed, incredulity and confusion coloring her tone. She was not used to men walking away from her, only to her. "Are you serious right now?"

Laughing to myself, I responded, "Yeah I am. Look, I get that you're super-hot but real beauty doesn't idolize itself. And there's a *real* beauty I need to talk to. Enjoy your night."

Without waiting to see her reaction, I walked away and left her to carry on with her drugging and selfie snapping behavior. I felt proud of my decision but uncertain about what would happen next. Looking directly across the bar at Averi, my heart sank. The man she was talking to was one of the most popular pickup coaches on the internet, one of the guys *I'd* watched and taken notes from when I was first getting started.

"Shit," I thought to myself, "I wonder if he's the real deal?" For a moment, my self-confidence took a hit. Even after the fun little faux elopement earlier, did I stand a chance against such a seasoned pro? Then, as if answering my question, she glanced down at her watch and proceeded to twirl her cocktail napkin mindlessly, barely even glancing in his direction.

I stepped up fast and spread my arms, greeting her over the din of the music and offering a hug, acting as if she was a long-lost friend. It was a bold move, but it paid off. She all but fell into my arms.

"Thank god you're here," she whispered into my ear.

"Don't worry. I got you," I responded, picking her up and spinning her away from the pickup coach. "I'm your fiancé, remember? I'll save you from the boogeyman!"

She held my arm tightly, protecting her from the dangers of unwanted pickup artistry. We had fun, laughing and dancing. At one point, I yelled out loud, "Let's run away like tigers and lions trapped in a zoo!"

To this day, I still don't know why I said that but, hey, it sounded fun and we were in an emotional state, not a logical one. She laughed hysterically, "You're so different, but I like it..."

At this point, it's worth mentioning that—as beautiful as Averi was—she wore an aura of innocence about her. Like she was the kind of woman who wouldn't *kiss* a guy until the third or fourth date. As such, our dancing remained relatively tame.

I made advances, got closer, went in for a kiss. Every time, she would lightly push me back, keep dancing, and give me a playful smile that said, "I like you, but I'm not that kind of girl." A few songs into this playful but frustrating dance session, I noticed the pickup coach creeping around the corner. He was eyeing us like a hungry lion waiting for an injured gazelle. I could tell he hated rejection as much as I do. It made him livid. He walked right up to us and tapped her on the shoulder in the middle of our dance, there to conquer her and win her from me. She turned, saw him, and couldn't help but start laughing. Her expression was worth a thousand words, but she whispered to me all I needed to hear: "Get me out of here! It's the boogeyman again!"

I picked her up and spun her around to another part of the dance floor—her hero once more—and naturally assumed this was the right time to attempt another kiss.

But she dodged away from my advances once again, though still smiling. I thought to myself, *what is going on here?* She's enjoying the night, dancing close to me, holding me, expecting me to be her hero in Vegas, but constantly evading my attempts to escalate. *Maybe I had gotten ahead of myself?*

She was leaving me with just two choices. I could withdraw and move on, or stay Grounded and continue having fun, offering value to her and seeing where the night goes. Perhaps she and I still had potential. With this beauty, I decided to do the latter. The pickup coach was lurking right around the corner, continuing to persist and pester us to the point where his advances were bordering on sociopathic. He took every chance he had to slide into our interaction, seemingly coming out of nowhere unable to understand the situation and accept rejection.

The next time I saw him coming, I leaned in for a kiss at the very same time. It backfired, she moved away, spinning away from me and accidentally right into him. In that moment, he considered it as his opportunity. He didn't acknowledge me and pressed into her. I saw her disappointed look and gave a slight shrug, then took a risk by saying, "Okay, I'm going to back to the hotel, come with."

It wasn't a bluff. I was ready to leave, with or without her. It had to be true or I would have come across as needy. For a few tense moments, I went to the booth and said bye to Jameson and his new friends, settled my bill, and started to walk towards the exit. And just as I started to reach the exit, I heard her voice, "Andrew, where are you going?" I spun around, contentment rising in my chest, to see Averi's relieved face, "I'm coming with you. I'm over this venue." She flashed me a smile that, for the first time, was indeed seductive.

Our friendly neighborhood pickup coach was fuming as he watched me walk her out from a distance. "I couldn't stand that guy," she said, looking back at him anxiously. "Everything he said felt rehearsed, he didn't listen to a thing I said, and the way he kept aggressively touching me..." She shuddered.

"Oh, come on," I said with a laugh, "the boogeyman wasn't *that* bad, right?"

"He so was," she said. "You could tell he was only trying to get laid... and trying *way* too hard."

"You know," she continued, "I was pretty surprised when you walked away. I didn't really expect that."

I shrugged. "It's been a long day and I've gotta get up early tomorrow. You're pretty cool but I couldn't put a hold on my entire night for someone I just met, despite our shenanigans about getting married." She heaved a sigh of mock anger. "Hey! I'm your freaking fiancée, at least for tonight!"

We both laughed. "I guess you are," I said, draping my arm around her and continuing to walk towards the curb outside.

Then, as if on cue, we heard someone behind us. "I've been looking all over for you! Where the *hell* have you been?" It was Lacey, much looser and more relaxed than she'd been when we first met, but still none too pleased to see Averi walking out with me. Worried that Lacey might ruin the interaction and put a halt to an otherwise grand adventure, I responded, "And now you found her! We were just heading back to the hotel, let's get out of here already!"

Lacey shot me another puppy-killing mean face. "Come on Averi, let's leave," she snapped, clearly signaling that she did *not* want her friend to spend the night with me. I opened my mouth to respond. But before I could, Averi did it for me.

"Don't worry," she told her friend, "He's cool. He kinda saved me from a creep and we've been having fun."

Lacey seemed unconvinced. Flashing a smile, I extended my hand, "I promise I'll be on my best behavior, alright? Your friend here is a rare gem. I get why you're protective." Slowly but surely, she met my hand and rolling her eyes. "She is, and you seem chill. Let's go." And we happily obliged.

When we arrived at the hotel, I kept my arm around Averi and continued the fun, flirtatious conversation until we almost passed the elevator to my room. It wasn't entirely clear if Averi was coming up to my room. After all this, I didn't want the night to end just yet. She looked beautiful, and it had been a while since I'd felt such an instant and intoxicating connection with a complete stranger. I felt like there was more to unravel and explore.

Committed to taking the night to its highest point, I stopped the group. "Hey, this is me. I'm really enjoying getting to know you. Why don't you come up for interesting conversation, drinks, and the view?"

Lacey gave a quick girlfriend check-in with her eyes and I attempted to allay her fear, "I've saved her over a dozen times tonight, so I promise I'll bring her back safe." Averi gave her a nod—*she wanted this too*—and I could tell she was as excited by my confidence as I was by *her*.

Lacey softened and flashed us both a smirk, instructing us to "have fun" as she walked off towards her room. I could feel Averi's excitement grow as she put her arm around me and squeezed my hand. I could tell it was exciting for her to be a little bad. Maybe it was new for her. Either way, I was going to be sure we had a memorable night.

As soon as we entered my room, wasting no time, I turned her around and gently pressed her shoulders against the door. Looking into her eyes, I started to gently kiss her lips and she slowly dodged it yet grabbed me closer to her. Our breathing intensified in unison. I playfully nipped at the bottom of her ear before trailing my kisses down her neck. She breathed in heavily when I picked her up as she wrapped both of her legs around me. For the first time, she was fully accepting my advances without reservation. I carried her across the room and gently laid her down on the bed. She gave me a look like an awakened animal that had been caged for far too long. It was my job to unravel her.

She fascinated me. All night she'd denied my advances, dodged attempted kisses, and made me assume she was interested in the purely platonic. Yet here she was. In my bed, eager and ready to experience a rather pleasurable night. In times like these, I always think to myself, "I can't believe I learned this."

The next day, Jameson was ecstatic and all high-fives. He was amazed but a little confused about how the night had gone for him. "How the heck did you do that last night? You walked away from literally the hottest woman in the entire club and then left with another beautiful woman who was being hit on by one of the most popular pickup coaches online. What gives?"

I shrugged. "I mean, the first woman was hot, but there was no connection. She just wanted to snort blow and take selfies. Averi was very special. And who knows, she's moving to San Diego soon and, assuming she passes the tests, we might connect and see each other again."

He shook his head and looked at me. "You know, very few men in the world could do what you did last night. You know, that right? You should teach this stuff. So many guys want to know what you're doing and how you think."

I respectfully declined. "I'm nothing special, just a regular guy who's learning and growing like everyone else."

"No way. I talked to more girls than you did last night, and everything eventually fizzled out. You seem to always find the right ones you know."

Here's the difference:

He might make girls laugh, but I make them want me. If I don't escalate, I'm doing the woman a disservice. Every woman wants to go on an adventure with a Grounded Man, so I take her on one.

You don't have to be a good-looking millionaire to do that. You just need to have fun and lead the way. Jameson was at a level that many men reach and struggle to move on from. He was adept at the approach and engaging women in lively conversations, but that's all he knew how to do. He just entertained them. I do the same thing but take it a step further and take a risk to show a woman that I like her, want her, and that I'm interested in both her intellect and her beauty. Women appreciate a man who knows what he wants and isn't afraid to let that be known.

I laid that all out for Jameson, and it only made him believe it stronger. "Dude. Yes. You have to write a book!" In that moment, I realized that men struggle with transitioning from a fun social conversation to being more physical and sexual. So I listened to Jameson, and I made sure to include this critical phase in the book.

And here it is…

HOW AND WHEN TO PHYSICALLY ESCALATE WITH WOMEN

You're having a good conversation and you're probably wondering when should I get physical? The answer is right now! If you don't touch her lightly and playfully early on in the interaction, you're indirectly hiding your intentions and sliding closer to the friend zone. If you've approached, hooked, tested, been tested, and she's still talking to you, it's clear she's interested in more than just a friendly conversation. When she responds positively, then have fun with it and you can move forward to physical escalation.

Sometimes, especially when you're first beginning your journey into the dating game, it can be difficult to gauge whether or not a woman wants you to escalate the interaction and get physical. However, there are five common signs that she wants you to move forward and escalate the interaction.

Specifically:

1. You've developed a man to woman vibe, and the tension is increasing.
2. She is holding strong eye contact with you.
3. She is talking to you and sharing herself with you, beyond just normal conversation.

4. She is smiling, laughing, flirting back, and responding well to your conversation.
5. Her body language indicates arousal, e.g. her hips are pointed towards you, she's leaning in your direction, she's playing with her hair, licking her lips, and trying to stay close to you.

If she's doing any of those things and you don't physically escalate, you're basically saying, *"I'm not interested in you,"* and your lack of escalation will make *her* feel rejected.

She'll wait a while and chat with you, but if you don't escalate, then she'll slowly start pulling back and think that you're only interested in her as a friend. She'll think to herself, "Wow! He's an amazing guy but he's not advancing on me. I guess he's just fun and flirty, but he must have a girlfriend or not find me attractive."

She's not going to tell you, "Hey, will you touch me now?" It's your job to take action, pursue, and physically escalate. You have to display your sexual interest to her in a playful but respectful way. Here are the different types of physical escalation:

Platonic: Close proximity, rubbing, arm touching, shoulder touching, lower back touching.

Dominance: Picking her up, spinning, grabbing her hand, kissing, dancing.

Sexual: Hips, butt, thighs (when she clearly likes you and feels safe with you).

Relationship: Holding hands, arm around each other, sitting on you, cuddling.

Go in that order: platonic, dominant, sexual, then relationship, then switch it up and use a combination of all of them throughout an interaction as things progress.

An enjoyable thing to do when you first meet a woman that elicits a positive response is to reach your hand out like you're going to shake her hand, but then, you spin her around. Another one of my favorite things to do is the hand clasp, where you put your hand up almost like you're taking an oath, but your fingers are spread out. As you reach out and she makes contact with your hand, then you close the hands so you're holding hands, which lets you bring her close to you. From here, you have the man-to-woman vibe perfectly in place. I'd suggest staying close and having some conversation for a minute then doing a fun move such as a spinning hug where you pick her up below her waist and spin her. Set her back down and remain close and continue having conversation.

Another fun thing you can do later in the conversation is to bring her close to you, put her arm around your neck, take her hand, and waltz for a few steps then turn around and go in the other direction. Search "waltz dance" if you're unclear of what that is. Hold on, you're probably thinking these silly moves are so immature, right?

Attraction is an emotional response, not a logical one. When you do these fun physical gestures, you spike her emotions and stand out from other men who would never dare to take such bold risks. You'll display your desires in a polarizing way.

Women often say things to me like, "You are so crazy!" or "Where did you come from?" while wearing the biggest smiles. I know some of these actions probably sound weird or obnoxious. But I promise, when you actually put them into practice and see the huge smile or hear the uncontrollable laugh from women, you'll get what I mean and think differently.

Now, continue chatting and talking and allow her to feel comfortable with all of this emotion. If it's too much too soon, she'll freak out and leave so you have to do these physical moves slowly, pepper them into your conversations and learn when to let go and slow down.

These moves are not the main course. Remember you are The Grounded Man, but these moves elicit very high positive emotions and add to the fun of the interaction. Think of yourself as the filet mignon and these physical moves as the sides. It helps make a great meal, but without it you can still do well.

If you are getting close with a woman, you want to make sure that you aren't staying connected at all times. This will make you seem needy, too try hard and overly clingy. Instead, let go of her, enjoy conversing with her, trust that she'll come back and re-engage in physical contact.

If you've followed the steps up to this point, she *will* come back, hungry for more. Ideally, you'll want to follow a "two steps forward, one step back" approach in your escalation. This will give her the opportunity to reciprocate your touch and give you a chance to uncover whether she's really interested or not. Let her relax a bit, continue to have stimulating and meaningful conversation, and then come back to being more physical.

If you touch her on her lower back when you're whispering a joke and then she responds a few minutes later by leaning against you and whispering something to *you*, then it's safe to say that she's interested.

And at this point in the interaction, a kiss is a possibility. Although there's nothing wrong with going in for a kiss as soon as you can, I like to wait and build the tension to make her chase me for the kiss. Always create tension then release the tension with the kiss, then repeat but with longer kisses as you go. The greater the tension, the greater the kiss.

For instance, I typically build up to it by getting really close, holding her body, and pulling her in close to me so my lips are just about three to six inches away from hers. They almost touch, but before they do, I look confidently at her, I may whisper something witty, and then pull away.

At this point, she'll want you to kiss her and is licking her lips, but you don't give it to her. You continue playing, talking, and when the moment is right, you go for it and give her a good kiss, but keep it short and be the first to pull away.

You are the prize. Keep her wanting more. Allow her to chase by not giving all of yourself to her so early.

For instance, if she goes for the kiss, maybe you dodge her and nip at her neck instead, then whisper into her ear, "Patience my dear".

From here, just have fun getting to know her while being physical and enjoying the interaction. It's a beautiful dance of physical, emotional, and intellectual stimulation that women find irresistible. This sets up the man-to-woman frame perfectly, making it very clear that you're not a friend but rather someone who wants her.

You will have significantly better interactions if you use a small amount of physicality over a long period of time, rather than an intense amount of physicality in a short amount of time. Be light and physical while you're talking to her, since it demonstrates that these are natural behaviors to you and not a fake, rushed attempt to force the interaction. That way, you're able to establish physical rapport with the woman. It's really about being very comfortable being close together in a sensual, challenging and playful way that intensifies attraction.

But don't escalate too quickly until you're in a position to go the distance. If you give her the full experience right away, then she has little to imagine in the future. You want to keep her guessing, as it leaves a bit of mystery and uncertainty to the interaction. You want her thinking, "Why isn't he going further with me when I know he could?"

This is more challenging and gets her to invest more into the interaction. Give her enough space to realize, "Yes, I like this guy and I want him to like me more." If a woman is with a Grounded Man over a sustained period of time and a man-to-woman vibe is established, then attraction will naturally build. Eventually, she will want to be intimate with you if the time and place is right.

The more you combine stimulating, meaningful conversations with fun, sensual, and physical escalation, the more aroused she will become. That volume knob will keep turning to an uncontrollable level of, "I want this man now."

At this point, things are going great for both of you. You've followed all of the advice from chapter 4, you're having fun, playful, and stimulating conversations in combination with light physical escalation, but now you're thinking, "What's next from here?"

Well, you have a wide variety of enjoyable opportunities to choose from, it all depends on her logistics for what you should do next. Failure to understand the importance of logistics will ruin any chance of further escalation, even if she really likes you.

DETERMINING HER LOGISTICS TO TELL YOU WHAT TO DO

Once you have approached a woman, hooked her interest, and positioned yourself as a lover-to-be instead of a friend, you need to figure out her logistics in order to determine how and where to lead the interaction next.

If you aren't doing this, then you aren't playing to win. Period. You don't want to stand in one location for the entire interaction. If things are going well, it's your job to escalate accordingly. You want to escalate to either:

1. Going to your or her place to be more intimate.
2. Going to another venue to continue the interaction and build a deeper connection.
3. Exchanging contact information with the intention to meet later in the week to eventually do one of the above.

Work in logistical questions like:

- Where are you from?
- What area do you live in?
- What area are you staying at (if out of town)?
- What are you doing this weekend?
- Who are you with today/tonight?
- What are your plans for the rest of the day/night?

You'll want to include these questions in your regular conversation. Don't wait until the last minute when she has to leave and bombard her with all these questions at once. It comes off as trying too hard and gives an agenda-seeking vibe, which puts women in a defensive state.

The answers to those questions tell you what to do next. If you think that she's open to an "adventurous" night with you, whether that means a one-night encounter or going to a new venue together, here's how to make that happen.

STEP-BY-STEP ON HOW TO
LEAVE A VENUE TOGETHER

Once you've determined a woman's logistics and realize that there is potential to escalate the interaction, your next step is to move around the venue together then eventually leave together.

You want to do this *before* you consider escalating the interaction to anything more intimate. By leading a woman around an existing venue and to a different location, she will become more comfortable following your lead. Here's your step-by-step guide to leaving a venue with a woman who is attracted to you:

1. When She's Solo

She's looking for a fun night out and you're the guy to bring it to her. This is probably a best-case scenario, yet quite rare. If she's from out-of-town, this is the only night you will ever have with this woman.

If you really like her and want to take it further, then the one-night encounter is your best option. By asking, "What are you doing this weekend?" you'll learn whether she's here for the weekend or going back home.

If she's solo and from your town, then you have the option of getting her phone number and setting up a date later or a one-night encounter tonight. Both are good options, yet I would always push to make most of the interaction since the emotions are the highest right now.

She may forget about you if you just get her number. It may take a lot of effort to get her out again, but right now you are already with her. Plus, you have to consider that there are other guys pursuing her, as well. However, right now, she's with you, so make the most of it.

2. She's with Friends and From Out of Town

In this scenario, you will have to either have a one-night encounter if this is her last night, or if she is here for a few more days, you have the option of getting her phone number now and following up with her to hang out later.

However, since you're already together now, it makes most sense to make the most of the night. If she's visiting, it's going to be difficult to get her to leave her friends to go with some guy she just met. She has social pressure to stay with the group and will most likely ignore you even if she did like you.

3. She's a Local Who's Out with Friends

Then it's a one-night encounter or get her phone number. Her friends will be a logistical barrier you have to work with in order to get her out. It helps to have your own friends with you so your friends can mingle with hers. Then it becomes a fun party.

When you want to leave the venue, you can either take her with you or bring the friends with you, which is usually the case. Now, I know what you're thinking: is this all about one-night encounters? I thought this was about finding the woman of your dreams?

No, this is absolutely *not* about only one-night encounters and I am a huge proponent of being with one incredible woman. This is about making the most of your night, having fun, and gaining the most experience in the shortest amount of time possible.

Remember, women want sex, too. You want sex. I'm just making it very clear, so you know what options you have. That way, you don't waste any of your time when you go out and miss out on opportunities. If you are a Grounded Man who's followed the proper steps, then you are experiencing a wide range of emotions. The end result of all of that is naturally sex if the logistics work out.

I'm giving you the tools here to safely move the two of you from the venue to a place where you can be more intimate. Sometimes sex doesn't happen, which is perfectly okay, because you had a really fun, adventurous time together; maybe it even got a little physically intimate. It still leads to a higher chance of staying in contact and seeing each other again. You'll stand out from the other men and be more memorable this way versus just getting her phone number after fifteen minutes of so-so conversation. When in doubt, lean towards more adventure, more experiences, and more fun.

Once you've determined her logistics and you know that she's going to be up for leaving with you that night, it's time to take the lead and get the party on the move! Start leading her around the venue, to the bar, to the dance floor, to the table, to the lounge area, and if you aren't at a bar type of venue just lead her around wherever you are, so when it's time to leave, she already has a history of following your lead and it won't be a big leap of faith for her when you want to leave. It's important to plant the idea of leaving with you in a playful way without actually leaving together just yet. For instance:

"It would be fun to do X with you, but I just don't know if I can trust you."

"There's this other place I really like but I don't know if they would let you in."

"You like X too? I know the best X nearby, I'm probably going to go there soon."

You're basically giving subtle hints that you could leave together and do something fun in the future, yet not outright. If she responds positively and plays with it, then you have successfully planted the idea of leaving together rather than suddenly suggesting that you leave together, which is a big ask for anyone.

When you do that, she'll naturally shift into a defensive mode and give you more resistance, even if she likes you. Often, you'll escalate physically, and things will be going great. You're ready to leave and she may be too, but there's a lot of social pressure for her to fit the "good girl" stereotype.

So you want to reduce the pressure of the interaction by saying something like, "I really can't be up all night, I have to get up early," which does three things:

1. Makes her realize that you aren't chasing her all night like most guys have in the past. It says that you're okay walking away.
2. You're okay with the interaction not ending in a more physical way, which means you value your time more than her.
3. The idea of sex is somewhat out of the picture for her and if you two leave together then you are genuinely leaving together to go do "this thing," whether that is to get food, drinks, or dessert, or just be more private.

At this point, when I'm feeling ready to leave, I'll throw out a question like, "Are you adventurous?" This creates intrigue and she'll typically respond with a challenging, "Why?"

You can confidently and slowly grab her hand or have her hook your arm and start walking out of the venue. If you're on the street order, a shared ride or head toward your car or a taxi. If you have done the above well, then about fifty percent of the time, she'll follow you and won't say a word because she likes and trusts you and wants to experience more of an adventure. The other fifty percent of the time, she'll ask, "Where are we going?" or "It depends..."

This next part is very important. You want to respond with a challenge by making it hard for her to continue the interaction with you, like she can't come anymore, suggesting that you've gotten ahead of yourself. For instance:

"You know what, forget it, we're not going to do it anymore."

"I was getting ahead of myself, I only do this with people that I really know or trust."

"I'm sorry, I have a really good reputation over there, but I think I could get you in… maybe."

The goal is to get her to invest more and qualify herself to you that she is worthy of whatever adventure you have planned. This flips the script. She is trying to get you to *let* her come with you rather than you having to persuade her to come with you like a professional negotiator. Again, we want win-win, so let her qualify herself to you to make it her decision about leaving with you, not solely yours.

She might say, "Shut up, I want to come. It's getting boring here anyway." Then once she qualifies herself, you accept, be straight to the point and say:

"Alright, let's get drinks/food."

"Alright, follow me..."

"Okay, since you asked so nicely…"

Then grab her hand or have her hook her arm around yours and lead her out. If you fail to do the above and just abruptly out of nowhere say, "Let's go," it may work, but it could reduce the quality of the interaction because she feels like it's not win-win.

You want to have a build-up to leaving together by planting the idea first, reducing the pressure, and getting her to qualify herself before asking to leave with her.

One *horrible* phrase to avoid at all costs is, "Let's go to my place." This just *screams,* "I want sex!" Even if a woman wants to be intimate with you, she won't respond well to this type of advance because it can make her feel shameful for her desires.

You want to make it feel like things "just happened" in the adventure, maintaining the fun and spontaneity of the interaction. However, before you can successfully lead this interaction elsewhere, sometimes you'll need to handle any friends whom she's already with.

Here's a simple way to do this.

HOW TO HANDLE HER FRIENDS

If she's with other people, then she'll respond with, "What about my friends?"

1. You can say, "We'll be back soon."
I'll usually set a deadline of about one hour. I'll look at my watch and say, "I'll bring you back by X time," and gently extend your hand and let her voluntarily grab your hand then continue walking out.

As you walk out, ask the doorman if there is reentry into the venue. Most of the time, it's "yes" and he'll stamp your hands. I do this because it tells the woman that she can easily come back into the venue and meet her friends whenever she wants to.

2. You can say, "Introduce Me!"
It feels empowering to let her lead the way in this case. Her friends need to see that she likes you, trusts you, and is enjoying her time with you, but more importantly, that you aren't annoying her or creeping her out. Simply introduce yourself, ask them how they know each other, and chat with her friends. Then let them know you're going to this "other place" for just a little bit.

Often her friends will actually be rooting for you. Maybe she's been looking for a good guy for a while. It's the same way that you'd be rooting for your friend if he was leaving with an attractive woman that he liked.

3. Organize a party

If you both have friends with you, then you can organize a party where everyone can go to another venue or take it to whichever friend's place is closest.

Now, if you go to another venue, plan on spending no more than an hour there. Going to different venues together is very powerful. It creates that feeling of togetherness between the two of you, so I urge you to go to one to three different venues when you're with a woman you just met or even on a date. Inside the new venue, you want to continue having meaningful and stimulating conversation, physicality escalating, and then mention something like, "I'm heading back for some drinks to relax since I have to wake up early. Come with."

That's it. Be straightforward and to the point. Don't keep rambling on and on. You'd be surprised at how many women won't say anything because at this point, they want this to happen as much as you do. All you have to do is lead the way. It is your job, not hers. You can skip going to multiple venues if you feel she's really into you, but sometimes she needs to spend more time with you before she feels safe and trusts you enough to go somewhere more private. The whole time you're in transit to your house or the next location, you must remain the confident, relaxed, and fun guy she was with earlier.

If you change frames and start getting overly excited, nervous, or anxious, you might stop talking or flirting. She might start to feel a bit of distrust or even a little unsafe, so continue to keep her emotions high with fun, sensual, and positive energy. The guy you were earlier needs to be the same guy she is with while leaving. If there's a sudden switch in frames, it creates a sense of suspicion leading to resistance, doubt, and uncertainty. Now, I'm going to pause here and come back to the topic of going back to your place later in the chapter. Don't worry, I *will* spill the beans and share what to do when you bring her back to a more private location. What I'm going to share with you works, whether it's the first night or the third date.

But for now, let's backtrack a little bit and discuss what to do if you're unable to escalate the interaction to your place this quickly (which will be the most common scenario).

THE BEST WAY TO GET HER PHONE NUMBER & SOCIAL MEDIA WITHOUT FAIL

Let's say the logistics weren't working out for you, or she liked you but wasn't going to leave her friends. Or maybe she has to be up early for work the next day, had to leave the venue early, but made it clear that she's interested in you.

This is very common. Although you can stay with her longer, build more rapport and flirt and try to leave together later, which can work, but you have to assess how much you like this woman. The Grounded Man thinks abundance. He knows there are plenty of women he can talk to. So, always ask yourself, is this one person worth more of my time and energy?

If she is, then always challenge yourself and stay with her to bring the interaction to its highest point of adventure. If you're on the fence, then get her phone number while keeping in mind this is a risk. You may not get a response from her via text/phone or see her again, especially if it was only a so-so interaction.

With the proliferation of social media and the inescapable connectedness of modern existence, a phone number is no longer what it used to be. Just a few years ago, women gave away their number only when they actually intended to follow up. But today, women have access to an infinite number of men through various social media channels and dating apps; you are only one of many. Without first creating a memorable experience, your number will get lost in an endless sea of DMs, text messages, and right swipes.

If you don't first set yourself apart and give her a *reason* to continue the interaction with you, then the phone number is useless. A phone number does *not* mean the connection is moving forward. It doesn't even mean that she actually wants to connect later. You just have a form of communication to contact her later and she may or may not reciprocate.

Always aim to have an adventure first, then stretch the interaction out as long as possible while sharing as many positive emotions together. Ultimately, you want to end up in a private location where you can be more intimate because this will be more memorable. Sex does not have to happen in order to be memorable, although it certainly doesn't hurt.

> **The phone number is never your main goal. It is not a piece of social validation or a sign that your "skills" are improving. The phone number is a tool to help you continue the adventure at another time and place.**

When you ask for the number, be casual and relaxed because it's not a big deal. Your body language is communicating how you feel on the inside. Any nervous activity will show her that you're not safe or have low value. At this point, she should want to give you her phone number because you have demonstrated enough value in your interaction. Here's how to ask for a woman's phone number effortlessly:

"Hey, let's exchange phone numbers real quick."

That's it. "Let's" is a "we" statement and "exchange" is a mutual swapping of value where she gets your number and you get hers. You're not taking value from her, but she is also receiving value as well.

The phrase "real quick" and having the phone out increases compliance since humans grab whatever you hand them. Once it's in her hands, she's going to start entering her number. And after exchanging numbers, add in something fun and challenging like, "Wait, you're not going to be calling me every night, are you? I have things to do, goals to achieve, you know."

This "frame reversal" is a fun and uncommon way to increase compliance and her sense of security. It suggests you're not like the "other guys" who will stalk her with texts and phone calls.

Instead, you're coming from a grounded frame, playfully setting the standard that *your* time is valuable and is not something to be taken lightly. Say all of this in a light but assertive voice, as if you were talking to an old friend. Before you give her your phone, be sure to navigate to the "Add Contact" screen.

You want to eliminate any friction of her trying to figure out how to use your smartphone. As an important note, when you are getting her phone number, have her input her name and number herself instead of you asking what it is and you typing it in awkwardly yourself. This creates more compliance on her end and helps in case you forgot her name, too, which can happen when you're talking to many people in one night.

If you've gotten this far in the interaction, this will work about eight out of ten times. If she seems hesitant, don't react to that. Just casually say, "It's just a phone number, I promise to only send you funny things and subtle flirtations. If not, no worries." Or, "Hey, I thought there was a connection between us, and this would be the next step to getting to know each other better. If not, no worries." This states your intent of why you want her phone number and implies you're not trying to take value from her but give her value. Usually, she'll just start typing. If she is still hesitant to give you her number, then this says there is a lack of trust or genuine connection, or she just doesn't view you as a high-value man.

Maybe you were too self-amused and "gamey." Maybe she thought you were a funny entertainer like my friend Jameson in the earlier story, but you failed to show clear interest, listen to her, or show her the more authentic, calm, and relaxed side of yourself.

If you get denied, use my last resort option: give her a ten-second elevator pitch about yourself so she gets a better idea of who you are and what you are about. For example, I'll say something like, "Relax, I'm normal. I'm sure you've had a lot of creeps annoy you before. I'm not like that, just a guy from San Diego, a writer, a podcaster, I love traveling, working out, doing yoga, journaling, and I read everything I can get my hands on about self-development. I want to travel the world and play frisbee with dogs all day on the beach. That's it."

Basically, you're throwing out who you are, what you like, and something funny or quirky at the end to reduce the tension and get her to relate with you more. This is a fun way to make the woman feel safe giving her number to you.

If she still is hesitant after all of that, then bow out gracefully and respectfully. It's done and it's time to move on. You should never have to beg for a phone number. Anything you do further from this point is trying too hard and being too needy. Even if you get her phone number, she's likely to flake or not respond. She's not interested. She has a boyfriend. She just got out of a relationship. Who knows, and at this point, who really cares?

If women are hesitant to give you their number, then you need to establish more trust. The best way to do this is to add a little more authenticity in your interactions and dive back into the stimulating, meaningful conversations from the previous chapter.

And sometimes women will test you while exchanging phone numbers by asking, "What's my name?" If, for whatever reason, you do get caught and forgot her name when she asks you, just be honest and say, "Listen, I've had a long day. I know you are (insert 3 things you learned about her in the conversation) and I think you're awesome, but I did forget your name."

Say whatever you remember about her to show you were listening. Then simply apologize and ask for her name. Don't lie or make weird excuses, just own your mistakes and be straightforward about it.

If you have a decent social media account with fun activities going on, you can use this opportunity to get her social media handle. You can look at her account and see interesting things she does for fun and create talking points while you're exchanging information.

Social media gives women the unprecedented opportunity to get an overview of your life. A strong account filled with photos of friends, events, and adventure will instantly increase your social proof, set her mind at ease, and create a sense of trust and familiarity.

Inversely, if you do *not* have a strong social media presence, then skip this step as it will decrease your social value. Although I understand that many of you do not value social media and possibly consider it to be a negative influence on your life and society, I encourage you to reconsider your stance. If she asks why you don't have a high follower count then own it and say, "I'm too busy living an epic life to take selfies, maybe I'll consider it, so what's the best angle to take selfies for the most likes?" then proceed to actually roleplay with her and take a selfie.

Posting semi-frequently and allowing your social media accounts to serve as an adventure reel of the fun things you're doing with your life is a very powerful way to meet and stay connected with high-quality women.

It's very "try hard" and approval-seeking to tell people how successful you are in life, and it's socially frowned-upon to overtly brag about your success. But social media is a way to bypass this since she's the one looking at your profile and viewing all of your successes on her own.

A woman who follows you on social media and sees your ongoing posts is more likely to respond to your text messages because she is an active follower of your social media… and in many ways, your life. It's a way of indirectly communicating to all the women you meet and keeping you top of mind as she goes about her daily life.

I'd recommend the general theme of your social media posts be adventure, fun, doing things you naturally enjoy, success-oriented, good times with friends, cute pets, and occasionally family. Basically, paint yourself as a lover with light elements of the provider. This creates a sense of trust and safety since she can see that you are a forward-progressing man, someone with friends who has an adventurous and well-balanced life.

Finally, you want to avoid making the mistake of leaving her the second you get her number. Continue the interaction for a few more minutes before saying goodbye. Stand there and text her your name and maybe something funny with humor from your conversation so she can put a name to your number right away.

You can increase the chances of her responding to your text or phone call if you stay with her for just another minute after you get the number and then bow out gracefully on a high note. In fact, I'll often ask for someone's number early in the interaction as a form of compliance then continue to have fun and escalate. She becomes more comfortable with me and doesn't feel like I was just trying to "game" her.

For a lot of guys, texting is a problem. They simply don't realize how powerful a tool it can be for getting more dates with girls. Go download my step-by-step "Texting Guide," and learn *exactly* how to go from getting her phone number to the first date. You can find it here: knowledgeformen.com/dating-toolkit

Once you've successfully followed up with her and scheduled a first date, let's talk about how you can keep up your momentum when you see her to make sure that the date is progressing forward in a fun, playful, and sexual way.

AVOIDING THE COMMON MISTAKES HOLDING YOU BACK FROM SUCCESS

I know lots of guys who are great with women socially. They're confident and maybe downright hilarious when meeting women. But then, when they finally get around to the first date or two... and they screw everything up. Guys who are solely good at meeting women initially and "pickup" are rarely good at dating in the long term for one simple reason:

When men start to build a good connection with a woman they like, they often slowly give away their power. They become less grounded and are willing to compromise to gain approval.

When you feel yourself beginning to "fall" for a woman, you must remain the Grounded Man more than ever. Be a rock, not a leaf in the wind easily swayed by a pretty face. Maintain the frame that she first found attractive. You are the prize. She equally wins, if not more, by entering your life. Remember who you are and what you've been through on your journey. You have so much value you can offer to her.

Until you've known a woman for several months and get to see the "real her," you should not be so easily won over no matter how attractive she is or how lonely you may be. If you want to ensure that you enjoy an abundant dating life *without* making the mistakes that keep most men single when everything started out good, pay very close attention.

1. Going from 0 to 100 Too Fast

It's easy to meet an amazing girl, enjoy your first successful interaction, and then believe that she's "the one." She's not. Until you've been with someone for many months, you don't really know them. You still don't know if they're actually a good fit for you and the overall vision of your life. So take it slow and hold the frame that says, "I like you, but I'm not quite sure yet."

Don't get into a relationship just because she's attractive and you've had a few good interactions. Ask yourself, "If I had the ability to date my *ideal* woman, would I date *this* woman?"

Because after reading and applying what I've shared in this book, you *do* have the ability to date your ideal woman in time. If the answer is not an immediate "yes," then keep meeting other women while casually dating the one you're with now. Keep getting to know her but don't rush into a relationship too quickly. Remember, it's more emotionally engaging for a woman when she wins over a Grounded Man who has other good options.

2. Getting Too Excited and Settling Too Quickly

When you get too excited about any new woman, it's easy to settle too quickly and fantasize about a future with her. Maybe you've had a few successful intimate encounters and casual dating experiences. Great! Now keep going, relax, continue being social, and having fun in your life. When you make her the only source of your happiness and validation as a man, you are also welcoming disrespect, second-class behavior, and loss of attraction.

Remember, this isn't *just* about finding your dream woman. This is an opportunity to grow into the strongest version of yourself and find the best possible woman *for you*. Don't settle just because you've had some early success and you're tired of this journey. Date several women at once, have lots of exciting experiences, meet as many women as possible. You really don't know what's possible for you until you put yourself out there for a while with consistent effort.

If you settle into a relationship out of scarcity, one that you weren't a "hell yes!" about, it will fizzle out and be a very painful experience.

Instead of wasting time, spend that time and energy on growing as a person and finding the woman that you *know* is right for you.

3.   Dating Only One Woman at a Time

Until you've been with someone for at least six months and have both agreed to be exclusive, you do not need to date only one woman.

Have several women that you're dating or at least talking to at all times. This isn't about ego or being a macho man, it's about abundance, eliminating scarcity, and setting yourself up for the best possible win-win relationship. High-quality women often talk to and date multiple men at the same time, and there's no reason you shouldn't be doing the same thing.

Best of all, you won't become needy because you know that you have options. If you decide to get into a relationship, you can do so from a place of abundance and certainty, knowing that you are not settling and that you're making the decision because you *want* to not because you're afraid, tired, and lonely.

4.   Losing Your Power

In the beginning, you spent so much energy chasing her that you never gave her the opportunity to chase you. She knew she had you from the beginning. Basic human psychology states that humans value what they cannot have and what they have to work hard for. Humans do not value what they can easily have and what they do not have to work hard for. Are you easy to get or hard to get?

Women want to chase you. If it's not challenging, then it's not valuable and emotionally engaging. There is less tension and excitement around you. In your first few dates, you're basically just building tension up to a release point, either through physical intimacy or to see her again.

Women respond well and are quick to get back to you when there is a lot of sexual tension; when there is no tension, then you are in line with everyone else. The longer you stay in line, the more likely you are to become her friend. Remember, this isn't because she's a bad person but because *you* are allowing her to take advantage of you. You're giving away your power in return for short-term validation from her.

The quality of woman you can attract is proportional to the quality of woman from whom you can confidently walk away from.

Again, you like her but you're not sure yet. She must earn a place in your life. Remain a challenge and make her win you over while also giving her positive emotions, having fun, and sharing more of your life over time. It's a balancing act. The more she chases, the more she values you and invests into the relationship.

Here are a few strategies to help you create this dynamic on your first few dates.

WHEN YOU MEET UP FOR THE FIRST TIME

When you set up the date, arrange it at a place where you would have fun *even if you were alone*. You don't want to be in a place that you are uncomfortable. You want to be in motion, doing something fun and not standing in one spot for too long. I do one of these three things on my first date:

1. Happy hour drinks/light food
2. Yogurt/dessert
3. Coffee/tea

You meet at one of the above locations, and then, after about thirty minutes to an hour, you go for a walk in a busy social area like a shopping center, park, or mall. You want a wide variety of things for you to do in a place with a nice view, plenty of people, and lots of scenery. Stay away from taking a woman out for dinner and a movie during your first three dates. It's boring, expected, and worse—it's incredibly difficult to have a meaningful conversation in any of these places.

When setting up a first date, opt for a Tuesday, Wednesday, or Thursday in the evening between 6:30 and 9:00 p.m. Why so specific? Friday, Saturday, and Sunday should be avoided for first dates since you should already have fun things going on during those days. Those days should be reserved and protected for the people who are closest to you. She is not there yet and should not have such priority in your social life on those days.

And, just to make this point clear, I pay for everything on the first date, but I rarely pay more than $40 on the initial meeting. If you ask a woman out, then you pay. It's nice if she offers to pay, but respectfully decline and cover it. Respond with, "I'll let you get the tab next time around," implying that you expect to see her again.

Remember, all dates must be fun, adventurous, interactive, and on the move. Ideally, you want to go to a location that's close to where you live. This makes it easy to bring her back to your place and escalate the interaction more intimately. But at the end of the day, an amazing date is really just an extension of the first interaction you shared together. You'll be using the same conversation strategies and general principles you used during your approach to deepen your levels of intimacy and build more connection with one another. Remember, you're not her boyfriend... yet.

Too many guys assume that if they act like a boyfriend to be, they will automatically become the boyfriend. But in reality, you're skipping one of the most important parts of the entire dating game: being chased.

You *want* her to chase you, to put in effort, to prove herself to you and demonstrate that she is worthy of having a place in your life. This is what allows your kindness, caring, and loving nature to be received as value versus appearing weak, approval seeking, and needy. She's passed your tests and proven herself and you've passed hers, so now she's feeling safe and trusts you.

At this point, you haven't done any of these things to the extent that is necessary. Just because you had an emotionally charged conversation, danced, kissed, or even had sex (although sex does accelerate the dynamic faster), that doesn't mean you're in a relationship or you should act as such. You have a different job to do in your first few dates.

She may test you, and you still want to look for that hook, get her qualifying herself to you, and then get into having a stimulating and meaningful conversation. And of course, be physical; if you can kiss her, go for it or at least tease the kiss. If you're at a venue, do not sit across from the girl. Sit next to her so you can be close to her and be physical.

I recommend changing venues at least once. That's why I love getting coffee, yogurt, or having a drink at a trendy bar because they are simple and there isn't too much stress about the date since it's just coffee or a drink. Then, go out into the streets or to a park where you can enjoy the area and be together. Once you're together, focus on building comfort, getting to know her, and being physical.

The frame is that you want her but you do not need her. Right now, is her opportunity to impress you.

WHAT TO TALK ABOUT ON THE FIRST DATE TO LEARN MORE ABOUT HER

The goal of the first date is to have fun, be your "best self," and build a connection together. If you do this, then the second date is inevitable. To take some pressure off of yourself, remember each of you have fifty percent responsibility for the conversation. It's not all on you like in the initial approach, but you can navigate the conversation in a way that builds a stronger connection in the shortest amount of time possible.

In addition to the stimulating and meaningful conversation previously discussed, here are some fun conversation starters I like to talk about on first dates:

"So, you told me you did ___ for a living. Tell me more about that."
"What do you enjoy most about that?"
"What were you like in college?"
"If money wasn't an object, what would you want to do or be?"
"I have a scenario for you. I can give you one plane ticket to anywhere in the world... where would you go?"
"What book would you bring with you?"
"What movie can you watch over and over?"
"What is your favorite way to spend the weekend?"
"Were you a trouble maker or good girl growing up?"
"What's the boldest thing you've ever done?"

"What are your guilty pleasure TV shows?"

"Would you like to be famous? Doing what?"

"What would make a "perfect day" for you?"

At the end of each of these questions, be sure to answer the question yourself to share more about who you are and stay on that topic for a while, diving deeper into her answers to peel back the layers and see her for who she really is.

The key here isn't to play 20 Questions, but to get her talking about herself so that you can get to know her better. For example, if you asked her what would make a "perfect day" and she said, "Waking up, going to a yoga class, enjoying a lazy coffee with a good book, and then hiking with friends," you should follow up with something like, "That's interesting, have you ever thought about becoming a yoga instructor or opening up your own artisan coffee shop?"

These types of questions will allow you to go far deeper than generic, "What do you do/where are you from" back to back questions. Refer to the stimulating conversations section in chapter 4 for more on this.

WHAT NOT TO TALK ABOUT ON THE FIRST DATE

I'm going to keep this really simple. Don't complain or be negative about life, politics, religion, money problems, illnesses, family problems, or your ex. It's not that these topics aren't important to discuss later, but right now on the first date she doesn't care enough about you for it to be a meaningful conversation that would add value to the date.

Instead focus on having meaningful conversations, physically escalating, building a strong connection together, and going to multiple different venues or locations to have a wide variety of new experiences together in a short amount of time.

If you do that, you'll be golden on your dates.

HOW TO KISS ON THE FIRST DATE

You want to focus on slowly escalating things physically from the moment you see her on the first date. Start with a hug, then move on to touching her lower back, to having your arm around her lower back for a short while. The more you build up these light physical touches, the easier it will be to transition to a kiss.

The less light physical contact you have, the more awkward it will be for the first kiss. The best time to kiss is in the middle of the date when the emotions are spiked at the highest and there is tension. This is better than at the end of the date when it may feel inauthentic, assumed, and forced. Here's a simple step-by-step process on how to kiss a girl:

Get close to her.

Put your arm around her or leave both hands touching her waist.

Make eye contact.

Make a statement about her, how you feel, and tell her what you're going to do. For example:

"You're beautiful, I'm having fun with you. I'm kissing you."

"You're adorable, I'm enjoying the night with you. I'm kissing you."

"You're so cute, I'm excited we met. I'm kissing you."

"This view is just too damn beautiful, I'm going to kiss you."

Then go in slowly for the kiss.

Now, don't make the first kiss a crazy make out and shove your tongue down her throat. Just a nice, warm, gentle kiss that she can remember. Leave her wanting more and be the first to pull away.

If she rejects your kiss, then you may not have been physical enough throughout the date. I start off with my arm gently touching her lower back as we walk. Open doors, for example, while always being a gentleman and leading her with this kind of contact. Slowly, move your arm around her back for a few minutes, and then take it off. Switch back. Tease her hands, hold her hands, pick her up and lift her, carry her, spin her around.

Now that you know how to physically escalate, set up a date after your first meeting, and then ensure that your date goes *perfectly*, let's discuss how you can escalate the date back to your place...

HOW TO BRING HER BACK TO YOUR PLACE

Towards the end of the night if you just met (where we left off earlier) or on a date, you may want to bring her back to your place. If you've done everything right up until this point, this is actually easier than you might imagine.

To start up the conversation, simply mention you have something fun to watch or see, or maybe a view. It's just something to do at your place that is fun and entertaining. Using humorous references from the date can come in handy here. You want to have a reason to bring her back to your place.

If the date is moving forward well yet she's not responding to going back to your place then say, "I'm heading back for some drinks to relax since I have to wake up early. Come with."

If the first date was near your place, I usually go for a walk. When you get close to your place, just say, "Hey, I live right over there I can show you ____ (something that you talked about) real quick."

If she resists going back with you and it's a very serious "no," then remain unreactive and just continue enjoying your time together, finish the date, bow out gracefully, and repeat the texting steps to set up another date. Then, repeat this process until you can get her back to your place on the next date.

If it's a playful "no" or she says something like, "Well, what are we going to do?" Then, just assure her you really want to show her this thing or do what you talked about at your place and be honest with that. You can also say, "You're not getting lucky this soon, I just want to show you this thing."

Basically, don't make a big deal out of it if she doesn't want to come back. It does not mean she doesn't like you or is not interested in seeing you again. It simply means she's not ready to come back to your place in private yet.

If you get upset by this, it will ruin the date and she might think you're only after sex. Sex is not the goal, but it can be a natural extension to an adventurous and stimulating date. Your goal is to get to know her better, have fun, and lead the date as far is it can comfortably go for both of you. If sex is a part of that fine; if not, that's fine too.

All in all, dating is fun so just stay in touch and add value to her through a text or phone call. Work on setting up another date and enjoying your time with her. Spread out your first three dates to one per week. Once you've dated more than three times, then you can start opening up your weekends to her and seeing her more often if you like.

Don't overwhelm her with text messages and phone calls. Just relax. If she's responding to you after the first date, then calm down. She likes you. Stay grounded and trust that you're enough. She'll respond positively the next time you ask her out.

WHAT TO DO WHEN YOU BRING HER BACK TO YOUR PLACE

Let's say you get her back to your place for the first time, whether you just met on the initial interaction or if it's the first or third date or more. Once there, the key is to immediately make her feel comfortable and safe.

Before you leave for the date or go out for the night, you want to ensure your place is clean and that you have drinks and snacks readily available. I have a setup on my phone that syncs to a sound system so I can play music as I'm entering my home.

I can create that fun vibe immediately. I usually give a quick tour of the place to make her feel comfortable while turning on lights to make her feel at ease. I have bookshelves of books that I have read and cool art on the wall that can give her a taste of who I am. None of that stuff is for women, it's for me, but women tend to notice it and it gives them a deeper glimpse into who I am, creating a sense of familiarity and safety.

Also, gentlemen, clean your bathroom before the date! She's going to use it as soon as she walks through the door. If she intends to get intimate with you, she will most definitely want to go and freshen up, so keep your bathroom clean.

If you're having drinks, then make the drink in front of her and make it the same amount of alcohol as your drink, but always have juice or something to mix the drink with if she prefers. I have a cabinet of juices, sodas, and soft drinks specifically for women. Keep in mind neither of you are getting drunk here. You're basically just holding drinks to create a fun, social vibe.

The drinks establish that she's staying with you for at least fifteen minutes. If she's not into alcohol, use a different beverage or throw something into the oven, maybe a snack or light meal if your date didn't involve one. The goal of all of this is to make her feel safe, comfortable, and at home. A woman cannot fall into her feminine if she feels unsafe, therefore no intimacy is possible. She will be on guard and defensive, which benefits neither of you.

I like to take the drinks and show her the view from my balcony. I get a little physical, touching, joking, teasing, and light kissing, then we move to the couch in the living room and I will begin to dim the lighting. I keep folded furry blankets on the couch, for example, and often women will just grab one and put over them. That's good because it means she's getting more comfortable and relaxing with me.

I usually throw on a show and might pop some popcorn and put on something funny, but never put on something that you're seriously interested in watching like a serious drama as it will distract from the interaction and chemistry that you're building with her. The goal is to not watch a show that's going to keep her fully engaged, but to put on something that's just on in the background while the two of you are talking and being close.

Instead of putting your arm around her, I usually pick up her legs when she's sitting and put them over my lap so she's laying on her back with her legs over me. You want her comfortable, relaxed, and enjoying herself. At this point, I'll say, "Hey, no shoes on the couch," and I'll take them off for her, which most women will usually respect since it's your house and your rules.

While talking to her, start lightly massaging her legs on and off and go in for the kiss periodically, always being the first to pull away. Remember the golden rule: always leave her wanting more. When you feel she is emotionally engaged and she's already laying down, move over, slowly get partially on top of her, and start kissing. Things can heat up from here.

You might have to kiss her, then watch the show or continue chatting, then kiss again. The pacing of your escalation should be determined by the quality of her reactions. You want her to feel comfortable and safe and *never* feel like you are pressuring her into anything. By pulling back, you're going at a pace that's comfortable for her and slowly turning up that "volume knob" of attraction she has for you.

Escalate and lead the charge, but always give her room to set the pace and determine the speed of the interaction. From here, you're in a very good place to move things to the bedroom and get more intimate. But I'm getting ahead of myself...

Sometimes, she won't come back to your place, but she *will* ask you to drop her off at her place. When you're dropping her off—whether you're in your car, shared ride, or in a taxi—ask if you can use her bathroom. Women will almost always oblige and allow you to enter her home with her without any friction.

After using the bathroom, I'll typically say something like, "I've got to wake up early tomorrow, but while I'm here put on your tour guide hat and show me around real quick." While she's showing you around, she's going to show you her room and then you can get close to her when she's near the bed and start kissing and lean into her until she falls back onto it. If she doesn't show you her room, do this on the living room couch.

Although this is an amazing place to be, many men, especially guys who don't have a lot of experience with new partners, can struggle to truly enjoy the interaction because they are stuck in their heads worrying about their performance or the size of the gentleman downstairs.

And, with the advice I'm about to share with you, you can increase your confidence in bed, reduce anxiety, and enjoy great sex with new partners. But first, we need to address and increasingly important topic that can save you from doing anything stupid that you may regret for the rest of your life.

HOW TO BUILD SEXUAL INTIMACY SO IT'S WIN-WIN

Before we go *any* further, I want to make one thing very clear. You are never under any circumstances to engage in any sexual act without complete consent. Equally, never take advantage of a woman who is overly intoxicated or under the influence of anything that alters her mind. She can still say that it wasn't consent and was taken advantage of after the fact. She will remember what you did and her trust in you will be diminished if you intend to see her again.

If you don't know if you have consent, then you don't! Nothing will ruin your life, future relationships and career faster than an allegation of sexual assault *even if* you thought you had consent. Always err on the side of caution, be slow, respectful, and use protection. Let me repeat myself here. If the slew of sexual assault allegations and dozens of high-profile celebrities and politicians being accused in the "MeToo" movement isn't enough to scare you into gaining explicit consent, then allow me to do it for you: never force yourself onto a woman in any way. You do not have any right to a woman's body. Expensive dinners, gifts, and dates do not entitle you to any sexual acts from her.

She has the right to say "no" from the second you start the interaction to the moment before you stop having sex. This is serious and one wrong step could have serious consequences that will, quite literally, alter the trajectory of your life negatively. It's always better to play it safe and escalate at a pace that is comfortable for her. You avoid this dilemma altogether when your interactions, flirting, and sexual tension are so heightened from your interaction that she is the one who is making it clear she wants sex. And you are the one who determines if you want to have sex with her or not.

You want her being the one jumping all over you, ripping her and your clothes off, starting foreplay on her own and making it very clear that she wants sex. Now, if she's not fully sexually aroused but is still enjoying being in bed with you, kissing you, in your arms, and maybe light humping, you may still rightfully be concerned about whether or not you have consent.

The key in these scenarios is to not get thrown off, scared, upset, or angry if she does not respond positively to your escalation. It's not necessarily a rejection, maybe she just needs more time with you to establish more comfort. She needs to feel safe and to trust you because sex is a very intimate and potentially risky act. Relax and go back to stimulating her and having meaningful conversation. Get to know her, have fun with her while slowly physically escalating. You're not in a bad place since you're alone and intimate with a woman, after all.

If she's not feeling it right away then, think of this as a "time out" where you're taking a break from escalating. This gives her time to re-evaluate her decision, and you should allow her all the time she needs. If she's still in your bed or lying down with you on a couch, she may be considering having sex. If she's getting up, putting clothes back on, or slipping into her shoes, then just let it be and don't get upset. If it's a playful "no", that may likely be her logical mind saying, "I just met this guy, I shouldn't. Society says I shouldn't hook up so soon, I don't want him to think I'm a slut."

From here, slow down, take a step back and remain calm. The worst thing you can do when she's not in the mood is to get angry and upset with her. The second worst would be to whine, beg, or act needy. Do not try to logically convince her why you should have sex, listing all the things you've done for her recently or ask her if she still likes you out of desperation, or think there's another guy.

Any form of insecurity, neediness, and approval-seeking behavior when intimate will end any chance of further intimacy.

All will kill the mood. Just relax; be okay with the situation, let it be, and continue playing with each other. You want to take two steps forward, one step back. If I sense she's not sexually aroused, then I slowly transition into massaging her and caressing all parts of her body while she's laying down, speaking to her slowly and intimately. Dedicate about fifteen to thirty minutes to massaging, then start kissing and touching her sensually over her entire body while purposely avoiding her pelvic area and breasts. Get close, but don't touch. Tease and don't give her what she wants just yet.

By this time, she will usually be in a more open sexual mood and will have verbally told you or shown you she's ready by taking off clothing or asking if you have a condom on hand. If she doesn't verbally tell you, she may physically tell you by her grabbing you, bringing you closer to her, or putting your hand over her pelvic area. From here, you can continue moving forward, but take a step back, move forward, and then step back again. You need to build the sexual tension by giving then taking it away and making her want sex more than you. Continue this until you feel she's ready. Simply grab her hand and slowly put it near your lower belly. Does she go down further, or does she pull back?

If she's not ready yet, then lead her into her sensuality and continue massaging and caressing her entire body while kissing her and repeat. This process (surprise, it's called foreplay for a reason) can last thirty to ninety minutes. It really just depends on how much you want to invest into this. Be patient, relax, and be the Grounded Man. Take your time and let her relax and fall into her feminine with you. This is supposed to be fun, so slow down and enjoy the moment.

Always use protection when having sex. Never do anything she doesn't want to do. Be safe!

If sex does not happen that night then remain calm, confident, and carefree. You can slowly approach her, look her in the eye, and tell her that you respect her decision. Go ahead and tell her that you would never do anything that she doesn't want to do, then kiss her and pull back completely.

She will respect you for that and may reconsider her decision. At the very least she may be more open to the idea of sex with you at a later time. Women want to know that you care about *their* experience of being with you as much as you care about your own. When you focus only on sex and it's clear that is all what you want from her, you are coming from a taking position rather than giving. It doesn't feel like a win-win scenario for her, she feels like she loses, and you win, which creates distrust and resentment.

The goal is not to have sex with women, it's to connect, have fun, be intimate, and enjoy the experience together. Sex is a natural extension of stimulating emotions while being physically intimate and alone together.

Now all of the above information is making the big assumption that you're a champion in the bedroom, that everything is working well and you last long. But inevitably, there will be time where you're being intimate with a woman and things just don't seem to go your way. To do all the work it takes to meet a woman and get to this point and not be able to perform is a real struggle for many men. Don't worry, this is more common than you might expect and it's a lot easier to handle than most guys realize.

Let's talk about this now.

EVERYTHING MEN SHOULD HAVE LEARNED ABOUT SEX (BUT DIDN'T)

If you were anything like me, you didn't *really* learn about sex in school or from your friends or from, well, anyone. Instead, your "sex education" likely consisted of a few (hundred) hours of porn as a teenager and maybe a perfunctory glance at a few books that didn't make much sense.

I want to give you the foundations of how you can deepen and improve the quality of your sexual interactions, whether with a brand-new or existing partner.

1.   Great Sex Begins Outside of the Bedroom

First, great sex is entirely dependent on great health. If you're a heavy smoker, alcoholic, regular drug user, overweight, or out of shape, then the quality of your sex life will drop drastically. You'll struggle to have or maintain strong erections and won't be able to give her the loud, body-shaking, toe-curling level of sexual performance that she desires.

The solution here is relatively simple. Clean up your lifestyle and intentionally spend time improving things that improve your health and well-being. Lift heavy weights three times a week and sprint to strengthen your body. Regularly stretch out your pelvic floor, hips, abdominals, and lower back, and practice yoga to improve blood flow into the pelvic region. If you sit all day, then standing more, opening up, and loosening your body will all make a huge difference. Eat a diet that is primarily whole, non-processed foods and avoid things like cigarettes, stimulants, and alcohol as they often reduce sensitivity and blood flow to your pelvic region and damage your overall health.

If you will do these few things consistently, the quality of your sex life will improve by leaps and bounds. But the second way in which great sex begins outside of the bedroom is in the way that you psychologically arouse the woman throughout the day. Most guys rush into sex too quickly or fail to plant the seeds of desire earlier in the day. But if you want to enjoy truly mind-blowing sex, you must begin seducing your partner *before* you are even alone together.

Although this tip applies more directly to women who you have already slept with and are dating, if you're bold enough, you can use it with new partners just as effectively. Throughout the day and during your date, you want to begin planting seeds of desire in her mind. For example, send her texts like:

"I can't wait to ravish you later tonight."

"Wear that black dress you had the night we met. I won't be able to keep my hands off you."

"Excited to see you tonight, I can't promise I'll be good though."

"Can't wait to see you and pin you against the wall and kiss you."

"Have you been a good girl or bad girl this week?"

All this illustrates that you want her, and it gets her thinking about you intimately before you're even together. It builds the intensity for when you do finally see her, there will likely be a greater release of tension. Even while you are on your date, regularly pull her in and whisper similar phrases into her ear, saying things like, "I love your outfit. I can't wait to rip it off of you when we get back to my place."

Tease then push away. Women's attraction is a volume knob, not a light switch. So seduce her *psychologically* throughout the day to slowly turn that volume knob up and increase her desire for you at the end of the night.

2. Let Go of Your Ego and End Anxiety

Many men struggle with some form of sexual anxiety or dysfunction. It's a relatively normal part of life and is something that any woman you're dating has likely encountered before. But I'm going to let you in on a little secret: things like erectile dysfunction and premature ejaculation don't matter nearly as much as *how you handle them.*

While you're sitting there feeling anxious about your performance issues, she's probably wondering what *she* did wrong or if she's not attractive enough. The key here is to remove your ego from the equation and embrace sexual problems as they arise.

For example, if you are unable to maintain a strong erection, instead of freaking out or losing your grounded frame and saying something like, "This never happens" (which you both know isn't true), simply own it. Laugh at yourself and make light of the situation saying something like, "Well, it looks like I wore my soldier out. He won't be rising to salute tonight. All is good, I have other ways to satisfy you."

Often, all you need to remedy the problem is a little bit more foreplay and the sound of *her* finishing. Besides, even if you still can't get it up after helping her orgasm, she will appreciate the selflessness and likely think to herself, "If this is what he can do while he's having problems downstairs, I wonder what'll happen when he's at full mass?"

This same principle applies to premature ejaculation. If you finish too quickly, don't freak out, apologize or get upset about it. Instead, laugh it off and reframe it as a *good* thing. Tell her something like, "Wow! That doesn't happen very often, you just rocked my world. I'm getting us water and let's do round two."

Despite what most men think, women are often *turned on* when they make a man finish quickly, *especially* if he's a grounded or more "alpha" male. It's a boost to their egos to know that they are so desired, so sexy, or so good in bed that men simply can't control themselves.

Remember, whatever you feel, she feels. If you feel anxious and uncertain, then so will she. And if you approach the issue from this frame and blow it off as if it's no big deal (and it isn't since you'll likely be ready to go again in 20 minutes), she won't think twice about it. She'll likely be even more aroused when you have sex next time around.

3. Focus on Foreplay and Get Inside Her Mind

If there were ever two areas where most men fall short in the realm of sexuality, it's foreplay and talking seductively, aka dirty talk. Remember how I said that men are turned on quickly like a light switch and women are turned on slowly like a volume knob?

The same is true in the bedroom. Women need time to become comfortable with you—after all, they're opening themselves up in the most intimate way possible—and the more time you spend on foreplay and the better you can stimulate her emotions with dirty talk, the better the sex will be.

Ideally, you want to make her wet through foreplay and dirty talk *before* you actually have sex. This will dramatically reduce your anxiety and performance issues since you've already tended to her needs and she will be horny. To do this, you need to take things slowly, like ten times slower than you've likely taken things before. Spend five to ten minutes doing nothing but running your hands over her body and kissing her without ever touching her pelvic area. Get close, tease her, whisper into her ear, but gradually pull away.

The more tension that you can build up during foreplay, the more excited and aroused she will feel whenever you actually have sex. The intensity of her breathing and soft moans will be a sure sign she's ready, and will arouse you as well. So take it slowly. There's nothing wrong with spending thirty minutes or longer warming up and having incredible foreplay. Put on intimate music in the background, dim the lights, connect with her, and enjoy being this close with her. As you're engaged in foreplay, you'll also want to stimulate her emotions by describing what's going on now in detail and what you want to do to her later very vividly, through dirty talk.

Most men are quiet as a mouse when they're having sex and this often makes women feel like the man isn't enjoying himself or that she's doing something wrong. Instead, unveil your dirty thoughts and tell her exactly what you want to do to her, tell her what you *are* doing to her in an erotic and dominant way.

Be masculine, dominant, and feel no shame for your sexual desires. The key to good dirty talk is that you have to *own* it and make her feel what you are saying. Tell her what you like and want. Tell her how beautiful her body is and how much she turns you on. Even if you're thinking something that's kinky or taboo, *tell* her in a dominant way and you'll often be surprised by how she'll respond.

Awaken her wild feminine and believe me, even the nicest and most sincere women have a sexual side to them that you wouldn't believe. When she is in this state, and you'll know when she is, she will have the best sex of her life. She'll want to continue having sex with you if you're the rare man who can get her into this sexual state. It's your job to open her up so she can experience that, otherwise, sex is all about you.

If you don't get the response you intended, then revert back to the level of comfort and dirty talk that you had before and continue from there. Don't get sad, complain, or ask why. She must feel safe, at ease, and respected while dirty talking. The first few times you try this you may not get the wild outcome you're expecting, it may take some time but as you keep practicing this, you'll notice sex getting better and better as she is becoming more comfortable tapping into this primal side with *you.*

4.   Be Dominant and Fully Present

The final key to great sex is to be dominant and fully present in the moment. Sex is a primal act where two people become wild animals for a moment in time. You want to get out of your head and into your body. Really feel every aspect of your bodies together as if you were becoming "one."

It's a natural thing for *most* women to want the man to take control in the bedroom. Of course, there are exceptions, but I've rarely encountered it. There can be times when she's taking a lead role, but I'd guess around eighty percent of the time you're in control of the positions and twenty percent, let her do her thing.

Throughout the experience, it's important to realize that not all women are sexually experienced or comfortable with every act and position you may want to try. Many women will be unwilling to try something new or "kinky" simply because of embarrassment, previous bad experiences, or a fear they won't be good enough to please you.

Despite what most men believe, women have sexual fears, insecurities, and anxieties, too. To alleviate them, it helps when you share with her how she makes you feel and which positions and acts you enjoy. You may even have to slowly overtime teach her how to engage in certain acts or positions. Always be considerate and respectful with a desire for mutual pleasure and excitement, saying something like, "I want to try something with you that I think you'll really like. Let me show you."

Small actions like this one will set you apart from other self-centered lovers she's experienced in the past and create a more dynamic and exciting sexual experience for you both. The more you lead, let loose, the more she'll do the same. You two will experience a side of each other that may have never been shared with anyone else.

It's the ultimate form of the masculine and feminine dance, where all the tension built up over time finally gets released together in a ravenous physical act. Take the lead, make noise, breathe deeply, spank her, pull her hair (softly at first then harder if she enjoys it), and she'll follow suit. Relax and enjoy the intimate experience.

Now that you understand some of the finer points of enjoying a more fulfilling and impactful sex life, there's going to be a lot of women vying for your attention. In the next section, we're going to discuss how to date multiple women at the same time, so you have clear expectations, no one gets hurt, and you're being honest with all women.

This is how you enjoy a rather, copious dating life...

HOW TO DATE MULTIPLE WOMEN WITH INTEGRITY UNTIL YOU FIND THE ONE

This is the period usually within the first six months where you are seeing a woman regularly, having sex, and going out on fun adventures together. You're not exactly official, but it's clear that there is a lot of potential for both of you in the future. You're not opposed to being official, but the conversation just hasn't happened yet. You want to slowly draw her into your life by having fun and sharing a wide variety of experiences together, while making it clear that you do like her and there is room in your life for a girlfriend, but she still needs to earn it.

Just because you're having sex regularly doesn't mean that she's earned that position or that you are obligated to see her or call her every day. Stay focused on improving your life, career, and goals, while spending time with the important people already in your life.

Having a strong social life, hobbies, and passions will reduce the need to see her often and reduce your neediness and any approval-seeking behavior that repels women. Grounded Men do not revert their life's purpose to make a woman they recently met their girlfriend, no matter how attractive and incredible that woman is. It will have the opposite effect and act as a repellent that pushes her away. The moment you show any signs of weakness is the moment she starts second guessing you as a potential partner.

When you become exclusive too quickly, you are not allowing her to chase you. You are depriving her of the exhilarating opportunity of winning over a Grounded Man, which is a critical phase that should never be skipped at the onset of a new relationship. The key is to remain a Grounded Man with the internal mindset and understanding of what women want. If you do, then you will succeed in transitioning from dating to a relationship—if that's what you want.

Now, after a few months, if you haven't labeled the relationship, these questions or something similar will come up from her: "Are we together?" or "Are we exclusive?" This is a positive sign because it's showing interest in wanting a relationship with you and moving to the next step. Many men might not be ready to settle down, so here's the best way to handle it if you're not sure:

"I wouldn't put a title on it, but I want to keep getting to know you to see if this can be something more. I'm really enjoying getting to know you better (Insert 3 things unique about her that you like). I'm always going to be honest about how I feel about us, and so far, so good."

The key is to speak the truth and not lie. It's not a trick or gimmick. Just share with her how you feel about her, where you're at, and that you are interested in the possibility in something more. As you go through the 90-day sprint, you'll be meeting and inviting many women along for the journey and creating an abundant dating life. By the end of your first sprint—if you take the appropriate actions—you'll have many women in your life with whom you're occasionally going out with that you like. Eventually, as you select the best ones there will be three to five you connect with deeply and would consider dating more intentionally.

I know this might sound like a lot, but you need to remember that you won't be seeing all (or any) of these women on a daily or even weekly basis. Due to the hectic nature of life and busy schedules of professional individuals, you'll date some of these women for several months while only seeing them once or twice a month. This is why you'll want to casually date multiple women at once, so that you're going out and connecting with at least one or two different women on a weekly basis. It's important to remember that these are not serious relationships where you're sharing your undying love for each other.

Once you've achieved this level of abundance, your goal now is to narrow down the group of women you're interested in to the three highest-quality women. Again, this puts you in a position of abundance and power because *you* are now selecting which women you'll allow to stay in your life.

As a side note, I'd encourage you to never seriously date in the long term (e.g. going out once a week and regularly talking throughout the week) more than three women at once. Short term, yes, you'll have to until you find the right ones to go deeper with, but in the long term it's too stressful and it will detract from other important areas of your life and drain your energy. But here's the deal... Until you have found that one woman who makes you say, "OMG! I want to be with you and you alone instead of all the others," you're still consistently going out, having fun, and bringing new women into your life.

This will allow you to continually improve the quality of the women in your life until you find the ONE woman who is the best fit. And yes, this *does* mean that you will regularly have to let good—but not great—women go who do not meet your criteria for long-term dating and relationship material.

As harsh as it might feel, you need to remember that you're doing the women *and* yourself a huge favor. By being honest about your feelings and experience, you're saving them from the inevitable pain and heartbreak of wasting months or even years in a relationship that you secretly knew was never going to last. This is not being a Grounded Man, but rather a selfish man acting out of scarcity.

Now, I want to make something very clear. Over the past few years, our society has vilified and demonized masculinity at every turn, and with it, they've attempted to convince men that dating more than one woman at a time is "wrong", "unethical" or "immature".

As with a lot of things society says, this is incorrect. As long as you have not committed to any one woman, it's not only okay for you to be dating multiple women at a time, but it's *healthy*. As a strong Grounded Man, it is natural to have a burning passion for and appreciation of feminine beauty–and to want to express that passion and appreciation by sharing adventures and experiences with as many women as possible while you're still officially single.

To restrict this energy is to restrict the very essence of your masculinity. To spiritually castrate yourself, hold back your truth and make the decision–conscious or not–to channel this energy towards unhealthy behaviors and habits. By having an abundance of women in your life while searching for the "one", scarcity, neediness, and weakness will be eradicated from your life and then, should you decide to pursue only one woman, you can do so from a healthy and abundant place that women are more receptive towards. Okay, let's say you do suddenly meet your ideal woman and you haven't been intimate with a woman in months or years, then honestly, it is going to be near impossible for you to consistently have backbone, be challenging or call her out on any second class behavior. All of the things that women find attractive and make you stand out from the other desperate men that surround her are non-existent since you wouldn't dare do these things and you need this interaction to work out, but to your own detriment. You will enter the interaction from a place of taking value vs giving value since you need her more than she needs you. How do you eliminate needing anything from her?

Simple, you already have high quality women in your life that fill this need which allows you to be fine with or without her. It's from this frame where you can you show up in a truly value giving way without any expected outcome which women find irresistibly attractive. Ughh you're probably thinking, "well how do I get her then damnit?" First, stop the scarcity-based thinking. You slowly build up to this by using your unique traffic strategy to bring one woman, then a second and maybe a third into your life that you genuinely enjoy spending time with. Then you increase the quality of these women by removing lower quality women who are not a good fit for your life and adding in higher quality women over time as you continue meeting new women utilizing your unique traffic strategy.

Brother look at it this way: attractive women have more options than the average man today and can more easily select and date their ideal partner from a large pool of eager men. If and when she shows interest in a man, he without question jumps at the opportunity to date her. Why is it that men can't enjoy this level of abundance too? As long as you are honest and up front about your intentions and desires with women (I'll explain in detail how to do that in the next chapter), dating multiple women at a time finally levels the playing field with high quality women, removes approval seeking behavior and allows *you* to show up more powerfully and attractive when you meet new women. This makes women respond to you in a way that very few men have ever experienced, where you are at the cause (strength), not the effect (weakness).

In the same way that you don't want to settle with a woman you don't find attractive, who shares no chemistry, or has conflicting values, women have no desire to settle with a weak man who has no other options. They want to be in a relationship that is their best possible option and feel like they won the best man out of a pool of many, in this case, you. And the best way for someone to "win" you is for there to be other women also legitimately desiring you. She will value, respect, and appreciate you *more* when she prioritized, worked and put in effort to equally win you over vs being like the majority of every single man today: a weak, desperate and value taking man plagued by scarcity.

Inversely, when one particular woman is your only option—regardless of your perceived status, financial or professional success—the parasitic effects of neediness and approval-seeking behavior will slowly permeate your behaviors and drain you of your ability to hold your power and remain grounded aka you lose your attractiveness. In sum, you are able to date the highest quality women in the world by not needing them because you are fulfilled with women, a social life and passions already in your life, but you are open to the idea of meeting new women should they adhere to your standards.

Remember, you just met these women. You don't know them. They don't know you. And neither one of you has any idea if you're compatible romantic partners in the long run. No one is cheating on anyone since there is no official relationship established!

Unless you are actively lying to one or all of the women with whom you're involved, you should feel no guilt or shame about having several women in your life (because I can all but guarantee you that she has multiple men in hers). But what if a woman asks if you're seeing anyone else? Then you must be honest and say something like, "I do have other female friends that I hang out with from time to time, but it's nothing serious."

This is honest truth! You go out with other women because you're a social guy who has friends and you're not exclusive with any of them, but you have options. The position of "girlfriend" is still open, but you haven't yet decided on any one woman yet. This dynamic does a few things to women that very few of them are used to experiencing. First, let me just make it clear that women will rarely, if ever, in the moment be excited to hear that you're "seeing" other women.

But their unconscious attraction for you will increase over time because they will realize that you are a man who is desired by other women. Remember, pre-selection is one of the most powerful drivers of human attraction since humans value what other humans value.

The second way this dynamic will influence their behavior is that it will create a greater sense of urgency in their minds, making them more responsive to your calls, less likely to flake, and more eager to impress you. When you invite her out on a date, she will respond faster because she knows that if she doesn't accept the opportunity, another woman will.

When you have multiple women in your life, *this* is the dynamic that you're creating. And I can tell you from personal experience that this is one of the greatest feelings a single man can have, true abundance of high-quality women vying for his attention. After dating for a few months and having several women that you are highly interested in, it's now time for you to determine if you want to continue casually dating new women or become exclusive with one woman who seems to be the right fit for your life.

If it would be helpful to have additional support with getting to this point in your dating life then, watch this presentation and learn more about how I can guide you further: knowledgeformen.com/live

But the question remains, how do you decide which woman to pursue when you have so many good opportunities.

If you don't take this question seriously, you can easily end up in a long relationship that goes nowhere and leaves both of you miserable and wasting finite time. Worse, you might end up *marrying* the wrong woman out of scarcity and then going through an eventual divorce, only to spend the rest of your life mired in custody battles after losing half of your net worth. So how do you select the best woman out of so much opportunity?

I've got you covered in what is likely the most important chapter of this book. I will teach you the exact process to filter the women you date so that you can find the best possible woman for your life. You want a woman who will add tremendous value to your life and encourage you to become a better man, someone you are equally *excited* about possibly spending the rest of your life with.

Let's dive into that process now.

CHAPTER 6

ENTERING INTO A RELATIONSHIP WITH THE RIGHT WOMAN

"Don't waste your love on somebody, who doesn't value it."

- SHAKESPEARE

"Sir?"

The words knocked at the door of my mind, insufficient to open it. My thoughts were elsewhere, lost in a daze of blissful reminiscence of a past era.

"Sir? Are you—"

The voice continued, unable to capture my wandering mind. I was replaying my own highlight reel of wild debaucheries, the gentle touches, subtle flirtations, and unforgettable connections I'd experienced. The thrills. The chase. The lust. The love. The laughter. The adventures. The life I'd left behind and was now— "Andrew! Pay attention."

My girlfriend's voice jolted me back to reality in a dimly-lit restaurant in Pacific Beach, San Diego. Mellow jazz buzzed in the background. Our waiter had been patiently trying to capture my attention. From across the table, my girlfriend was shooting me a confused look.

Now, my thoughts turned to her. I'd shared four years with this woman and, for the most part, they were incredible. Unlike many of my prior relationships, I didn't "stumble" my way into her life by some stroke of dumb luck or feel as if I was settling with a woman who brought no value into my life other than her physical features.

No. When we first met, I was where you will soon find yourself, in the midst of multiple casual relationships and a place of true abundance. From the midst of that abundance, I had chosen *her*. She was the one to whom I decided to commit. A stunning, tall blonde with a fit body sculpted by hours in the gym and on the yoga mat both as a student and an instructor.

There was so much more to her than that, though. She was one of the few women with whom I deeply connected. Her playful, free spirit intoxicated me. Her sarcastic wit kept my life interesting and, occasionally, exhausting. Other men swooned over her, placing her high atop a mind-made pedestal. They attempted to win (and later steal) her through all forms of flattery, but she was with me. She chose and chased me because I did exactly the things I've shared with you.

I had wanted her but didn't *need* her. I had other women in my life when we met. I sought to take nothing from her but share as many positive emotions and exciting adventures as I could. More importantly, I stayed grounded and had the backbone to tell her "no," calling her out when needed. As she once put it, "I'd never dated a man who was able to walk away from me."

So why now, four precious years later, did I find myself unable to focus on her or appreciate *any* of it? Why was I reminiscing about what I'd left behind? You see, right before my nostalgic and rather distracted date with my girlfriend, *I was writing this book.* Crafting the right stories to share, reviewing the lessons to be taught, and thinking back on the past decade of my life in hopes of finding inspiration to fill these blank pages.

As I sat alone in my office typing the very words you're reading, I felt a gnawing sensation in my gut. Something was wrong. My fingers froze on my keyboard as I caught my reflection in the computer screen, completely stunned. I wondered, *"Am I following my own advice?"*

The answer was more elusive than one might imagine. There were no red flags signaling the demise of our partnership. Our relationship was not marred with infidelity or blatant deception. I still found her attractive. We had great sex, shared similar interests, went out and had fun together often, and had a *good* connection. But that was the problem. Things were just *"good."*

Our relationship no longer inspired me. It no longer fulfilled or challenged me to grow into a better man. It simply drained me of my time, my energy, my resources, and happiness. In that moment, I knew *I* was settling. I'd ignored these feelings for so long because I didn't want to go through the pain of starting over, the maze of finding new love, the woe of being alone. She might be as good as I would ever get and maybe I was crazy to think I could do any better. More importantly, I didn't want to hurt *her.*

Although I was beginning to realize our relationship had run its course, I still wanted the best for her. I still cared about her future. I wanted to see her happy, to see her smiling and laughing like she always did, freely and without reservation. I knew that if I continued down this path, the relationship would slowly turn toxic and implode or worse, we'd both spend "till death do us part" resenting one another instead of going out and finding the love and connection we both deserved. I knew something had to change, for both of our sakes. *Deciding* to end the relationship, however, was not a simple choice. It never is.

A few nights later, we had another unusual night. It wasn't because we were arguing about which show to watch—that was a fairly common phenomenon—but rather because of the silent tension in the air. There was an anxiety and awkwardness discoloring every conversation we shared. We both felt it.

In exasperation, I finally let her choose a movie (that I didn't want to watch) and slumped back into my corner of the couch. We used to hold each other tightly on this couch. Now we sat at a distance, cold and reserved.

A few minutes into the boring film, I heard the crash of a shattered wine glass and my girlfriend screamed. I looked over to see she had spilled wine all over the couch and floor. Sighing to myself, I stood up and told her, "Don't worry, I'll get it."

After retrieving a set of towels and stain remover from my kitchen, I got down on my hands and knees and began cleaning up the mess. As I vigorously scrubbed, I looked up and saw her lost in her own world, scrolling through her phone on social media and completely oblivious to my effort.

Unable to control my agitation, I snapped, "Would it kill you to help out? I wish you wouldn't act so entitled." Her demeanor changed in the blink of an eye. Looking at me with disgust, she retorted, "I am so *sick* of this shit! I'm always doing *something* wrong with you." I threw my hands up and fired back, "Well, whose fault was this? You spilled the damn wine! I just wish you would stop taking me for granted and show some appreciation. This is just who you are!"

Exchanging scathing glances, I continued in as understanding a tone as I could muster, "A simple "thank you" goes a long way, you know." She abruptly leaped out of her seat and began furiously collecting her belongings around the apartment and stowing them in her bag. "I'm done with this," she said to herself, barely glancing at me as she began lacing her boots.

I couldn't believe it. How far was this about to go? "Are you fucking serious right now? Look... if you want to make this relationship work, you can't just run away from problems. We have to work on them *together.* " She began walking towards the door, refusing to acknowledge what I'd just said, so I stood and stepped in front of her. I gently put my hands on her shoulders and looked her square in the eyes. I said softly, "Please. Don't do this. Don't go."

Her eyes began to tear up as she pushed me aside and placed her hand on the doorknob. I laid my hand on top of hers and began shaking my head. "Stay, let's work through this." Unable to contain herself any longer, she started crying and breaking down, blurting out, "What happened to us? Things used to be so good." I knew that was exactly the problem, but I attempted to console her. I put my arm around her and whispered softly, "I know we're a mess, but we can do this."

She slid away from my embrace and looked at me coldly. "Maybe you can, but not me. We're always fighting, and I can't keep doing this." Tears streamed down her face as she turned the knob. I lowered my tone, but the words were firm as I looked at her one last time. "If you walk through that door, that's it. I love you, but I can't fight for a relationship alone." We stood in silence. Seconds passed, both feeling the tension increase. Then she turned her back to me and pulled on the doorknob. The creak of those hinges has never sounded so loud. I started following her out, attempting to reconcile one last time, "It doesn't have to be this way—"

I was cut short by the door slamming in my face. Through the window, I watched her walk away without a glance back, each of her steps bringing me back to the times we'd shared together. Her naked body wrapped around mine as we laid under the sheets and felt the sun pour through the windows on a lazy Sunday afternoon. The vivid sexual intimacy and connection we shared in the bedroom, feeling as one. Our morning yoga sessions on the bay where she led the flow as I witnessed her beauty and feminine aura radiate around me. The late nights we'd spend at quiet venues, laughing until it hurt.

Step. Flashback. Step. Flashback. Step. Flashback.

Then she was gone. Not once did she look back. To me, that symbolized the end. We'd done this before—at least twice a month for the last three—but in that moment, I knew. I loved, respected, and admired her greatly, but I couldn't keep doing this.

Our relationship, as amazing as it had once been, had run its course. It felt forced, heavy, and unnatural. It was like walking around with a dumbbell tied around my neck all day. My thoughts were cut short by the blare of my phone's ringtone. It was her. Picking it up, I let out a heavy sigh and answered. I could hear her sobbing uncontrollably on the other end. "Is it really over?" She barely put the words together. "It can't really be over, can it?" I paused. I had to be careful here, and strong. She cried aloud, "Andrew, answer me!"

In the flash of that moment, I thought about my future. Where I wanted to go. What I wanted to achieve. The life I wanted to live. Most importantly, I thought of who I wanted to live it with. *Would she amplify my life experience or bring it down?*

Then I thought about her. Our relationship. The good and the bad. I thought about the problems we were facing and fast forwarded a decade into the future. *Was that the life I wanted?*

The answer terrified me, yet I had to live in alignment to my values and act upon them if I was to truly be a Grounded Man. Though I knew it would hurt in the short term, I also knew it was for the best for both of us in the long term. I responded firmly, "Yes. It's over."

The dissolution of our four-year partnership brings me to this very moment, this chapter. That breakup led me to pause the writing of this book for several months and even considered scrapping the project entirely. Honestly, it felt inauthentic to be writing about finding your "dream woman" while in the throes of a serious breakup and emotional meltdown.

Then I thought about you, the reader. I knew there were lessons I'd learned that were worth sharing and that, putting my ego aside, I needed to share them with the world if I was going to help *anyone*. The imperfection of my own romantic life was no excuse to abandon something that could provide value to other men.

When I started this project, I had no idea that I would completely rewrite this chapter in lieu of my breakup. I couldn't have known I would have this fateful story to share with you. I never expected to be in the midst of a breakup while trying to help other men meet the women of their dreams.

After intense journaling, however, I realized I *had* practiced what I'd preached. I'd enjoyed (and now continue to enjoy) an abundant dating life. I'd selected one woman from a pool of many and a place of true abundance. We'd shared many wonderful memories and experiences together and I wouldn't change the four years that we enjoyed for the world. In the end, however, I knew it was time to move on. The relationship had run its course.

And it made me realize that maybe the point of all of this isn't to find just the one love of your life, but to experience as many loves as possible, filling your life with as much intimacy, connection, and love that you can while you're here.

A part of me worried that letting you in on this part of my life would make you wonder, "Is Andrew a fraud?" Some of you might think so. After all, here I am teaching you how to date the women you want while in the middle of a breakup myself. I can't control what others think and, fortunately, their opinion of me does not decide my self-worth. The proof of my authenticity can be found in the answer to just one question: *Did I find and date the woman of my dreams for years?* Yes, I did.

I now continue the journey of a lifetime, dating more woman than I can count, enjoying experiences I thought were reserved for rock stars, after spending several happy years with a woman that I will always cherish. Yet, I broke up with her, lifting myself out of what was no longer working so I could say yes to the next chapter of my life instead of living in indecision and later regret. The fact that our relationship didn't end in marriage, a house with a white picket fence, and 2.3 kids does not mean it wasn't a success. After all, if permanence is the factor upon which we predicate success, we are all ultimately failures.

But if you want to find "the one," and say "I do," I respect that. And this book will give you the edge you need to make that a reality. It will open up the opportunity for you to select the woman you want from a place of abundance, power, and freedom. You'll have the ability to walk away from the partners who aren't a good fit so that you can pursue the ones who are.

The following pages are my notes to prevent you from wasting time, energy, and resources with the wrong women who enter your life. If you ignore what I'm about to share, you may spend the rest of your life settling from a place of scarcity, forever stuck in a vicious cycle of toxic and demoralizing relationships that will leave you feeling emasculated, spiritually castrated, and incessantly asking yourself, "Where did I go wrong?"

Use this chapter as a guide to help ensure that you are moving forward with the right partner so that you can either move on or deepen your existing relationship. If you follow this advice, you'll be set up for a life of more happiness and fulfillment, sharing your days with the woman of your dreams, smiling in the morning when you see her sleeping next to you, and truly feeling like you've made it.

Let's begin...

SETTLING IS WORST CASE SCENARIO

Divorce rates are nearly 50% in America. Acclaimed anthropologist Helen Fisher recently partnered with Match.com to conduct a massive survey regarding the overall satisfaction of singles and couples in America. Alarmingly, her research found that men are now openly admitting—in larger numbers than ever before—that they are not in love with their wives and are instead opting for a partner that is good enough. Even the most perfunctory look at the couples and spouses around you illustrate the simple fact that most couples are settling in their relationships. They aren't in it for passion or romance, but to find a glorified roommate of the opposite sex.

Why do most men settle? They don't realize the *true cost* of settling. They think to themselves, "Yeah, she's not really the woman I want to spend the rest of my life with but..."

- The sex is frequent.
- She's attractive *enough*.
- I don't want to put in the extra effort to find the "right" woman.
- I'm focused on my business or career, so I don't have time.

They can easily identify the short-term *benefits* of settling (regular sex, companionship, ease, and comfort) but they never stop to consider what is *really* at stake in the long term. To truly understand the cost of settling, you must train yourself to think like an investor, not just financially, but with regard to the opportunity cost of any big decision in your life.

When men are in relationships that aren't right for them, they often fail to consider the time, attention, and energy they are investing into an underperforming "asset." It's like investing all of your money in a company that is losing value and headed towards bankruptcy. Any smart investor would pull out immediately to save whatever funds they can, yet ironically, men don't act this way in their relationships. And at the end of the day, money you can regain, time you cannot. You know staying in the relationship is not the right decision. You intellectually realize that you're hurting yourself, you're hurting your partner, and you're holding yourself back from meeting other women who would excite you. Yet you're too complacent to go through the work of finding the right partner, so you settle for less than you deserve.

When you are settling, you are stealing from your future self to pay for today's comfort.

Whether consciously or unconsciously, you are making the definite choice to invest in a relationship that you *know* will not serve you in the long run. What's worse, by making this decision, you are also making the decision *not* to pursue a relationship that would truly fulfill you.

If, on the other hand, you make the decision to *never* settle—to find joy in the journey no matter how long it takes, to commit to becoming your best self, and to seek out your ideal partner—everything changes. Instead of putting all of your assets into a company on the fast track to implosion, you diversify. Eventually, you might find the one "company" that matches all or the majority of your criteria. You feel it's going to grow further and so you bet big and go all in, profiting wildly and living the life you want as a result. Dating is the same way.

The woman that you allow to hold the most important position in your life is a direct reflection of who you are as a man. With a perfunctory glance at the woman on your arm, the world can immediately determine your self-esteem, self-worth, and value as a man. When a man settles with a woman of low-quality and poor character, it reveals his own insecurities and the value he places on himself. His fear of rejection and fragile ego are palpable, and he is unwilling to face the uncertainty and discomfort required to succeed with the women he *really* desires.

Inversely, when you find a man with a high-quality and attractive woman in his life—a woman who is beautiful and amplifies every area of his life—his confidence, self-worth, and self-esteem are obvious. It's clear that he has high standards and he abides by them.

However, a man who settles for a low-quality woman does not *always* mean that he has low confidence or self-esteem. In fact, I know many highly confident and incredible men who are simply too nice to hurt their partners feelings. They've built a codependent relationship where they've taken responsibility for their partner's happiness at the expense of their own. This is *much* more common than you might imagine, so let me be really clear.

Staying in a relationship for the wrong reasons will hurt your partner significantly more later, than leaving today.

Settling is failure and it will wreak emotional havoc across every other area of your life. Because of the emotional stress of your relationship, you'll be more likely to suffer physically, becoming susceptible to drinking or drug addiction, binge watching television, emotionally overeating, or drowning yourself in endless work to mask the root of the problem.

You'll feel less invigorated and excited by life, making you less likely to take risks and be more courageous in your own life. Instead of starting that new business or going for that promotion, you'll simply continue wasting away in a job that is below your potential because your physical and emotional energy are being drained in a relationship that isn't serving you.

I know this might sound like a bleak doomsday prediction, but it's important that you understand what's really at stake here. This isn't just a relationship we're talking about, it's your one life.

If you're currently settling in a relationship (and you know it) the rest of this chapter will help you escape the trap of settling, achieve the abundance of women you desire, and reclaim your power to *choose* the person who is right for you. If you're single and trying to avoid the common pitfalls of relationships, this chapter will give you the tools and strategies you need to fully assess the women in your life, determine whether or not they are the right fit, and then decide how to either end or escalate the relationship from there.

My goal is not to *scare* you out of a relationship but to *empower* you to live in abundance and do what is necessary to experience the relationship you deserve. Decisions are always better made when you act from abundance instead of scarcity. When you live in abundance, you will experience more joy and fulfillment because every decision that you make is a decision that you *chose* to make, not one that you were forced to make.

But how do you know when you're living in abundance, and more importantly, how do you actually achieve abundance?

You will know that you've achieved abundance when you arrive at a point in your journey where you no longer feel like the pursuer but rather the selector.

Instead of bending over backwards for women with a nice body and pretty face, you will carefully examine *who* a woman is before allowing her a place in your life. When you complete your first 90-day sprint, when you go out and interact with new women, you won't be trying to *get* another woman, you will have women chasing *you*. Women will be begging to spend time with you, date you, and enjoy the pleasure of your company.

The work that you invested into becoming a Grounded Man will allow you to select your partner based on your goals, vision and values instead of what's available in front of you. I know this might sound like a distant dream right now. You might be saying to yourself, "That sounds great, but I just want *one* woman to like me! I'm tired of living a single and sexless life."

And I get it, when you are living in scarcity, your only focus is on surviving, not thriving. But I promise you, it's possible. Many men who have read this book and took action before you have done it, and you can too. What one man can do, another man can do. If it's been done before, it can be done again.

Let's start with the biggest mistake 99% of the population is making and, more importantly, how you can avoid it...

THE #1 REASON THAT MOST RELATIONSHIPS FAIL (AND HOW TO AVOID IT)

The main reason that most relationships fail is not that couples suck at communication, are unfaithful, or don't have the right therapist. It's that most people do not have any sort of "filtration system."

They don't have rules regarding what values and behaviors they will and will not allow in their life. They don't test new partners to determine the quality of their character. They are more concerned with sexual chemistry than they are with values and emotional compatibility. As a result, they waste years of their lives trying to fix unsolvable problems with someone they never should have dated in the first place. This is especially true of men. Since childhood, we've been conditioned by society, biology, and the media to pay attention to a woman's physical beauty and outward appearance. Men don't look at a lingerie model and think to themselves, "Huh, I wonder if she's a good person?"

Instead, most men will quickly say, "I want her," without pausing to ask whether the woman will improve or impede their quality of life.

We are instantly attracted to a woman who has a symmetrical face, firm body, and perfect hip-to-waist ratio, but our biology is incapable of seeing the bigger picture and asking the important questions on its own.

Let me ask you something. If you were the CEO of a billion-dollar company and you were looking to hire an operations officer to handle the day-to-day operations and grow your business, would you settle for the first job applicant that met the minimum requirements?

Of course not! You would rigorously filter out and test every single applicant to make sure that they were the best possible fit for the job. You would potentially turn down *dozens* of great candidates until you found the *one* amazing applicant who was the perfect fit.

Your decision would be made from a place of abundance, power, and authority. You would feel no qualms about turning candidates down because you know that what you're offering is the opportunity of a lifetime. The wrong hire would cost you millions of dollars and countless hours. The right hire, on the other hand would save you time, help you earn more money, and create more freedom in your life. So why don't we extend this attitude to the most important decision in our lives: who we choose to spend the rest of our lives with?

It's funny how casually most men treat their relationships. They will spend days, week, and months deliberating over decisions in their career or business. They'll test drive different cars for months before deciding which one to buy. Heck, they'll even spend half an hour debating over which TV show to watch. These decisions are meaningless. And yet these same men won't spend a single day in solitude carefully asking themselves, "Am I with the right woman?"

Yet, if you get into a relationship with the wrong person, especially if you *stay* in that relationship for years, you are giving up your time, energy, and money for something that is not serving you in the long run. And if the relationship isn't *that* serious? You're still wasting the only non-renewable resource you have, your time. By following the steps I'm about to lay out in this chapter and creating a filtration system for the women in your life, you'll do all of the heavy lifting up front and increase your odds of success.

80% of the work in your relationship is in finding the right partner to begin with and 20% of the work is in keeping her.

I am not saying that there is no effort, stress, or frustration after you find the right partner. These are inescapable realities when two people decide to share their lives together. But when you have the right partner, these factors will be significantly reduced, allowing for greater relational success.

Most relationships are the opposite if someone settled quickly with an incompatible partner from the start. They spend the majority of their time trying to fix problems with each other that cannot be solved. Men often allow themselves to be led by their fears, insecurities and sex drive instead of their goals, vision and values which leads them into a relationship with a woman who is a terrible fit for their lives and future.

Relationships are only hard when you don't filter out the wrong women and settle with a woman you should have befriended within months of meeting and continued meeting new women. If you have never friend zoned a very attractive woman, then you've likely always entered your past relationships from a place of scarcity and weakness.

Sure, conflicts and problems will always exist in any relationship. But you should spend the majority of your time in a relationship expanding and growing together as a strong couple, and a minor part of that time working on the relationship and trying to resolve issues and differences. I want to encourage you to actively turn down the "so-so" and even the "good" relationships that come your way and only enter relationships that are "great" or have the future possibility of becoming "great."

Your overall life may be going well, but when you have zero women in your dating life and you meet one who finally is interested in you romantically, it's very difficult for you to hold your power and have backbone. This is a serious problem in the early stages of the relationship, which sets a weakened frame for the entire relationship moving forward.

The more time you invest in becoming the strongest version of yourself, building your life, and regularly interacting and flirting with women, the better opportunities will come your way. You're probably wondering how you actually go about filtering out partners and finding the right person.

Let's start by addressing two important misconceptions that confuse many men...

THE TWO MOST DANGEROUS BELIEFS ABOUT WOMEN & DATING

There are many misconceptions men hold about women and dating, but none are more dangerous—for either men or women—than these two:

Misconception #1: The "one" exists. There is a "perfect" woman out there for me.

Misconception #2: I've known her for a month and I'm in love. First, let's tackle the topic of the "one." Many men still buy into the belief that there is only "one" woman out there for every person. Let's just be real here. There are nearly 8 *billion* people on planet Earth. Do you really think that the universe hand-picked *one* single person to complete and fulfill you? Of course not! There are thousands, if not millions of women who would fit perfectly into your life and with whom you could fall madly in love.

Throughout this journey—if you take it seriously—you will undoubtedly meet many amazing women who actually *do* fit perfectly into your life. But an all-too-common scenario is that they will fall into the category of "right girl, wrong time."

Maybe they're moving to a new city. Maybe you're in the process of getting a graduate degree or starting a business and don't have time for a new relationship. Maybe you both just got out of a serious break up. There are myriad reasons that you might meet the right woman for you at the wrong time. You can't force a relationship onto a woman when it's the wrong time for her and vice versa.

As such, you must always remember there is no such thing as "the one" or the "perfect woman," there is only the right women at the right time.

Next, you must learn to differentiate between love and lust. Most men who have never experienced abundance with high-quality women often mistake their feelings of lust for feelings of love, especially during those exciting first few months of a relationship. Sure, if you've been with a woman for six months, you "love" them—a.k.a., you are lusting after them. But you do not have enough data and information to both logically and emotionally be in love with them.

The problem is that your biology, as magnificent as it might be, cares more about the survival of your genetic material and less about your long-term happiness and romantic satisfaction. According to anthropology professor Dr. Helen Fisher, during the first stage of attraction (known as lust) your brain releases a slew of pleasure chemicals, specifically serotonin, dopamine, and norepinephrine. This is similar to what you'd experience after snorting a line of cocaine.

In other words, your brain is driven to have sex and procreate at any cost. Your biology is not aware of marriage, divorce, sexually transmitted diseases, and a slew of the other negative effects of being with the wrong partner. It's not interested in making sure that you choose a suitable life partner in the 21st century. It just wants you to get your rocks off and do it again soon.

According to Dr. Fisher, after twelve months, these pleasure chemicals begin to die down and suddenly you'll start to see your partner for who they really are. It's only at this point that you can start to talk about "love" and have it actually mean something.

Understand this timeline. Don't rush into things just because your emotions are going haywire. Stay grounded and think about the neurochemistry at play before you make any life altering decisions like moving in together, buying a wedding ring, or having unprotected sex.

As a general rule of thumb, I recommend:

1. Casually date multiple women until you've found one very special woman
2. Live separately until you've been dating exclusively for at least twelve months
3. Avoid decisions like marriage, moving to a new city together, or children until you've been together for at least one year, preferably two or more years.

If you can remember these two things—there is no such thing as "the one" and there is a big difference between love and lust—you will avoid making rash decisions. You'll set yourself up for much greater success and happier, longer-lasting relationships that benefit both of you. Now, you're probably thinking, "How the heck do I determine if she's the right or wrong partner for me?"

Let's dive into the actionable steps to make this crystal clear for you...

HOW TO FILTER DOWN TO THE BEST WOMAN FOR YOU

When it comes to filtering out the wrong women and finding the right ones, it's not that the signs aren't there from the beginning. It's that most men aren't even aware of the signs they should be looking for.

They have not conditioned themselves to pay attention to red flags, shared values, and high-quality relationship indicators and so they continually find themselves in troubled relationships, wondering, "What went wrong? Are all women crazy?"

This section will change that. Instead of blindly falling into relationships with the wrong partner, you will have an acute awareness of the traits and behaviors you should look for when filtering women. You will reclaim your power and learn exactly how to find the right person for you by paying attention to the right signals and signs. And to do this, we must start with ourselves and get in touch with the things that make us who we are...

Know Your Values or Be a Blind Man Walking

The experiences you will have will largely be determined by what you value. This doesn't make your experience any more or less valid than another person's, it simply makes it *your* experience. The experience of a man who values primarily financial freedom, achievement, and contribution will differ greatly from a man who values adventure, love, and excitement. It doesn't make one better or worse. It simply means that the type of woman each man will thrive with may be different.

Before you go any further in this chapter, I want you to sit down for a minute and ask yourself, "What do I really value?" If you have never done this exercise, then this is likely the leading cause of your past problematic relationships.

For example, again here is a quick list of my top 10 values:

1. Aliveness
2. Adventure
3. Love
4. Fun
5. Financial freedom
6. Friendship and family
7. Health
8. Personal growth
9. Impact and contribution
10. Creativity

Therefore, what I value in women is:

- She has clear goals and is moving towards them.
- She loves to travel and experience new cultures.
- She has high standards for herself and the people closest to her.
- She's close with her family. Her parents are happily together.
- She adventurous, free-spirited and willing to take spontaneous risks.
- She has her own hobbies (outside of partying, drinking and getting stoned).
- She can hold her own socially.
- She does something that impresses me or that I admire.

When you know your values and you meet a woman who meets those values, then you may have found a woman worth investing in. Without shared values, you have no basis for a relationship other than you like to hump each other naked. You have no common ground to build a life and future together and are asking for problems and more stress. This is an immediate sign that you must friend zone this woman, continue to meet new women, and carry on.

Investing any time in a woman with whom you share little to no values with is a recipe for disaster and is a symptom of scarcity.

Values are the bedrock of any successful relationship. They are the foundation upon which the castle of your life will be built. It's important that any time you meet a new woman, you are actively observing her actions, personality, and history to determine if the majority of your values are in alignment.

Remember, there is no right or wrong here, only alignment and misalignment. However, before you can filter out a woman *based* on your values, you must first *define* your values. Until you know precisely the answer to that question, you do not have a strong basis to filter women, let alone other people, in your life.

A basic starting point for men can look like this:

- A woman who challenges you to become a better man.
- A woman who makes you come alive and makes every day experiences more exciting.
- A woman who shares your values and who has aspirations that match or support your own.

Who you select as a partner is a direct reflection of how you see yourself as a man. Before settling down with a woman, always ask yourself, "Is she a good reflection of the man I am and the man I want to become?" Answering "yes" to this question can indicate that she may be a good fit and answering "no" may indicate that she is best suited as a friend.

Additionally, there are several other key factors that you must consider before deciding that she's worth pursuing in the long run.

THE FIVE "GREENLIGHTS" OF A HIGH-QUALITY WOMAN

Now that you understand what you should *avoid* in a long-term partner, let's examine the qualities that make for an exceptional relationship. Again, there is not just "one" woman in the world for you, there are many "ones" that exist in the world. If the woman you're dating has some or all of these five characteristics, then your relationship and life will be infinitely easier.

1. High Self-esteem

The first and most important trait that you can look for in a long-term partner is high self-esteem. Nearly every red flag about a woman is a result of low self-esteem.

The woman that you're dating should value herself highly. She should *want* to be with you yet be entirely happy and content whether or not you (or any other man) are in her life. At the end of the day, all humans need validation and they will either give it to themselves internally or try and get it externally from those around them. If you date a woman with low self-esteem, she will constantly be looking to you for approval. She will feel paralyzed by making even the simplest decisions and be prone to fall into codependency.

However, when you date a woman with high self-esteem, she will push you to be a better man, she will not tolerate low-class behavior from anyone, and she will value herself enough to be honest and set strong boundaries with you.

Ultimately, high self-esteem in a woman is the bedrock that determines a high-quality woman, which will make for a much richer and fulfilling relationship.

2. Happy and Positive

Emotional states are contagious. If your partner is a happy, positive individual who can find the silver lining in the storms that life will throw at you, your entire world will be brighter and happier. If she's negative and unhappy, nothing you can do will fix this and she will find a way to ruin even your best of days. You can't expect her to be this way all of the time, but you want her to bring more positive emotions into your life than she does negative ones.

Remember, the goal of your relationship is to *amplify* the experiences in your life, not dampen them. If you are in a romantic relationship with someone, they should have a default emotional state that improves the experiences you share together. If your partner is unable to be happy and positive, then you should consider moving on until you find someone who is or else, you'll soon be just like her.

3. Sexual Compatibility

Sex is one of the ultimate forms of human connection. It's an intimate, highly pleasurable experience that forms a strong pillar of a romantic relationship. As such, it's important that any woman you date seriously is sexually compatible with you. Ideally, you want to find a woman who has a slightly higher sex drive than you do.

Nothing causes more problems in a relationship than feeling like sex is a chore or that you're taking from your partner every time you want to be intimate. It shouldn't feel like she's making a big sacrifice and you now owe her.

Find a woman who wants sex just as much, if not slightly more, than you do, and your relationship will be better for it. Be aware that if her sex drive is *too* much higher than yours, that can cause just as many problems as dating a woman with a low sex drive. Great sex does not solve the major problems in a relationship, but it can add fuel to the fire and cause the relationship to fail.

4. Healthy and Fit

Beyond the desire to have an attractive partner for years to come, having a healthy, fit, and active partner is essential to your relationship's success for a number of reasons. Women who exercise regularly are less likely to develop depression and anxiety. They tend to be happier, healthier, and more positive individuals. Their sex drive will be higher, they will be more attractive to you (and there's no reason to feel shame about this), and they will have higher self-esteem.

A woman who is healthy and fit *now* will age better, be less stressed, and remain sexy to you. You don't want a woman who is very attractive today then, a few years from now she lets herself go with bad diet and fitness. Although she may check a lot of boxes internally and you will always love her, you will silently resent her and be prone to looking at other women. And it goes both ways. If you are a fit and healthy man (as every Grounded Man should be) then you have every right to have a partner that has those same qualities. Don't feel any shame in wanting your woman to remain attractive to you and more importantly herself. At the end of the day, everything's better when you and your partner are fit and healthier.

5. Growth Mindset and Self-Awareness

A woman with a fixed mindset is a woman who will sabotage your hopes, dreams, and goals for the future. She will want you to stay complacent out of fear that if you grow, you will leave her (men do this, too).

A woman with a *growth* mindset is a woman who will constantly push you to be better, who will be open to new ideas, and who will help you live your best life. She should make *you* better by challenging you, calling you out on your bullshit, and encouraging you to grow in positive ways—as you should with her, too.

Women with growth mindsets tend to be happier, more positive, and more self-aware. They are making strides towards improving their lives and demand that the man they date does the same. Life is never a bore as she is pursuing goals, hobbies and passions of her own as you are too.

But now that we've established the positive characteristics you should look for in a partner, let's flip the script and take a look at the subtle (and not so subtle) red flags to be aware of. If a woman possesses any of these characteristics, then I encourage you to heed the wise words of the '90s philosopher Jenny and "Run Forrest, RUN!"

RED FLAGS TO BE AWARE OF (IGNORE THESE AT YOUR OWN PERIL)

In this section, I'll share the eight biggest red flags that men often overlook, to their own detriment. Most of your past break ups are likely a result of ignoring a few of these red flags.

1. She's Rude to those "Beneath" Her Social Status

This reveals who she is at her core and how she views herself. If you're on a date with a woman and she treats the service staff poorly, walk out. Dead serious. I've been on many dates with women and there were more than a few instances where the woman I was out with acted mean and rude towards the barista, bartender, or server.

Without exception, that same woman turned into an absolute nightmare of a girlfriend and made my life a living hell. Do not spend time with women who treat other people with disrespect, vulgarity, or contempt. She's not worth your time, no matter how hot she is, because this same attitude will soon be directed at you.

We all have bad days every once in a while. But if someone you're dating *never* says "please" or "thank you" for anything, it's a sign that she's overly entitled and spoiled. Neither of these are attractive traits in a partner. Call her out on this and see how she responds; her answer will tell you what to do.

2.   She Has Low-Quality Friends

Her friends are a direct reflection of her. It will be hard for her to improve her life when those closest to her are stagnant, downright bad influences, or try to bring her down out of fear of losing her. If they sense her life is improving as a result of being with you, then her friends can turn her against you. You'll be fighting an uphill battle as the relationship progresses. Yes, people can change and get new friends, but you should be paying attention to the quality of people she spends most of her time with.

After you've been dating for a few months, host a dinner and have her invite her three best friends, people that she spends the most time with (and be sure to invite yours). From here, you can learn so much about who she really is and how she spends most of her time when she's not with you. Her closest friends will bring out her true colors. This will help you "shortcut" the filtration phase and allow you to better gauge her character before wasting any more time and energy on dating further.

3.   She Has No Passions or Vision for the Future

If all she does is go out, party, do drugs, go shopping, and watch the latest popular television series, then she's not a valuable asset in your life, but instead is a liability that will bring your life down.

When a woman has passions and a vision that she's actively working towards, she's more alive and engaged in life. She's not letting life happen to her, she's actively creating a better life. It's not an instant deal breaker, of course, since people can change. You can help guide her, but if she refuses to do anything with her life or says she'll change but takes no action, this is a sign that she will slowly bring you down, too.

During the first month of dating, ask her about her vision and her passions for the future. Then, over the course of the following weeks, pay careful attention to whether or not she takes any *action* towards that vision or her passions. Don't listen to what she says, her actions tell you the truth.

4.   She's Overly Nosey and Often Jealous

If you find your girlfriend snooping through your personal items, reading your journal, looking at your text messages, or browsing your search history, this is a sign she has serious trust issues, low self-esteem, and no personal boundaries. Some jealousy is natural and even healthy in a relationship. But extreme jealousy, the kind where you can't even look in another woman's direction without incurring her wrath, is a sign of deeper-rooted problems. A woman who cannot trust me to be faithful to her is a woman who will make my life miserable in the long run. It's simply not worth it.

5. She Has Mental Health Issues That She Isn't Taking Care Of

Unlike some of the other red flags on this list, this one doesn't have to be an instant deal breaker, but you need to not overlook this and pretend like it's not that big of a deal. It is a very big deal that will affect your life.

There are many amazing women out there who are legitimately, medically predisposed towards depressive or anxious patterns. They are not damaged, bad, or unsuitable as a partner. They are also not incapable of controlling their emotions or behavior and growing from their challenges into a stronger woman.

However, you need to be fully aware of what you're getting yourself into. If she rocks your world, is aware of her medical challenges, is on the path towards being healthy, and has her life together despite her medical condition requiring prescriptions or therapy, this is a positive sign you can make the relationship work. In fact, it may become stronger because she knows what it means to face adversity.

Yet, if this level of control over a serious medical issue isn't there, you may be in a relationship with a victim of past circumstance who is simply unwilling to grow and get help for her challenges. That can place a serious burden on the relationship, one that includes excuses for bad behavior and an unwillingness to shoulder responsibility.

If that's the case, you are signing yourself up for problems that aren't necessary when you come from a place of abundance and could choose a woman who doesn't have these issues. You are not her therapist or her counselor, and if she isn't taking care of her mental health as well as her physical health, this isn't the woman for you.

6. She Was Abused Growing Up

Similar to the last point, there are many women who were sexually, emotionally, and physically abused in their past who take that pain and use it to grow stronger. Unfortunately, they are typically the exception, not the rule. Most problems and limiting beliefs in people's lives today are a result of unresolved past trauma.

Be aware that past abuse and trauma can manifest itself in unexpected ways in your relationship. Again, it is not your job to be her psychotherapist and fix her problems. If you fall into that role, you are creating more problems than solving. You can support her, but she needs to take a proactive lead role to heal her past trauma.

However, if these past issues are an excuse for why her life isn't going well, why she lashes out, why she exhibits trust issues or jealousy, or any other second-class behavior, then she's not in a healthy place to be in a relationship and will drag you down with her. Many people have faced abuse in their pasts—some of it unimaginable to those who've never endured it—and they've become strong, successful, resilient people. If that's not who she is, then she hasn't recovered enough to be a suitable partner at this time.

Support her, love her, and listen to her, but don't feel like it's your job to solve her life's problems. Again, if she's worth it, this doesn't have to be a deal breaker, but be aware that it can create a lot of extra work, stress, and drama for you that isn't necessary.

7. She Can't Communicate Effectively and Isn't Willing to Improve

If she can't open up, share how she's feeling, and speak her truth, you will likely never have a relationship that grows past surface-layer lust. There will always be a problem left unresolved or unspoken. You won't even know it, but you'll "always" be doing something wrong and she'll be silently frustrated, holding back and making you pay for it in covert ways.

Equally, any woman who cannot admit when she's wrong and apologize is a woman that is unable to learn and grow as a person. If she always has to be right and you find yourself up late arguing about nonsense, you're dealing with someone who can't communicate effectively (men do this, too).

Nobody's perfect. A woman with a superiority complex who believes she can do no wrong, or who can't open up and tell you what's really going on in her life, is a recipe for a relationship that will always be based on surviving and rarely thriving.

8. She's Overly Self-Absorbed

If a woman is constantly taking selfies, always on her phone, talking about her followers, addicted to chasing likes on social media, or generally so self-absorbed that she misses what's happening around her in the real world, just take off running in any direction. You'll benefit more from the sprint than you would with any more time with her. I've dated many of these women and can tell you from experience they are intolerable in the long run. This red flag in particular is a growing trend among younger women. You deserve a woman with high self-esteem *and* the humility to match it.

Now, at this point, I know you're probably thinking, "Wow Andrew! After all of these red flags, there won't be any women left to date!" But it's this very type of scarcity-based thinking that has kept you single or in the wrong relationships in the past. It's likely that you've entered into relationships with women who had these red flags, ignored them, and then struggled through constant problems and the inevitable breakup occurred.

Despite what you might believe from your friends, family, and modern media, this is *not* normal or healthy. To live your life to the fullest and experience incredible relationships, you *must* learn how to identify high-quality women who will add to your life and low-quality women who will detract from it.

Most men judge women ONLY on their appearance. And as a result, most men spend their entire lives in toxic or just mismatched relationships. They aren't willing to walk away from an attractive woman and, as a result, they waste years with the wrong person and slip into scarcity because they believe "This is just how it is" and accept the status quo.

But... One of the dangers of the dating game is that it's all too easy to put your best foot forward during the first few months of a relationship. Men and women can easily hide their true colors and fool even the most perceptive of partners. That is, *unless* their partner knows how to effectively test them to find out who they really are.

HOW TO DETERMINE IF SHE'S RELATIONSHIP MATERIAL

If you've ever applied for a car loan or mortgage, then you are undoubtedly familiar with the bank's tedious and often invasive examination process. From credit checks to income verification to utility bills to DNA swabs (ok maybe they don't do the last one yet), the average bank will have an entire team spend days, sometimes even weeks vetting you to determine if you're trustworthy with such a large sum of money.

Now imagine if they *didn't* do this. Imagine if they simply believed everything that new applicants said and accepted nearly everyone who applied for a loan (sounds familiar to the 2008 Great Recession, huh?) Oh, you want a $500,000 mortgage even though you only earn $25,000 a year and you just got the job? Well, you *claim* that your business is about to take off! Sign here and here.

It would be chaos. A disaster. A complete mess! Yet when selecting a romantic partner, arguably one of the most important decisions you can make in your life, this is exactly what many men do. They invest all of their time, energy, and resources into a woman without fully knowing who she is or properly vetting her to determine if she's the right fit for his life or find out when it's too late.

If you want to have a healthy, happy relationship, then you must test women the same way that they test you. You need to put yourselves in situations where her true colors will be revealed in order to determine if she's a long-term fit. Treat these tests the same way an employer would treat a mock project for a prospective employee. You know that the person *might* make a good fit for a position in your company, but you want to put them through a test *first* to give you sufficient data that you're making the right decision.

A common phrase after a break up or divorce by both sides is "he or she was not the person I thought they were." A test is not manipulation, it's simply gathering information before you commit to something more serious. For example, when I'm dating a girl, I'll take her on a simple weekend trip together to have fun and connect like so many couples do. However, I'm also paying attention to how she reacts in different situations.

A trip typically messes with people's diet, sleep, and patience. If during the trip she is overwhelmed by the stress of sitting in traffic, there is a problem with the hotel room, or she becomes very cranky and rude without eating at the right times, these examples indicate the type of woman she is under stress. It's neither good nor bad, it's simply more data for you. It's important to see how someone acts under stress so you don't have any surprises later.

If, on the other hand, she jumps at the chance to go on an adventure, is grateful for the invitation, excited by the opportunity offered to her, and handles stressful situations with ease—or better yet, relieves you of your stresses—these signs show more of who she is and gives you more data to make a better decision.

You should test a woman from the moment you start dating until the second you decide to commit. Otherwise, you run the risk of getting into a relationship with someone before they ever revealed their true selves. It's easy to put your best foot forward on scheduled dates for just a few hours (especially if consuming alcohol), but harder to maintain a false front for long periods of time and under stress.

While the spontaneous weekend getaway is one of my favorite tests, there are many others that you can use to discover a woman's true character. You want to create tests that mirror your own values, but here are a few ideas:

- Intentionally leave a $100 bill at her house in a place you were sitting and see if she tells you about it or takes it for herself.
- The next time she asks you to hang out, tell her that you already have plans with your friends and see how she responds.
- Leave your wallet in the car and see if she voluntarily pays for the bill at a restaurant.

- Leave your phone unlocked nearby while you go to the bathroom and see if she respects your privacy or starts snooping through your private life.
- Spend a week or two working significantly longer hours than normal to see if she supports your drive and ambition or becomes irate, overly clingy, and needy.
- Buy her a book on something she says she wants to do or work on and see if she reads a few pages or if it sits on the shelf.

The more thoroughly and effectively you can test a woman to determine her true character, the more information you will have when determining whether or not you should commit further. Equally, you are saving her from wasting time and energy if you commit to her without knowing who she really is.

If you don't have enough data, you can't possibly make a good decision about anything in life. And again, relationships are one of the biggest decisions that you will make so it would make sense to gather all the data you can before fully committing. Once you've tested the woman whom you're dating, you will now be able to accurately determine what type of relationship the two of you should have moving forward.

DETERMINING WHERE SHE FITS IN YOUR LIFE

In this section, I'm going to help you determine what to do with each woman based on the criteria we've discussed in this chapter. Then, I'm going to give you a general set of guidelines for determining if and when you should settle down and commit to one woman. You must realize that just because a woman is a good fit in your life does not mean that you necessarily need to be in a committed relationship with her. Conversely, just because a woman isn't necessarily relationship material does not mean that you should remove her from your life entirely.

As you go through the 90-day sprint and take action on your custom traffic strategy, you will have women calling *you* asking for dates, and have potential relationships that you could pursue. So how do you actually decide what to do with each woman? Well, if you've successfully tested the women in your life and compared their actions, behaviors, and mindsets to the criteria listed earlier, you will have a very clear roadmap for what to do next.

1. Friend Zone Her

If you're not actively friend zoning women, then you're letting your penis run your dating life. Any woman whose open to dating you should not instantly jump to the "potential relationship material" zone ever. You need to protect that zone with the highest regard and only allow the best to rise to the top.

If you've met a woman who you're not interested in sexually, doesn't match your values, has too many red flags, or is missing one of your non-negotiables, this doesn't mean that you should immediately cease all contact with her. In fact, if she's a cool woman, shares positive energy, and is fun person, then having her as a friend is one of the best things you can do for both of you. Women tend to be friends with other women whom you may be interested in, and you can exchange value through people you can introduce her to.

This is one of the most grounded things you can do since you are still finding ways to add value with each other and make it win-win. When you're able to introduce a beautiful woman to a friend without jealousy or fear, this is a sign that you've achieved true abundance. It's not all about you but offering value wherever you can because you want everyone to win.

If you feel that you should friend zone a woman, the sooner you do this the easier it will be. You don't want to drag this on when you know it's not going to work in the future. And this shouldn't be a problem since you'll have abundance and this book to help you continue building on it. Friend zoning women should be done within three months of meeting and casually going out. Here's a simple script of how to friend zone a woman whether in person or via phone:

"Hey, I really enjoy our time together and think you're an awesome woman (insert 3 things that support this), but I want to be clear that I'm not interested

in a relationship right now, yet I'm open to being friends and continuing from there if that's something you're open to."

That's it. That sentence alone will save both of you a lot of energy, time, and unnecessary stress. Use it often. Later, after a friendship is growing, you can add in that you'd like to introduce her to a friend that you know. After doing this, especially if she liked the introduction, you can ask her if she has any friends that she can introduce you to. Overall, if it's not a long-term romantic fit, but she's a good woman that you enjoy then view her as an ally on your journey.

2. Friends with Benefits

The vast majority of the women you meet will likely fall into this category since you're probably a horny guy who wants regular sex while you're single. Women that you're attracted to sexually but who have misaligned values should not automatically be removed from your life or ignored.

In fact, I'd recommend that you have one to two women in your life that are friends with benefits while you continue to search for a woman who is relationship material. You can still achieve win-win by engaging in a casual sexual relationship that allows both of you to get your needs met.

She wants to have more adventures, enjoy great sex, and connect with a strong Grounded Man. You want to have someone to join you on your adventures, enjoy great sex, and connect with even though you know that a committed relationship probably isn't in the future.

First and foremost, it's important that you are honest with the woman you're not fully exclusive with. Don't avoid the truth and make promises about a future relationship that you have no intention to keep. Tell her from the beginning that you are attracted to her and enjoy spending time with her but that you aren't looking for a serious or an exclusive relationship at the moment.

She will respect your honesty, and this will give her the ability to decide whether or not she wants to be in a casual "friends with benefits" relationship with you or just remain friends. On the other hand, never allow a friends with benefits relationship to spiral out of control and lead to a committed relationship with someone who you consciously know is not a good fit for your life. This should be done within six months of meeting and casually dating. I'd recommend doing this in person, so here's a simple script of how to form a friends with benefits situation:

"Hey, I really enjoy our time together and think you're an awesome woman, but I want to be up front and honest. Right now, I can't fully commit to anyone. Although I do value our connection, have fun with you and think we have good chemistry (insert 3 unique things that support this), would you be open to being friends with benefits for the time being?"

That's it. Now you can discuss what the boundaries are that work for both of you. These relationships can work in the short-term as long as both of you are on the same page and you have open and clear lines of communication. It's important that you continue meeting other women, otherwise you will fall into scarcity and may end up settling with her. As such, I recommend that you mentally set a "relationship deadline" with all of your friends with benefits relationships with an understanding that it is a short-term intimate relationship. It will be easier to end these interactions when you have an abundance of women that you are talking to and awfully hard if she's the only woman in your life.

After six to twelve months, you should be clear if this woman is relationship material and you want to continue dating her or move her to the friend zone and continue seeing other women. Having a friends with benefits relationship longer than twelve months will become very problematic and it is not recommended. You need to make tough decisions and trust your gut instinct based off the data that you have about her. This will ensure that you don't allow the relationship to go overboard or end up in a committed relationship that you didn't want, followed by an eventual painful breakup.

3. Potential Relationship Material

At this point you have filtration tools to help you determine if she is a potential fit for a committed relationship, or if she is friends with benefits material. But there is one final tool, a primal, uncomfortable, and wildly accurate tool that will allow you to eradicate any ambiguity you feel almost instantly. The tool to which I'm referring is a simple notion I call the "Ejaculation Test."

Assuming she is not using any form of contraception, would ejaculating inside of her be a good idea or a bad idea?

No. I don't mean would it *feel* good in the moment. Mother Nature has made the answer to that question inescapably obvious. I'm asking how you would feel over the following days if you came inside of her.

Would you wake up the following morning or the next week thinking to yourself, "I'm okay with her having my cum. She will make an amazing long-term partner, a good mother to my future children, and someone with whom I could happily do life with for the foreseeable future."

Would the act elicit emotions of commitment, companionship, and love? Or abject terror? Would you immediately wonder if you'd made a serious mistake and rush to your local pharmacy to purchase a morning after pill?

Again, the idea here is that you are *not* ready for or wanting children when this happens. Simply explore the hypothetical situation of whether or not being attached to this woman in the long term and raising a child with her would *ruin* your life or *amplify* it.

Simple as it may be, this exercise will bring the underlying thoughts and emotions you feel for this woman immediately to the surface.

Now, if a woman has all or many of the five essential traits of a good partner, is aligned with the majority of your values, doesn't have any major red flags (or you're willing to work on some of them), passes the ejaculation test, and is physically attractive to you, well congratulations. This means that she has the *potential* to be a long-term partner!

Keep dating her and building that connection while remaining grounded. However, just because she has the potential to be a long-term romantic partner does not mean that she *should* be or that the relationship will prosper.

There is one final determining factor that can make or break a relationship with even the most amazing of women. If you aren't aware of this early in the relationship, you could be setting yourself up for a lot of unnecessary stress, disagreements, and an eventual heartbreak.

Unfortunately, I see it happen all the time.

HOW YOUR STORIES AFFECT
THE SUCCESS OR FAILURE
OF RELATIONSHIPS

Once you've begun seriously dating a single woman, it's important that you understand how your individual stories will affect the relationship. Just because a woman has passed your tests, has the character traits of a good partner, and seems to be a good fit for your life does not mean that the relationship will seamlessly work.

The reason for this is often overlooked because we want the relationship to work and we become blind to anything that says otherwise. Everyone has different internal stories about what a relationship should look like since adolescence which will dictate the type of relationship they want.

For example, some men expect that their partner will be a stay-at-home mom and a motherly woman, whereas the woman you're dating might want to be a hard-charging entrepreneur or corporate executive.

Some men (and women) view marriage as an outdated contract designed to involve the government in their personal lives, while others view it as a beautiful public testimony of two people's love for one another.

Some women may want the man to be extremely involved in her extended family activities like the niece's birthday or her second cousin's soccer games. And the man may not have any interest in being a part of every single-family activity as he values his time and wants to spend it doing things he enjoys.

Some women have strongly held religious beliefs that are incompatible with your own. She might be unwilling to have sex outside of marriage or insist that her children be raised in a church that is fundamentally opposed to everything that you stand for (or vice versa).

Some women may want to have children and get married within three years, whereas the man may not be ready for marriage and children so soon.

And this is where deep conflict can arise in a relationship. When couples fall in love but then slowly realize they have different stories about what a successful relationship is supposed to be, problems come up. There is no right or wrong story. Everyone is entitled to their own version of a relationship, and no amount of convincing is going to completely change what someone considers a successful relationship.

You can do everything right and have what seems like the perfect partner. But if your stories are incompatible, then there will be an added level of friction to the relationship and things may not work out in the long run. As such, it's important that you understand the stories that you have and that your partner has before you commit to a serious relationship or get married.

So right now, you need to ask yourself.

1.   What type of relationship do I want?
2.   What are the stories I have about relationships?
3.   Which stories am I willing to change?
4.   Which ones are non-negotiable?

For example:

• Do you want to have children? If so, how many?
• Do you want to get married? If so, by when?
• Do you expect your partner to be a certain way (career drive, family oriented, lifestyle)?
• Do you expect your partner to share the same religion or adopt your beliefs?

The more clarity you can gain on your stories and their importance, the better equipped you will be to navigate the way that these stories affect your relationship. It's important that you have these conversations early on (ideally before you're exclusive) to avoid conflict in the future.

A friend of mine recently experienced this firsthand. My buddy, David, is a successful entrepreneur. He's in no rush to get married and saw no reason to even consider it until after the age of 35. The woman he was dating, however, was operating from a completely different story. She believed that she *needed* to get married by 26 so that she could have children by 28. She was unwilling to waver on her story.

Even though they were a great fit for one another and made a great couple, their stories alone were incompatible. As a result, the friction grew over time until it finally burst, leading the relationship to end seemingly out of nowhere.

Misaligned stories are often the root issue of frequent petty arguments that seem to make no sense.

If their stories had been aligned from the beginning or if they'd had an honest conversation about what their stories meant for the future of their relationship, they could have bypassed or significantly reduced the drama and heartbreak. They would have been on the same page from the beginning and worked through it or avoided it altogether.

Remember, there are no right or wrong stories. They are only *your* stories and *her* stories. The more compatible your stories are or the more you are willing to adapt and change your stories, the less friction you will have and the more likely the relationship will succeed.

Now that you understand the importance of filtering to find the right partner and *how* to actually filter the women that you meet, let's talk about transitioning your relationship from "just dating" to entering a committed, exclusive relationship.

TRANSITIONING FROM A CASUAL TO SERIOUS RELATIONSHIP

Congratulations, you've found someone you think, and feel is the right person at the right time for you. Here is how to properly transition from a casual to a serious relationship so that you can enjoy a drama-free dating life.

Men often invest too much in a relationship too fervently. Despite what society or pop culture tells you, to a woman, this is *not* a sign of love and affection but rather a sign of weakness. They will wonder why you are so quick to commit. They will assume that you lack options and abundance and wonder what other women know that she may not know. You'll be seen as clingy and desperate, *not* grounded. As a result, she will be repelled by your commitment instead of excited about it.

Very few women with an abundance of eager men to choose from (which is *most* attractive women) will be willing to transition to a serious or exclusive relationship within the first few weeks or months. So slow down and enjoy the ride brother. Dating is supposed to be fun and you're supposed to enjoy the process of building *up to* a relationship.

Rushing into a relationship, even if she likes you will scare her away and prematurely end what could have been an otherwise great relationship, if you had been more patient and slowly transitioned into the relationship. Sure, you've seen in movies, books and popular culture that spilling out your undying love for someone within weeks or months of meeting them leads to the fairytale romance you crave, but psychology doesn't work that way. Commitment that comes too soon, too fervently and with little effort on her part is not viewed as romantic, but desperation and weakness. And if there's anything you've learned from the earlier chapters – women despise weak approval seeking men like the plague. Of course, there's that random story from a loose friend where a couple fell madly in love with each other and it all worked out (or so they say), but for most high-quality women rushing into a relationship will only repel them. And in those rare cases where rushing may have worked, consider that if the couple didn't rush into things and slowly transitioned into a relationship it likely would have still worked out too. So, your odds of success with women are far greater when you slow the fuck down, enjoy your life while making steady progress into a relationship. But what's great about this is when you're casually dating and being intimate together, a woman is already attracted to you, so time now works in your favor, even when you aren't even with her. Overtime, the tides will shift and she'll be the one who wants to be exclusive with you and will do everything in her power to prove to you that she's the best fit and the other women that you're talking to are not.

Your resources—time, money, even mental space and attention—are not instantly her resources. Slowly allow her to gain more and more access into your world as she proves that she deserves it. Slowly begin to engage in more intimate connection and conversations after sex, introduce her to your network and friends, go on exciting trips together, and spend more quality time together.

The more intentional you are about transitioning the relationship, the more likely long-term success is. In fact, according to Dr. Scott M. Stanley and Dr. Galena Rhoades, researchers in charge of the Relationship Development Study at the University of Denver, partners who cohabitate (aka live together) before marriage "had more negative interactions, lower interpersonal commitment, lower relationship quality, and lower relationship confidence" and were more than twice as likely to file for divorce after marriage.

However, the reason given for this phenomenon isn't what you might first imagine. Researchers have found that one of the leading predictors of divorce with cohabiting partners is that they were not *intentional* about moving in together. It just suddenly "happened," mainly for logistical reasons. There was no real talk or discussion, and few boundaries were set.

If you want to avoid a toxic living situation, breakup, or divorce, then take things slower and really get to know someone before making any serious life altering choices. Having control of your life is about setting healthy boundaries and making important decisions intentionally instead of letting them just happen.

However, if you truly believe that she is the right fit for you and decided from a place of abundance that you want her in your life, then all that's left to do is have "The Talk" and establish the nature of your new relationship. Do it on a regular date in person, *never* over the phone, through text, or via social media. When you decide to introduce the topic, there really shouldn't be any reason why she would *not* be your girlfriend. The conversation simply hasn't been had yet.

She won't become your girlfriend because you asked her the right way or used the right lines. There's no trickery here. Also, making her your girlfriend will not fix any problems or compatibility issues that may exist. The goal here is to make the new relationship a win-win. It's not like you're getting a hot new girlfriend and she doesn't get anything in return. She should be equally excited about the idea of having a Grounded Man in her life who is willing to be exclusive with *her*.

So assuming that all of the aforementioned factors are established and in place, here's how to setup the conversation and sail smoothly into an exclusive relationship.

First, you'll want to be intentional regarding the environment in which you have this conversation. You should be laughing, connecting, sitting close together, and fully focused on one another. It should still be casual and fun (you're not asking her to be your wife, after all), but you want to make sure that you're not distracted by anything so both of your attention is solely on each other.

Share a few "we statements" to establish a sense of connection and recap some of the highlights that you've shared recently. This will set the tone and create a deeper level of togetherness. She should be nodding her head in agreement as you share, so when you ask the big question she's already been saying "yes" in her head multiple times.

For example: We've had a lot of fun doing those early morning yoga classes together. We seem to really connect with our visions for the future and where we both want to go. Our values seem really aligned. It's so easy dating someone who's also growth oriented. And then, as she's nodding in agreement, simply ask for monogamy and exclusivity.

You: "What do you think about being monogamous with each other? No more seeing or talking to other people?"
Her: "Yeah, I'd like that."
You: *Kiss* "Awesome… I'm glad I can call you my girlfriend now!"
Her: "I'm glad I can finally call you my boyfriend!"
You: Kiss her again and (if in private) make passionate love.

That's it. Don't fall for all of the cheesy weak antics you see online, e.g. "You will make me the happiest person in the world if you say "yes" to be my girlfriend… please tell me what you think about the possibility of that?"

This just screams "I'm needy" and highlights that the man benefits more than the woman. If she's putting in equal effort to see you, genuinely connects with you, shares sexual chemistry, and meets your major criteria, then she has the role, you just haven't made it official.

It's like someone who is happily working for free as a volunteer and doing an excellent job already. If the manager asked if they wanted an official title and compensation, the answer is easy and without hesitation. "Yes."

In fact, if you've done everything right up until this point, it's likely that she will initiate "the talk" herself and directly ask you where the relationship is going. This is ideal because it shows that she wants to move the relationship forward. However, many women are conditioned to expect the man to initiate serious conversations. And this is fine.

Before I end this section, I have a simple exercise that I want you to complete that is required for any man who wishes to engage in a serious relationship. When you find yourself debating whether or not you should get serious with a particular partner, I want you to have at least three deep conversations with men in your social circle, network, or family who have gone through a divorce or serious breakup.

I'm not talking about the guys who have become so jaded and broken after their divorce that they begin to despise women and submit to a life of singledom. I'm referring to a healthy, happy, well-meaning guy who, despite his best intentions, wasn't able to make his past relationship work. Sit and listen to him. Ask him what led to the divorce. Figure out what warning signs he ignored early in the relationship that could have saved him later down the line. What were things he would have done differently? I want you to do this for two reasons.

1. It will give you some much needed perspective on what's *really* at stake here. Talk face-to-face with a man who has lost pretty much everything because he settled early into the wrong relationship.
2. It will inform you of the subtle warning signs and potential problems to which you are currently blind (because of those pesky love hormones).

Get an outside perspective and an objective set of eyes on your relationship before making a big move forward. After all, this is your life we're talking about. Although I expect that you will be dating around for a few months to achieve abundance and make sure that you're with the right person when the time eventually comes for you to get into a more serious relationship, I want to make sure that you know how to conduct yourself and set yourself up for success.

With that in mind, here are the key principles to making the relationship work and grow when you eventually decide to date one woman exclusively.

TAKING CARE OF YOU OR LOSE YOUR POWER

Once you've filtered out the women in your life and gotten into a serious committed relationship, then there is still work that needs to be done. Although your relationship should be easier than most—if you've put in the hard work up front to find the right partner to begin with—this does not mean that it will be *smooth sailing with no problems whatsoever.* You must remain grounded, set and maintain strong boundaries, and ensure that you continue to act in the same way that attracted her in the first place.

Take Care of Yourself First

Men often think, "Now that I'm with her, I can be happy and show up in the world the way I finally want to." People look for things outside of themselves to fill the gaps of self-worth and validation. Your partner should not be the sole reason that you are happy and why you get out of bed in the morning.

A solid frame to enter a relationship is to have things that are more important in your life than being in a relationship with somebody else. Have friends, hobbies, passions and activities that you enjoy by yourself (long-term relationships slowly one or both parties sacrifice their identity and lose their interests and social life which makes you prone to needy behavior and less attractive) when you change your identity in a relationship, you no longer become the person your partner fell in love with.

People who don't improve their life tend to go from relationship to relationship and think they just need to find the right "one", when in reality they need to take more responsibility and work on themselves to attract the type of women they really want.

When you improve the quality of your life and take action going after the women you want then a great dating life and relationships is a natural byproduct of that life.

Prioritizing Time with Your "Boys"

One of the most important aspects of self-love is prioritizing time with friends and family outside of your relationship. There's nothing wrong with dating a woman that you want to spend *most* of your time with. However, it's important that you don't get so caught up in your relationship that you forget to make time for the other important people who have already earned their place in your life.

In a healthy relationship, both you and your girlfriend should want each other to have a healthy social life. She should *encourage* you to go out with your guy friends and you should equally support her spending time with her friends. It is difficult to maintain a healthy relationship without maintaining a healthy social life. You will slowly start to lose yourself in the relationship, become prone to approval-seeking behavior, and fail to uphold the same characteristics and qualities that attracted your significant other in the first place.

This doesn't mean that you should be out getting drunk with your friends every night of the week. It simply means that you need to prioritize time with your friends doing things you naturally enjoy. Personally, I try to go out with my guy friends at least one to two nights a week. I've noticed a direct correlation between prioritizing "guy time" and showing up more powerfully and masculine in my relationship.

You cannot expect to get everything you need personally and emotionally from your girlfriend since *that is not her job*. Male friends serve an important role in your life that is essential to your growth, overall wellbeing, which is something your partner will equally benefit from. She needs to respect and understand this.

Right now, I recommend that you set a rule for yourself that you will not let a week go by where you don't spend *some* time with a close male friend, either in person or at least virtually. It doesn't have to be a huge event or cost a lot of money each week, but you need at least an hour of quality "man" time to maintain a healthy relationship with your woman and more importantly yourself.

On Personal Responsibility

It's important to be the Grounded Man in a relationship to prevent you from blaming your woman for your problems or situation. Take full responsibility and accountability for any problems or challenges in your life. When you make a mistake admit it openly, ask for forgiveness, and move on. Learn from them and grow from them. Being a Grounded Man is why she fell for you, so the second you begin losing touch with that, she's going to slowly disconnect herself from the relationship, maybe not physically, but emotionally.

Although it may please her in the short term to have a man who lives for her, in the long-term it will be a detriment to your relationship. Any healthy woman wants you to respect and live your own life and purpose. You love your woman fully, but don't forget to love and respect your own wants, needs, and desires. Remember: true happiness comes from within, not from someone else. You alone are responsible for your own happiness. Not her. But sometimes it can be difficult to be happy when your partner is constantly unhappy, so you fall into the trap of trying to fix her.

You Are Not Her F*cking Therapist

I've shared this point multiple times for good reason. Despite what you might have inferred from romantic comedies, sitcoms, and terrible advice from your well-intentioned friends and family, it is *not* your job to fix your partner's problems...and vice versa. You are not responsible for your partner's actions or emotions and they are not responsible for yours. As noble as it might *feel* to try and take on your partner's problems—emotional, financial, maturity, or otherwise—it isn't your job.

Unfortunately, people are conditioned to believe that the more problems they have, the more attention they will receive and the more love and sympathy their partner will give them. On the other side of the equation, the "fixer" in the relationship often believes, "The more problems I fix, the more I will be loved and needed, and the more likely the relationship will last."

This becomes a vicious cycle where one party creates problems to get attention and the other party fixes the problems to feel needed. Unfortunately, the problems never end and the relationship fails to grow beyond this point.

People often blame their partner instead of dealing with the emotion or hurt that causes their desire to fix or be fixed in the first place. Sure, it feels good in the short-term, but we aren't actually changing anything in the long-term.

It's not your responsibility to make your partner happy or fix her emotional traumas of the past. You love and care about her, but you must accept that the weight of her problems does not fall on your shoulders.

You must both take full responsibility for your own problems and lives or the relationship will not succeed. It's easy for a man's logical mind to come in and attempt to fix her problems like a checklist and mold her into the partner that you want. But when you do this, you are subconsciously signaling to her that you are unhappy with who she is today – which pushes her even further away especially if little progress is made.

If you can't love her for who she is *now*, then you should reconsider being in the relationship at all. It doesn't mean anyone did anything wrong, but simply that you aren't as compatible as you once believed in the present.

However, the problem is often not that you and a woman are incompatible, but rather that she exhibits specific behaviors and patterns that violate your expectations and boundaries. If this is the case, the relationship *can* be saved. But you must stay grounded and willing to assert your truth even when it's hard.

SETTING HEALTHY BOUNDARIES AND STAYING GROUNDED IN YOUR RELATIONSHIP

The most overlooked key to a healthy, long-lasting relationship is to identify from the onset the exact type of relationship that you want and the personal boundaries you must set to achieve it. It's important to note that there is no such thing as a right or wrong relationship (barring physical or emotional abuse), only a relationship that is right or wrong *for* you.

For example, I know some guys who pay for everything and allow their girlfriends to quit their corporate jobs to work on their real passions while keeping the house in order (e.g. cooking, cleaning, and running errands). They're happier than they've ever been because those boundaries work for them and are congruent with the type of relationship they both desire.

I also know couples who sleep in separate rooms because they value quality sleep and having their own space. Or they only see each other once a week on a scheduled date night due to their busy lives. Or even not allowing each other to be angry and have unresolved arguments with each other before going to sleep. And guess what? These couples are happy and fulfilled in their relationships because those boundaries work *for* them.

Are those examples right for every single relationship? Of course not. They will be different for every relationship based on the beliefs, needs and wants of both individuals. But setting boundaries isn't a "set it and forget it" activity.

Boundaries must be reinforced, upheld, and reset on a regular basis. Without a willingness to enforce boundaries, you run the risk of a toxic (not to mention sexless) relationship or losing her entirely.

When entering into a new relationship, it's important to realize that you are not actually in a "real" committed relationship until a boundary has been stated, accepted, and respected by her. If she has not yet responded to a boundary that you've set, you are still friends with benefits even though you've discussed being together verbally.

If you do not enforce your boundaries early on and she knowingly or unknowingly acts in a way that is unacceptable to you (while you do nothing about it), she will lose respect. The tides of power will slowly shift in her favor and often turn sex into a scheme she can use to get what she wants which further reduces your power.

Until you have enforced a boundary and *meant* it, she is not yours. She has not committed to the relationship until she complies with a boundary verbally requested by you. If you are not willing to lose her in order to maintain the boundaries you have set for yourself and the people you allow into your life, she will never fully respect you. When her physical appearance and presence are held above your own values, boundaries, beliefs, and desires, you have ceased to be a Grounded Man.

And let me be clear, women do not want to surrender their bodies and open themselves sexually to a man over whom she holds power over. When your boundaries are tested, remain grounded. Stand strong. Respectfully, assertively, and empathetically uphold your values, even if it means an argument will ensue and risking the end of your relationship. She must accept that you are not like other men and that you will *not* tolerate second class behavior from her or anyone else. If she does not respect your boundaries, she will slowly but surely continue to push your hot buttons stopping just shy of your breaking point. Not because she is vindictive or malicious like most men would assume, but because she wants to know she can trust you. That your actions are congruent with your thoughts, words and emotions and that you are a man who says what he thinks and acts on what he says.

A general rule of thumb is to never tolerate behavior from a woman that you would not tolerate from a close friend.

If, after the reinforcement of a boundary, she returns to you, you will find a more committed, loving and serious woman who values you even more. She will open up her schedule, respond quickly to you, crave sexual intimacy, and respect you on a deeper level than the other weak men she dated before that she was able to walk over.

For your relationship to succeed, she needs to know that you are willing to walk away if you feel overtly disrespected. And if she doesn't know this, you will be taken advantage of for years and be subjected to low-class behavior from the very person who should be loving and supporting you most.

Now that you understand the importance of boundaries in maintaining a strong and healthy relationship, let's discuss a few strategies to help you cultivate an amazing, long-lasting relationship that improves for years to come.

HOW TO HAVE A LONG, HAPPY, AND LOVING RELATIONSHIP

After the end of my last relationship, I spent months mulling over what had happened and the lessons I could glean to improve my next relationship. As I was reviewing those lessons, I opened up an old journal filled with notes I'd made during my previous relationships.

They are not meant to serve as a coherent strategy or roadmap for relational or marital success (I will likely do a separate book purely on relationships in the future), but simply to serve as a guide or as key pointers to help you stay grounded and continue the positive trajectory of your relationship. The following are those notes...

The greatest killer of love, affection, and lasting happiness are *not* infidelity, anger, or abuse. It's complacency and taking her for granted. The second that you stop dating one another and begin taking each other for granted is the second that your relationship begins to die a slow, lengthy death. Never stop dating the person you're committed to.

Although the butterflies and nervous excitement you first felt for one another will fade, you should never use this as an excuse to grow complacent. There was once a time in your life when you would have done anything and everything to get the woman you're now with, and you have her, but you don't act like it and she can tell. It's easy to forget all the good that is right in front of you.

Commit to keeping the love alive and appreciating every phase of your relationship for what it is. Even if you can't recreate the excitement you felt on the first date, be mysterious and take her on excursions without telling her where you're going. Laugh until your stomachs hurt. Go on adventures together, step back from your busy life from time to time and appreciate her beauty. Stop taking everything so damn seriously and enjoy what's in front of you.

The key to a lasting and happy relationship is presence. No matter where you are or how busy you might be, when you are with her, *be* with her. Give her all of your attention. No TV, no smartphone, no social media, no email. Be with her, listen to her, and love her. She is giving you the greatest gift a person has to give—her time—the only resource she can never get back. Don't squander it on distractions and senseless entertainment that mean nothing to you an hour later.

Have wild sex together, again and again. Explore each other in new ways and fully open up and embrace your masculine desires and enjoy putting her into her deepest feminine. Ravish her, love her and play with her in all its grandeur.

Give her space. Let her do her own thing and support that she needs alone time as you do, too. Leave the bird cage open and the bird will always come back. She needs space to renew and get re-centered, to find herself, to grow, as do you.

Don't let money stop you from loving her and having fun adventures together. You don't need to take her to Tahiti to have a romantic getaway. You don't need to work eighty hours a week to make money so that you can take her somewhere and say, "I'm doing this for us." No, you're not, that's your ego. Get creative with your time together and how much you spend will not matter to her.

In disagreements with loved ones, deal only with the current situation. Forgive fast and focus on the present and future rather than carrying negative energy from the past. Strong relationships are not just about the good times you share, they're also about the challenges you go through *together* and the fact that you still say I love you at the end of it all. The first to apologize is the bravest, the first to forgive is the strongest, and the first to move forward is the happiest.

Always choose love. Relationships take work, and they require a commitment to grow together and a willingness to continually invest in creating something that can last. You're building a pyramid, it's going to take time. When you're done, it will stand as a wonder of the world where you will look at it in awe and be amazed by how beautiful it is.

Commit to being the Grounded Man and an epic lover. There is no greater challenge and no greater prize than being the man you were born to be, the man who makes his woman fall into her deepest feminine when she is with you.

For those of you who are struggling with women inside of the delicate 6 month phase of meeting and dating a woman. If you're constantly feeling like the pursuer, second guessing your every move with women and not feeling like the selector whom she excitingly responds to and chases. Then you may need more direct support from me so I can help you solve your unique sticking points and prevent them from sabotaging future possibilities with women.

Watch this presentation and learn more about how I can help you further so you're better equipped to enter into the highest quality relationships you've ever experienced: knowledgeformen.com/live

All right, guys... this is it for an incredible relationship. But before I leave you on your own and send you off to begin this journey, we must ensure that you can achieve lasting results and success.

You see, most books give you lots of great *information* without a clear plan or strategy for *implementation* moving forward to get results. I know what it's like to be confused and overwhelmed with the task in front of you. I have felt that frustration from knowing *what* to do but not *how* to actually get started or progress past the most basic levels.

And so, in the next chapter, I'm going to help you bring everything you've learned together and begin making real progress. It will give you a strategy, a game plan, a proven formula to achieve the dating life you've always wanted.

CHAPTER 7

THE PATH TO ABUNDANCE

"The fear of death follows from the fear of life. A man who lives fully is prepared to die at any time."

-MARK TWAIN

I couldn't breathe.

Sweat poured from my face onto the mat, pooling on the ground below me in a puddle of exhausted futility. Blood rushed to my head and I could feel each heartbeat pounding in my temples, as if someone was using my skull as a snare drum. My vision started to blur, and I knew I was only seconds away from blacking out.

My mind screamed, "Think of something, Andrew!" I tried to hold on, to fight, to keep breathing, if for just one second longer. The harder I tried to maintain my grip over my consciousness, the faster it seemed to slip away.

As my strength waned, the arm wrapped around my throat tightened even more. If I didn't do something, I knew I'd soon pass out—sprawled across the mat, a near-lifeless pile of failure and ineptitude laid bare for all the others to see.

My soon-to-be unconscious mind screamed, "Hold on. Don't give up now!" But it was too late. The heat of my assailant's body pressed against my back. His arms were locked around my neck in an unbreakable vice grip, an anaconda squeezing its victim to death. My body began to go limp, but I summoned all the strength I had left, lifted my hand…

… and tapped the mat three times loudly. In a split second, he relinquished his grip and let my nearly-dead body collapse to the floor. Relief flooded over me as I gasped for air and rested my throbbing head on the mat beneath me. I slowly lifted my gaze to the dozens of men crowded around the newly-minted victor standing proudly above me. They were dressed in white Brazilian Jiu Jitsu gis, expressions of primal delight across their faces from the carnage of my embarrassing match.

"Fuck this place," I thought to myself, coughing so violently I could taste blood. As I regained my composure, my opponent—a 35-year-old real estate agent who was four inches shorter than me and at least 40 lbs. lighter—said gingerly, "Good match, bro." As he walked off the mat, I couldn't help but despise him. "How does that little guy keep beating me? I'm stronger, bigger." Yet there I was, heaving to catch my breath, laid out on the mat spread eagle as I watched my sparring partners file out of the gym one by one.

I wanted to leave, to go home, to ice my wounds. Maybe I'd drown my sorrows and sore body aches in a river of tequila and lime. Anything was better than laying on that mat covered in sweat, shame, and self-pity at my appalling performance. First, there was something I had to do. Mustering what little energy I had left, I haphazardly peeled myself off the mat and staggered to the only person left in the gym. My instructor.

"Hey Coach," I said meekly, "I, um… don't think this is working out for me. I think I'm, um… done." I half-expected him to punch me in the mouth and then choke me unconscious himself, finishing the job for good.

Instead, he responded calmly and with a touch of disdain, "So you're just going to quit, huh? This is only what… your fourth, maybe fifth class?"

"Yeah, but I keep getting choked out by guys who are way smaller than me!" I replied in embarrassment. He chuckled. "So, what are you doing to prevent the other guy from choking you in the first place?"

"I don't know," I responded in frustration. "Then that's your problem," he replied sharply. "If you don't have a clear strategy to fix your game and avoid getting choked out, expect to get choked out. Right now, you're showing up aimlessly, just expecting things to magically get better. Andrew, working harder doesn't mean shit if you aren't working on the right things with a solid plan of action."

"Let me show you what I mean," my instructor said softly, motioning for me to come back to the mat. He worked with me on my weak points, pointing out the critical mistakes that I was making that led to getting choked out. We rolled, and I did my best to fix them and rehearsed the positions intently. I left nearly half an hour later feeling more confident, motivated, and ready for my next class.

When I returned, I rolled against the very same opponent. He looked me square in the eye and I glared right back. After the extra training I'd received, there was only one thought running through my head: "I am going to fucking destroy you."

Our instructor howled, "Begin!" We leapt at each other and clasped shoulders. I immediately started visualizing what I'd practiced the night before. *Okay, when he does this, you're going to do this and then go for—*

That thought was cut short by yet another vice grip around my bruised throat. I suddenly found my body sprawled out on the floor incapable of defending myself. *What?* I thought to myself, futilely trying to hold on before tapping out yet again. "Damn it!" I screamed as our coach instructed us to roll again.

So we did. Over and over and over again. I was choked out within minutes. I thought to myself, *this is bullshit! Nothing he showed me works. I'm just not meant to learn this. I'm quitting today.*

Then, as I settled on the idea of throwing in the towel, I heard my instructor's voice call out, "If you're in your head, you're dead. Don't think. Do." I barked back angrily, "What does that even mean!?! Of course, I'm in my head, I need to think of the right move, so I don't get strangled." My instructor walked away without looking back. "That's your problem."

Moments later, my opponent and I prepared to roll again. Clearing my lungs, I took a deep breath and fell into the moment. We squared up once more, peering into one another's eyes with primal intensity. I let my mind go blank as each heartbeat pounded in my ears, the passing seconds feeling like minutes. My opponent looked right back at me. His lips tilted upwards in a self-assured smirk that spoke so loudly words weren't needed: "You can't stop me."

Grinding my teeth against my mouth guard harder, I snarled at him, prepared to do whatever it took to bring the damn realtor down.

"Begin!" our instructor yelled as the buzzer ringed and in a split second, my opponent moved forward, grabbing my head and wrapping his hands and forearms around my neck in a tight clinch.

"Not a great start," I thought to myself as I instinctively tried to resist the downward pull of his clinch. Of course, the very act of resisting caused me to fall right into his trap as my upward momentum gave him the leverage, he needed to take me to the ground. He lowered his body, released my head, and rapidly shot forward, wrapping his arms around my knees and completing a flawless double-leg takedown. I gasped for air confused about what had just happened, as he effortlessly side-mounted me then took my back and placed me in a rear naked choke.

My temples pulsed with a fiery intensity. My vision blurred as I slowly saw a glimpse of the afterlife. Exasperated and on the verge of a breakdown, I tapped the mat three more times and collapsed to the floor (again).

"This fucking sucks!" I exclaimed as my instructor walked by.

Laughing at my misfortune, he responded smugly, "Of course it does. You're in a terrible state. So damn serious and tense on the mat."

"Well no shit," I muttered, gasping for air and becoming increasingly frustrated with the sport.

Looking down at me with an expression of pity-infused frustration, he snapped, "The whole reason you started training Jiu Jitsu is because it's supposed to be fun. So, if you're not having fun, you can leave my gym whenever you want."

In that moment, it hit me like a brick. Here I was, acting like I was some sort of soldier who would end up killed in action if I didn't get each move perfectly right. I was stressed, tense, and anxious, treating my training like it was a life or death situation. I'd forgotten the most important rule of training. It's supposed to be fun.

By enjoying the process—the good *and* the bad—and learning to fall in love with imperfect practice, you guard yourself from the siren's call of giving up. I returned to the mat, rolling with my opponent and once again, submitting within a matter of minutes. This time, however, I laughed it off. I shook his hand and replied with a smile, "That was great, but watch out. I'll be back next time."

I never did get to rematch him to avenge my losses. Weeks later, he quit. No one from the gym ever saw him again. I, on the other hand, stayed in the game and went on to win multiple medals competing in national grappling tournaments and consistently beating my opponents with none other than the same rear naked choke the realtor had beaten me with in the past. The very technique that caused me the most frustration had become my super power.

I didn't know it at the time, but those lessons I learned on the mat were the foundational principles that would later help me succeed with women and in life. The entire groundwork of my "game" was predicated on those three simple lessons my instructor shared with me:

1. You have to know precisely what it is you are working on improving, have a solid strategy and solution in place, then practice it.
2. If you're in your head, you're dead. Overwhelm your thinking mind with action.
3. This is supposed to be fun. If you're not having fun, you're doing it wrong.

In any worthwhile endeavor, it's easy to get lost in the trap of thinking that you need more information or more motivation before you can achieve the results you want. The real truth is that you often lack a *system* for success and a willingness to honestly analyze your weaknesses so you can work on or around them.

My goal in writing this book was never to give you an abundance of information that would sit comfortably in your head like classic literature on your bookshelf without ever being put into use.

In this final chapter, I'm going to help you break down your growth into manageable phases so that you know where you are, where you want to be, and how to break through the plateaus and obstacles that stand between you and the romantic life that you want.

You can't learn Brazilian Jiu Jitsu by reading a book or just learning about *theory* (if you think you can, I dare you to spar with even a white belt who has been taking action for a few months). No, like in any martial art, you will always fail with the women you want most if you aren't getting out of the world of *theory* and into the realm of *action and results*.

How often are you planting your feet and standing in front of an attractive woman? Expressing yourself, flirting with her, making your desires known? If the answer is once every few months, you are going to remain single, regardless of how much you *know* about women and dating.

How often are you inviting women into your life, asking them out on dates, creating fun and exciting interactions? If the answer is, "Um, once a year?" then you are going to remain single.

How often are you establishing a man-to-woman vibe and escalating interactions once you *are* out on a date? If the answer is, "I don't want to scare her, I want her to like me," then you're going to have lots of female friends who view you as their gay best friend.

Yes, becoming the type of man who is capable of attracting high-quality women and then *keeping* them attracted is challenging. It takes time, patience, persistence, and the ability to bounce back from rejection, but the rewards last a lifetime.

> **You have the ability to only master a handful of skills during your lifetime. Shouldn't meeting, attracting, and having incredible relationships with high-quality women who can support and love you be one of those skills?**

You have minimum standards that you uphold in the rest of your life. You are disciplined enough to keep a roof over your head, food on your table, and to drink clean water. I can tell you from my own experience and the hundreds of men that I've worked with that having a high-quality relationship is just as important as those necessities. Sure, a bad relationship (hopefully) won't kill you the way going without food or water would. But it will most certainly kill your spirit. It will suppress your masculine energy and castrate the fire inside of you. And to me, that is not a life worth living.

What's stopping you from achieving the romantic life you want is *not* a lack of information, riches, or good looks. It's an unwillingness to commit to mastery. If we manage to push forward, to make progress, to master the basics, we lay the foundation to face bigger challenges and progress to the next level.

As you grow, you'll begin to develop your own theories and strategies. You'll begin to create your own unique style and forge your own methods for achieving results. Eventually, you may feel pulled to deviate from this path. You'll believe you have everything figured out and immediately shift your focus to other areas of life the second you have the option for a so-so relationship. It may feel good to check the box "in a relationship" and move on with life in the short term, yet I encourage you to stay committed to the journey.

Your goal is not to get into a relationship with the first woman who likes you, nor is it to increase your "lay count." Total mastery and abundance in your romantic life are what you're moving towards. To truly, totally, and completely own your love life and have the ability to either enjoy a vibrant single-life, dating multiple high-quality women at a time, or being exclusive with one very high-quality woman that you *chose*.

No matter which of those you choose, I want it to be *your* choice and have it come from a place of power and abundance. That way, you'll *know* beyond a shadow of a doubt that the life you are living is the romantic life you want to live, not just the romantic life given to you.

Perhaps, one day, you'll have the opportunity to pass down these skills to a son of your own. You'll help reverse the trend of clueless fathers raising even more clueless sons who are lost in the world. This skill can serve as the catalyst to fix broken families that lack real love, connection, and support. It can create a generation of parents that deeply loves one another and raises their children in positive, loving environments instead of the toxic mess that is the modern American family. Therapists shouldn't be in abundance, Grounded Men should.

This skill is about so much more than *just* sex or women or ego. It's about ending pain, loneliness and suffering. And it starts with you.

THE ROAD TO MASTERY

You've made it. You've done something very few men will ever do and arrived at the end of this book, or the *beginning* of your road to mastery.

Throughout the previous six chapters, I've shared with you the *what*. You've set out on your path to becoming a Grounded Man, adopted the internal mindsets required to succeed with women and in life, and discovered what it is that women *really* want. You've learned the exact steps to approach, seduce, and date the highest-quality women, discovering specific strategies that you can tailor to your unique personality and lifestyle.

And now, having uncovered the *what,* I'm going to reveal the *how*. I'll break this entire system down into three manageable phases that will expedite your growth and give you the framework you need to achieve real results. The following strategy consists of three 90-day sprints, each one with different goals, focuses, and challenges.

It's important to note that, as stated in the introduction, you absolutely *can* have several quality women in your life after only one 90-day sprint. In fact, if you follow the steps I've outlined and put in more effort than is prescribed, I'm confident that you can achieve this goal much, much sooner. But my goal for you is not *only* to casually date a few attractive women and settle into a *good* relationship.

My goal for you is abundance. Pure, unbridled, unfettered abundance. I want you to wake up each morning knowing you are capable of dating the *highest*-quality women in your community. I want your phone to blow up with an endless stream of messages from these women, asking when you're available for another date or if they can come over to your place that night.

I want other men to pull you aside and ask, "How the f*ck are you doing this?" I want you to feel total confidence in yourself and your capabilities as a man, to know that you are powerful beyond measure and capable of achieving *anything* you want. But changes like this take time. You cannot expect to fundamentally alter the fabric of who you are as a man in only ninety days. But nine to twelve months of following the strategies of this book with a high level of commitment? That's ample time for a transformation of this magnitude to occur.

So yes. You can go through your first 90-day sprint, begin dating several attractive women that you enjoy spending time with, and then call it a day. But to achieve your highest level of abundance, you must remember these five simple rules to maximize your success:

1. **Always Be Learning:** Like any journey, this one will be riddled with missteps. When these things happen, don't get stuck in self-pity and negativity. Learn from them. Journal about your results, the good and the bad, throughout each 90-day sprint and constantly ask yourself, "What am I doing well? What is my sticking point? What can I do better to improve that?"

2. **Progress Is Everything. Failure Is Irrelevant:** The number of rejections you face and failures you experience is completely irrelevant. The *only* thing that matters on this journey is progress. Are you better today than you were last month? Even if you haven't achieved your goal yet, are you moving towards it in a tangible way?

3. **Small Shifts Equal Huge Results:** When most people begin this journey, they forget the incredible power of compound interest. When you make small daily deposits into your skills and mindsets, they will compound over time and help you achieve drastic change and results. They will slowly alter the lens through which you view the world. Thirty minutes of effort a day can transform your life in under a year.

4. **Trust the Process:** You will be tempted to try and chart your own path, do your own thing, and approach this journey *your* way in the beginning, but I encourage you not to. I've walked

this path before you. I've gone through the pain, the rejections, the breakups. This strategy is not one built from *theory* but from taking massive action, testing it, tweaking it, and finally getting consistent and predictable results. The system *works!* But you must work with the system.

5. **Play the Game and Laugh Often:** Every day, treat this process like a game where you are Player #1. You play, fail, learn, level up, and grow. You try new things and push the boundaries of how far you can go. Like any game, a "death" means trying again, getting a do over, starting at the beginning again. In that same way, a rejection means try again. You have unlimited attempts at this as women are in abundance. Every new level brings new challenges and lessons to be unraveled. And always remember, this is supposed to be fun.

If you are willing to implement the strategies in this book and adhere to these five simple rules, then you have a real shot at dating the highest-quality women in the world.

THE JOURNEY BEGINS: YOUR FIRST 90-DAY SPRINT

Before you can move into your first 90-day sprint (I encourage you to revisit the section in the introduction titled, "Your No B.S. Strategy to Dating the Women You Want"), it's essential that you have accomplished a few key action steps. If you have not yet downloaded the dating toolkit to assist you on your journey you can do it here: knowledgeformen. com/dating-toolkit

First, you must have completed the entire book *in chronological order.* It's inevitable that you skipped through some sections and chapters or jumped right to the parts that speak to you. I get it. But if this is you, I'd like to remind you that I strategically and painstakingly sequenced each chapter, section, and word to ensure that you're able to progress as quickly as possible. So read the whole damn book!

Second, you must have created and written out a detailed "traffic strategy" tailored to your goals and lifestyle as we discussed in chapter four. I know it might seem weird to journal out exactly how you plan to meet and attract high-quality women, but I can tell you from firsthand experience, this step is *essential* for your success. Without a clear plan, this is the end of your journey.

Third, get a friend and do this journey together and hold each other accountable. Have him get the book, read through it fully, and commit to completing your first sprint together. Any single guy who has a growth mindset, is willing to take action, and is a genuine, fun person will do.

Finally, you must remember that, as you begin to take action, your biggest win is simply following the process. It's staying consistent, showing up, and putting in the effort, even when you don't feel like it. This *will* be the hardest part of the entire journey, but also one of the most rewarding. If you can push through the first 90 days of rejections, failures, and ego blows, you will arrive at the other end a new man with invaluable lessons learned about yourself and a newfound skillset that brings attractive women into your life.

Your first 90-day sprint begins now.

DANGER: MASSIVE DISCOMFORT AHEAD

When you begin your first 90-day sprint, make no mistake, it *will* be uncomfortable. You will struggle with a host of psychological and social issues that may seem, at the time, insurmountable. I'm not telling you this to discourage you, but simply to ensure that your expectations are in line with reality. Your first sprint will be the hardest that you undergo, but it is also the sprint during which you will achieve the most growth. Think of it as your own personal bootcamp into an elite level of social and personal development that will never be *known* by 97% of society. During this first sprint, you will find yourself struggling with approach anxiety, holding engaging conversations, working on physical escalation, managing your state after rejections, and staying consistent with your unique traffic strategy.

You'll likely still see an attractive woman, start walking over to talk to her, and then resist at the last second, leaving you to walk away defeated. You may find yourself engaged in conversations with women and then, utterly awestruck by their beauty, be unable to think of what to say or how to escalate the interaction. You'll come home from a bad evening out, having been rejected by every woman you approached, and start to question your sanity, wondering if you'll *ever* risk going out again.

You'll be tempted to quit more times than you can imagine and for most men, these first ninety days are the equivalent of your very own Hell Week. And like the actual Hell Week endured by Navy SEAL candidates, the majority will not make it.

Again, this is *not* being said to discourage you. Rather, it is to give you a realistic set of expectations for your first sprint. If you *expect* to be rejected, to fail, to fall on your face, and make a fool out of yourself, you'll be less likely to quit because you've already accepted how challenging this journey will be before starting.

Quite frankly, this process isn't normal, and it isn't natural. You are actively fighting your biology and going against millions of years of evolutionary psychology. Your brain wants you to stay safe, to avoid rejection, and to stay in your comfort zone. But you want something else, something better, something much bigger.

Your goal is not to get everyone or every woman to like you, but rather to express yourself to anyone and everyone around you. Any time you're out, say "Hello" and strike up conversations with as many people as you can, then push the conversation to go longer than you normally feel comfortable. Give value by offering genuine compliments when meeting new people—men and women alike. Constantly be in motion, creating more social fluidity and reducing your reaction time between interactions with people.

The more you can condition yourself to be fun, friendly, and social with *everyone,* the easier it will be to be fun, friendly, and social with attractive women. This will reduce the pressure of thinking you need to flirt or escalate in every interaction with women. If it happens, great. But that's not how you gauge success in your first 90-day sprint. Your goal is simply to go out, have fun, and create more positive social reference experiences.

But heed this warning: one of the most common traps the beginner falls into is thinking that he needs more *information* to get better results. He thinks that the people getting results know something he doesn't or have some sort of unfair advantage. Maybe they have knowledge gained from consuming more content, attending an overpriced boot camp hosted by some "guru" or taken an online training course that was haphazardly put together in a weekend.

But the truth is, the difference between success and failure is rarely determined by information alone. It's determined by deliberate action and a commitment to the journey. The more real-world experience you can gain, the better your results will be and the more successful you will become.

GAINING MOMENTUM: YOUR SECOND 90-DAY SPRINT

After completing your first 90-day sprint, you should have one to three women you are dating and/or sleeping with on a regular basis. It's more than likely that you will have friend zoned a handful of women who didn't meet your standards for a relationship, and you're finally beginning to understand the real value that you offer as a man.

But before you begin your second 90-day sprint, it's important that you have taken action on a few key steps. Specifically, you need to spend time analyzing and reviewing your last 90-day sprint.

You regularly journaled about the process and the results you achieved, have a clear understanding of your strengths and weaknesses, and created a clear strategy to mitigate your weaknesses and double down on your strengths. Remember one of the key lessons from the story I shared earlier:

> **You must know precisely what you need to work on and have a clear strategy to improve it.**

Until you have done this, beginning a second 90-day sprint is futile. It will amount to little more than a social Groundhog Day where you repeat the same mistakes, achieve the same results, and arrive at the other side the same man. Yes, it will be fun. Yes, you'll meet new women. And yes, you'll probably experience *marginal* improvements in your development and social skills. But you won't make the big leaps forward and drastic shifts that you desire. Without a clear strategy and understanding of the gap between where you are and where you want to be, nothing will change.

So, once you've completed your first 90-day sprint, take a week or two to reflect on it. Analyze your progress. Determine *exactly* what you need to work on and then get ready for the next sprint.

THE INFAMOUS PLATEAU

Although you've undoubtedly made some remarkable progress since your first 90-day sprint, your second sprint will not be without its unique set of challenges and obstacles. One of the most common challenges that an "intermediate" will face is being clear in your intentions and owning your masculine desires with women.

After a bit of practice, it's easy to strike up a conversation and have a fun, friendly chat with even the most attractive and interesting women wherever you are. But making your desires known and clearly setting the man-to-woman vibe is far more difficult. You've been conditioned by society to play it safe and be the "nice guy," so asserting yourself and conveying your sexual desires in an effective way will not come easily. (Be sure to review chapters 4 and 5 to help you escalate your interactions more effectively).

Another challenge that you will face during your second sprint is that you will be tempted to stay in your comfort zone and continue your current habits and behaviors ad infinitum. Once you start to achieve results and can easily talk to women, it's tempting to simply stay at this level. To avoid the more challenging interactions, the more attractive women and stay complacent with the meager results you know you can accomplish.

However, to achieve massive growth and true abundance, you must face these challenges head on. Use fear as your guide and take action on something that scares you on a consistent basis. Failure to do this will extend the plateau period even longer. Some men will never break out of this, only doing what worked for them as a beginner and repeatedly playing a sheer numbers game that gets subpar results.

Challenge yourself to talk to groups of women. Talk to the "unattainable" girls at the venue or party, on the street, or in the gym. Strike up conversations with the *most* beautiful women and sometimes downright frightening women instead of the ones who seem easiest to talk to. Your fear will be your greatest teacher on this journey, showing you exactly where you need to go. Do not run from it. Instead, embrace it because it is your personal guide to the life you want.

And finally, during your second 90-day sprint, it will be all too easy to forget the fundamentals. You might rest on your laurels and think to yourself, "I know what I'm doing. I've got this." But never forget the habits and activities that helped you reach this point. Constantly revisit the foundations, mindsets, and strategies shared in this book and remember that, like in martial arts, a master is simply someone who has repeated the fundamentals over and over again until they become second nature.

ACHIEVING ABUNDANCE: YOUR THIRD 90-DAY SPRINT

By now, you've achieved results that most men will never experience in their entire lives. If your ancestors knew what you were up to, they'd set a bonfire blazing and pour gallons of their finest wine in celebration.

And the best part? You've done it in under six to eight months. You've successfully completed two 90-day sprints and are now enjoying the fruits of your labor. So before we dive into the outline of your final sprint, I want to pause and say, "Congratulations." You should be *very* proud of yourself. Well done and bravo!

But before you can move into the next stage of your journey and unlock higher levels of growth for which you've been striving, it's important that you have completed a few key action steps.

Specifically, and this should go without saying, you must have completed two whole 90-day sprints. You should now be at a point where you have multiple quality women in your life and have begun the process of filtering out the women who do not share your values or fit into the grander vision of your life (per chapter 6). Although it's likely some of the women in your life will be "friends with benefits," you may also be dating at least one woman who is "possible relationship material." As tempting as it may be to settle down and "ring the bell" because you're tired; don't end this journey prematurely and stop three feet from gold. I challenge you to continue this journey and push yourself to grow as much as possible and date even higher quality women who are a better fit for your life. The extra effort you spend advancing in your dating life at this point will pay off massive dividends for the rest of your life. You have to think long term and not be focused on today's comfort.

Take time to once again reflect on the previous 90-day sprints and the lessons that you've learned. Identify your sticking points that have the greatest opportunity for growth and continue to hone in on your greatest strengths.

Now you are finally ready to begin your journey to lasting abundance.

THE EVOLUTION

Unlike your first and second 90-day sprints, the challenges that you will face as you enter into your third sprint will actually be *good* problems to have. You will no longer struggle with approaching, knowing what to say, or escalating interactions. Approaches will be smooth. Flirting will become enjoyable. Sex will be a forgone conclusion of a stimulating interaction instead of a goal rarely achieved.

You will find yourself with a whole new set of problems that are indicative of your abundance and growing skillset. One of the most common problems that you will face at this point in your journey is having *too* many women in your life. It will be easy to lose sight of your major life goals and allow your focus on other areas of life to slip. Your newfound abundance will lead to a plethora of options, making it difficult for you to make progress in other areas of your life as you give a great deal of your time and mental energy to your dating and sex life. While this is an admittedly *good* problem to have, it is a problem, nonetheless.

Stay focused on your growth as a man and the things that undoubtedly attracted those women to you in the first place. Commit to yourself, your goals, your life, *and* the romantic abundance which you've strived to create. You *can* have it all, but you must stay committed to the big picture and refuse to allow sexual abundance to pull you away from your vision for a healthy, well-balanced life.

Find creative ways to blur the lines between your social, romantic, and professional life. For example, when you have an abundance of attractive women in your life, you can more easily invite other successful men into your circle by hosting parties and events instead of opting to go out alone as a lone wolf. Your romantic success will elevate your status with other men who are more successful than you in other areas of life.

While they may have invested years or decades into their professional and financial endeavors, your personal, social, and romantic development will give you unique access to something the majority of these men lack: aliveness, fun adventures and access to a social circle *filled* with high-quality women. Because of the abundance of women in your life and your ability to help *other* men achieve similar results that you now enjoy, other high-status men in your community will begin to take notice.

Your social and romantic skills coupled with your growing levels of confidence and self-esteem will naturally attract high quality men into your life. If you can offer value to these men by introducing them to and teaching them how to attract high-quality women, you will develop a symbiotic relationship that allows each party to have the best of both worlds.

They now have access to women who were previously "unattainable", and you now have access to the knowledge and resources of the affluent—namely job opportunities, investment capital, joint ventures, and powerful connections. The win-win of this relationship will compound in your life as your growing levels of professional success open up more doors and opportunities that allow you to meet and date higher quality women who directly and indirectly help you continue your upward professional growth. And it is in this cycle that the pinnacle of attraction and seduction lies that so many men who succeed in this journey miss entirely.

Not only are the highest quality women now available to you–but you are seen as a major "win" for them and become the target of *their* pursuits greater than ever before. You are a Grounded Man who is socially competent, alive, filled with positivity, and backed by a powerful social circle of high-status and successful men who respect and admire you. You have complete freedom. Not just socially. But financially, emotionally, mentally, and spiritually because of the rewards of this journey. You live as *you* have always wanted, pursuing your goals, your ambitions, and your desires, and bringing the people–both men and women–*you* desire along for the journey.

The process I've just described–although it may take many years to bring to fruition–is the ultimate evolution as a man. You are no longer a lone wolf, hungry, and on the prowl to feed his own belly. You are now the King of the Pride, seeking to add life changing value to everyone around him and ensure that those he cares about are cared for and flourishing.

But. The only way to achieve this perpetually virtuous cycle–a cycle I believe to be a great life hack available to the men who master this skill set–is to filter your platonic friendships with the same intensity and care you filter romantic ones. When you surround yourself with positive and high-quality people, you will slowly experience a simple but profound shift in your mindset. You will become less focused on *your* success and more focused on the success of your group. Seek to lift others up but remember to guard your circle fiercely. If you allow the wrong influences into your life, it is all too easy to fall prey to rampant drug and alcohol abuse, undermining your journey and ensuring that your success is temporary.

Remember, although this *journey* should be treated as a game, the women with whom you interact should not. The women you approach, seduce, and date are real people with their own feelings, emotions, desires, and visions of their own—not objects to validate your ego or challenges to be conquered. Never allow yourself to become so mired in your quick successes that you forget the importance of connection, respect, and empathy. The greatest "seducers" in the world were men who loved women and understood them, cared deeply about them. They took them on the wildest and most adventurous times of their life and left them with memories they would never forget.

Sure, this journey *will* lead to more adventurous-filled evenings than you can count. But don't allow your character and ethics to be corrupted by the pull of an easy lay. Respect the women who share themselves, their bodies, and their lives with you. They are entrusting you with the most valuable thing they have to give. Respect this, and they will respect you.

And depending on your level of commitment, effort, and existing social prowess, you may require more than three sprints to achieve abundance… or you may require fewer. Wherever you are and whatever is required to achieve success is fine. The only thing that matters is that you *continue taking deliberate actions*, learning from your mistakes, and staying committed to the journey. The more sprints upon which you embark, the more fun and adventurous experiences you will have. There's no need to rush to some specific outcome.

All that matters is the moment you are experiencing and *enjoying* right now.

CONCLUSION: THE GREATEST EPIPHANY OF ALL...

Towards the end of your third 90-day sprint you will experience a fundamental shift in your attitude and mindset, not only towards women and dating, but life. You will find that you are no longer concerned about your dating life. Much like the other habits in your life, being social and dating will simply become a part of who you are. You will no longer have to "work" at them.

As one of my readers once told me, "I honestly find it harder to see a beautiful woman and *not* talk to her than I do to plant my feet in front of her and say something. It's what I genuinely want to do." You will find that escalation with women becomes effortless and people will regularly ask you, "How long have the two of you been together?" even though you only met moments before.

But even more important than the results of your dating life are the results you will begin to experience *outside* of it. As you begin to apply these skills and mindsets into your health, career, family, and your platonic relationships, you will experience a radical divergence in the way you show up in the world. When you step into a room, people will light up. When you step out, your absence will be felt, leaving a void in its wake.

Challenges that would once have crippled you will now excite you. Opportunities you once believed were reserved only for the elite will open up to you as your new social skills, mindset and abilities allow you to network your way to the top of the social ladder. You'll be able to stare down a billionaire, a model, or even a celebrity with that sparkle in your eye that says, *I am enough. I am worthy. I am alive and happy...* and they won't be able to reciprocate.

Every aspect of your life will undergo a dramatic change because of the skills and mindsets you learned on this journey. The best days are here, right now, today. This is the beginning of the best time of your life and they will only get better from here. And the greatest epiphany of all will fall upon you...

This process, this hero's journey, was never about the sex or the romance or the thrill of new lovers. It was about mastery of yourself.

It was about becoming the man you've always known you were capable of becoming and harnessing your newly discovered power to live a life on your own terms. You have the power to mold, craft, and architect an existence so beautiful, vibrant, and alive you often wonder if you are living in a dream.

This, my friend, is the secret I've been wanting to share with you all along. And now, it's time to take that first step and embark upon the journey of a lifetime. The world now lays before you, open, ready, beckoning for you to show up as the Grounded Man. You will go forward and live a life which most men can only dream. You will not only date the women you've always desired but craft a life and legacy so remarkable you feel as if you've lived ten lives in one.

And you will live this life so fully and fearlessly that you can die without regret, knowing you gave it your all and left *everything* above ground.

THIS IS IT.

AFTERWORD

Congratulations! You now have the exact system, the *blueprint* you need to transform yourself from the inside out into a more powerful, purposeful, and confident Grounded Man. Although you *possess* the system you need, the thought of taking the next step and *applying* it to your life might seem a bit overwhelming.

I know this book wasn't exactly a quick read. You've just consumed the equivalent of an entire college course—Becoming a Grounded Man 101—so feeling overwhelmed is *normal*. The solution?

Make this book your friend. Mark it up. Bookmark the pages. Take notes in the margins. Revisit the sections related to your sticking points and read them again and again until you break through.

I challenge you to read this book three times. But a word of warning: do not become so mired in the *information* presented in this book that you fail to take action. The lessons I've shared with you—lessons I encourage you to review at least three to four times—are indeed powerful. But they are impotent without application. So follow this process and give it everything you've got. Read. Apply. Breakthrough. Read. Apply. Breakthrough. Repeat. Transform.

Remember, this is not *just* about mastering your social life and dating an abundance of high-quality women. It's about who you are becoming through this journey. It's about the process of becoming a stronger and more powerful man—not only the jaw dropping rewards that await you on the other side.

Now, all that's left is to commit. Go all in. Give your heart and soul to the vision that you have for the life you want. I can tell you from experience that you cannot even comprehend who you will become and what your life will look like on the other side.

Your new life awaits.

DO YOU WANT MY HELP?

By now it's clear that I help guys get unbelievable results with women they never thought would give them the time of day.

There is nothing that puts a bigger smile on a man's face than having approached an attractive woman, having a fun and playful interaction, exchanging contact info, following up with her where she happily responds, going out on exciting dates then finally releasing all the built up tension with wild sex. You'll go about your days with that special fire in the belly that makes you feel so alive, powerful and capable as a man.

And of course being able to bring her with you to fun dates with friends, family events and other social outings where everyone is giving you more attention because of this attractive woman by your side who respects you and the big smile you can't wipe off your face.

You just can't put a price on the feeling you'll get from having accomplished this journey and waking up with those rewards everyday. It's a very masculine feeling that is missing amongst most men today. I encourage men to take this area of their life more seriously and not treat it like a pastime hobby to put off until "someday" when they have more time or reach some arbitrary financial goal. All that will happen is you'll be older, bitter and less experienced with women which leads to settling for "good enough", and of course more frustration in a man's life later down the line. Let's not let that happen!

Don't get me wrong. Everything in this book is enough to accomplish your dating goals, yet if you want to get results faster, save time and work with the man who wrote the damn book and has been doing this for nearly a decade, I'm available to help you. There are a few hundred guys inside of my advanced men's group who take their personal development very seriously, have all read this book and are implementing it everyday at a high level and getting crazy results they too never thought they would have just months prior to joining.

Now I have to be honest I don't know for how long I'll be helping guys in this area of life. I might move on. I might get more involved in a new startup or real estate investments. Who knows...

The best way to figure out if I'm still working with guys is to watch this presentation: knowledgeformen.com/live

If the links work, the presentation runs and there's still an opportunity to apply to work with me, yay for you, then I'm actively helping guys. You should apply while you still can then schedule a call immediately after so we can chat to see if you're a fit for my selective men's community. If the link doesn't work, well then one of my ventures took off and I'm probably surfing in Costa Rica with a Mai Tai and a Latin babe haha.

Now for those of you who are willing to go ALL IN on your growth as a man, to achieve the results you crave even faster with me, and surround yourself with likeminded men who have mastered the contents of this book and can support you through each step and challenge of this journey... *THIS* is the next step to supercharge your journey!

Take action, put an end to procrastination and watch the presentation now.

THE MISSION TO IMPACT ONE MILLION MEN

It has been one of the greatest honors of my life to write and share this book with you. I don't take your time or attention lightly and I want to *thank you* for making the decision to invest in yourself, improve your dating life, and become a more Grounded Man.

I am on a mission to impact the lives of 1,000,000 men with this book—but I can't do it alone. So, if you've found this content helpful in any way, please pay it forward by leaving me a helpful review on Amazon (or wherever you purchased it) to ensure this book makes it into the hands of as many men as possible.

The more reviews this book has, the more men it can impact, and the greater dent we can leave in the world together. We can end the pain, suffering, and loneliness with which so many men are faced today, one man at a time. And with that...we arrive at the *end* of this book and the *beginning* of your journey. Make it count.

Stay Grounded,

Andrew Ferebee
Founder of KnowledgeForMen.com
Instagram @andrewferebee
Listen to the "Knowledge For Men" podcast on iTunes, Spotify or Amazon Music

GO OUT. LIFE IS WAITING TO MEET *YOU...*

Made in the USA
Monee, IL
20 February 2023

28364705R00187